6/98

 St. Louis Community College

Forest Park
Florissant Valley
Meramec

Instructional Resources
St. Louis, Missouri

THE KENNEDY OBSESSION

THE KENNEDY OBSESSION
The American Myth of JFK

John Hellmann

COLUMBIA UNIVERSITY PRESS   NEW YORK

Columbia University Press

Publishers Since 1893

New York   Chichester, West Sussex

Copyright © 1997 Columbia University Press

Library of Congress Cataloging-in-Publication Data

Hellmann, John, 1948–

The Kennedy obsession : the American myth of JFK / John Hellmann.

  p.   cm.

Includes index.

ISBN 0–231–10798–6 (acid-free paper)

1. Kennedy, John F. (John Fitzgerald), 1917–1963. 2. Popular culture—
United States—History—20th century.   I. Title.

E842.1.H44   1997

973.922'092—dc20   96-38203

                                                CIP

Casebound editions of Columbia University Press books are printed on
permanent and durable acid-free paper.

Printed in the United States of America

c 10 9 8 7 6 5 4 3 2

For Nick

CONTENTS

A week after John F. Kennedy's assassination, his widow asserted that "Jack's life had more to do with myth, magic, legend, saga, and story than with political theory or political science."[1] Jacqueline Kennedy also suggested that to understand the man, "You must think of him as this little boy, sick so much of the time, reading in bed, reading history, reading the Knights of the Round Table, reading Marlborough."[2] Her words call attention to the narrative impulse that drove her husband's self-presentation. Jacqueline knew the literary and artistic effort with which Kennedy and those aiding him had constructed his political career as the unfolding tale of a hero.[3]

The popular hero known as John F. Kennedy was a product, an image designed to both express and elicit desire. This object was constructed through a series of hero tales that, told and retold, produced a politician as the hero of an unfolding mythology. The effect was of American history taking on the contours of American mythology before the dazzled eyes of the public. Contemporary Americans saw the ideals of American mythology incarnated in a real-life reflection of a flesh-and-blood person. This modern American hero tale, the life and career of John F. Kennedy, is perhaps even the major American mythology of our time. It has spread out across a proliferating chain of contemporary texts, meditations of a culture attempting passage through its present doubt and confusion.

That mythology was produced by many hands. It was determined by diverse forces. The popular hero "John F. Kennedy" was mediated by institutions, by ideological codes, and by various "authors." But the contribution of the person John F. Kennedy, as one of those authors and certainly as the performer of the hero role, is where we must start. For the author and performer John F. Kennedy was himself a product of various forces, from the biological to the ideological.

This book traces the doubling of John F. Kennedy during his lifetime into something like a fictional character. It concludes by examining how and why Kennedy's double—the public image designed as hero—continues to live in the fantasy life of Americans more than three decades after Kennedy's death. The image was conceived by Kennedy and his advisers in very much the same terms as a literary or cinematic character. Over the course of Kennedy's spectacular rise to the heights of American politics and culture, the specific sites of the hero's construction included articles, books, and television. But the goal was to project the hero beyond the specific borders of these media. The text within which this popular hero was being characterized and performed was the unbounded cultural space, a kind of national screen encompassing the mass-communications network of the twentieth-century United States.

This "life" originates in the material and ideological worlds into which Kennedy was born. Kennedy's character and personality, his desire, were formed in his youth; and therefore our study begins with his youthful dreams, particularly as they are reflected in his reading. We will then observe how Kennedy was doubled into a work of fiction, a representation that was a projection of both his own desire and those of his readers. That fictional character was adapted to the visual media of picture magazines and then television, on which Kennedy was able to perform his role to elicit our desire. As President, he became the nation's romantic lover, the object of our projected fantasies who promised to return us to the scenario of our founding in order to relive the pleasures and heal the wounds of American history. With his assassination, Kennedy was transfigured into an object of religious longings. This book traces the interior dynamics of this plot, the dreamwork by which Kennedy became a great hero of our national mythology.

The historical Kennedy was the most important inspiration for this second self. He was a central creative force in the scripting of the image's character and story. He performed the role. Thus Kennedy biography contributes to this study, but only in the way that biographical material may contribute to a study of the relation of a literary or artistic work to its historical context. The image, or Kennedy hero, was constructed by moving back and forth between a cultural representation and a flesh-and-blood human being. It was also produced within the interrelationship of the material history and the cultural forms of the United States. I have thus focused on those aspects of Kennedy's biography, and of his and our times, with a discernible relevance to the construction of the Kennedy hero. The chapters move from the hero forming in the private imaginings of a boy, to the hero seen by the public in post-World War II America moving across the pages and screens of the mass media, to the uncanny return of the assassinated President as a character reimagined by Americans from our present knowledge and situation.

Among the primary materials used in this book are the articles, books, speeches, and television appearances that constructed the hero. These public materials are supplemented by manuscripts and testimony that reveal the processes behind the production of these texts and performances. Still other sources include the books that Kennedy read, especially as a youth. I bring to bear upon these materials the information concerning Kennedy's life and circumstances made available by biographers, historians, and political scientists, supplemented by my own investigations. Finally, my materials include the representations of Kennedy in the aftermath of his death, including novels, films, and the emulations of politicians.

From Kennedy's earliest imagination of himself to the most recent reimaginings by today's novelists, the image has always been a product of the tension between what is and what can be made out of it. The image has from the beginning been a working of nature and culture. The development of Kennedy's personality and character, within and against the shaping pressures of social and cultural forms of his time, is a complex dialectic that both precedes and parallels the production of Kennedy's image as hero. Preexisting forms—words, designs, and narrative formulas and genres—interacted with Kennedy's needs and desires in the projection of a persona that resonated for a large public. We can only fully appreciate who John F. Kennedy was and what he and his image have meant by studying the production of his image through a combination of the methods of biography and the methods of cultural analysis.

Certain concepts are central to this study, and it will perhaps be prudent to briefly discuss my use of them. By the term *image* I refer to a picture, representation, or impression made through either words or visual means. A *myth* is a story structuring historical event through the belief system that helps to define a group of people, such as the members of a nation-state. This belief system—the ideas, articles of faith, and values structuring a group's fundamental concept of reality—is often referred to as the *ideology* of that group. A complex of related myths, or stories, articulating the ideology of a group makes up a distinct *mythology*. Such a body of stories develops out of a related set of ideas and certain recurring images. A mythology might center on a specific landscape, series of actions, or hero. Some of the most important constellations of images and myths in American culture have formed mythologies around the ideologies of individualism, freedom, and success.

In modern societies a mythology is shaped, or even originally produced, by institutions and technologies of communication. The twentieth century brought print media—books, newspapers, and magazines—forward from the nineteenth, but added movies, radio, and television to create a *mass media* of tremendous power and speed that can fundamentally alter life and culture. It is in the cultural space constituted by this network of communications that variations on certain stories, or new stories set within a familiar landscape or involving the same hero, can be told and retold. The space around the campfire of primitive cultures has become this omnipresent cultural space of industrial popular culture. Kennedy's political career cannot be separated from the development of the mass media during the middle decades of the twentieth century.

People holding positions of power and influence in the mass media participate in shaping the myths of a modern culture. Elites, both artistic and economic, select, design, and promote the products presented to the public as information or entertainment. The interests and desires of these groups are crucial in determining the representations—from newspapers to novels, from the television news to movies—that are sent out to the public. Particular individuals possess special powers and idiosyncratic ideas or personalities that influence the products and their distribution, in a few extraordinary cases enormously. These artists or impresarios wield enormous power in the manufacture of a *mass culture*. Kennedy's father, certain writers, and Kennedy himself are crucial individual personalities who brought their talents to the production of an object that, like the star image of a film actor, proved to have tremendous power at the box office.

Yet the commodities of the mass market are strongly influenced, even in their original selection and design, by the consumers for whom they are intended. The producers depend upon previous experience, research, test marketing, and simple intuition in deciding whether to invest resources in the mass production of a designed commodity, whether it is a shoe or a film. Once the decision to distribute is made, advertisers and publicists strive to persuade people to buy the product. Even then, the public rejects most of the goods offered. Thus the products that make up the mass culture are strong representations of the popular. The populace has influenced their initial selection and shape and also made the ultimate decisions.

The imprint of the popular is elaborated by the simple fact that a cultural commodity is never passively consumed. Groups and individuals functioning as consumers both select and add to the meanings offered by these goods. They bring their own material conditions, felt desires, and dissatisfactions to commodities. They choose from among these goods, rejecting most. They respond to the products they choose by focusing upon certain aspects while ignoring others, or by investing ideas or thoughts not consciously, if at all, put there by the producers. Thus the public actually shares in the production of a cultural commodity.[4]

As we cross into the twenty-first century, the Kennedy hero journeys with us, the protagonist of a central American myth. This myth promises to play a role in the evolution of American identity in the twenty-first century rather like that played until the post-Vietnam era by the frontier myth. In the Kennedy myth the nation still sees the confidence that accompanied the period of westward expansion, but also the sense of limits and tragedy acquired through recent history.

ACKNOWLEDGMENTS

I have incurred many debts during the writing of this book. Among those who read the manuscript, in whole or in part, during different stages of its composition are James Phelan, Walter Davis, Linda Mizejewski, Richard Slotkin, John Carlos Rowe, Wayne Kvam, Robert Schulzinger, James Machor, Milton Bates, and Dan Lehman. Each made valuable suggestions.

As a member of the English Department of The Ohio State University, I teach at the Lima campus, where Violet Meek, the Dean and Director, and Philip Heath, the Associate Dean, have fostered an atmosphere supporting the symbiotic relation between teaching and research. The Ohio State University generously enabled me to travel to the John F. Kennedy Library and gave me time to write. While David Frantz served as Acting Dean, the College of Humanities awarded me a year-long leave in which I was able to serve as a Senior Fulbright Lecturer at the University of Bonn in Germany. While there I prepared lectures and seminars that furthered the composition of this book. My students, both in Germany and the United States, offered stimulating responses to those ideas I shared. Arthur Casciato and Gordon Hutner gave me an early opportunity in their journal *American Literary History* to work out some of my thinking on John

Acknowledgments

Kennedy and his image in American culture. The staff of the Kennedy Library were unfailingly helpful. William Johnson, chief archivist, and Allan Goodrich, in charge of audio-visual materials, deserve particular mention. John Hanks and Rick Ewig aided my use of the Clay Blair Papers in the American Heritage Center at the University of Wyoming.

I would like to give my special thanks to Kate Wittenberg, editor-in-chief at Columbia University Press. Her enthusiasm for my work and belief in this project sustained me during its more difficult periods. Also at the press, copyeditor Leslie Kriesel helped me streamline my prose.

My son Nicholas was a continuing source of joy as he grew along with this book, and therefore it is dedicated to him. I owe my greatest debt to his mother, Marilyn McKinley. After twenty-eight years she remains my wife, and as with my previous books she offered crucial suggestions and encouragement. More fundamentally, the gift of her presence helped form the perspective I brought to this book.

THE KENNEDY OBSESSION

Prologue: A Bedside Visit

The mythology centering around John F. Kennedy began in the dreams of a single person drowsing through a chain of sickbeds.

During his extended convalescence following a nearly fatal spine operation in October 1954, Senator Kennedy worked with his aide Theodore Sorensen in producing a book that would appear under the senator's name. The idea, which would result in *Profiles in Courage*, was to tell the stories of senators who at crucial moments in the nation's history had defied the wishes of their constituents for what they saw as the good of the nation.

One motivation for the book was the invalid's need for distraction from his suffering and enforced passivity. Since early childhood John Kennedy had turned to books during his many stays in sickbeds, and he welcomed the opportunity to examine his deepest thoughts on a subject that had long engaged him. Writing a book on courage could turn an otherwise dismal situation into a stimulating act of personal exploration and achievement.

A second motivation was the political strategy that had been under way since Kennedy hired Sorensen shortly after joining the Senate in 1953. Kennedy had been known primarily for his youthful war heroism and as the "boy" of the United States Senate. In producing a series of articles for

1

prestigious journals and newspapers appearing under the senator's byline, the two men had been announcing Kennedy's intellectual engagement with national issues. A book in which the recently married Senator Kennedy was seen contemplating acts of political courage by great senators of the past might dramatically transform the impression of youthful daring and energy into one of maturing seriousness.

Manuscript materials show that varying drafts were tried as possibilities for the opening chapter. One of these draft versions, deleted prior to publication, opens with a personal narrative that chronicles a mysterious visit to the young author's bedside:

Four strange men called upon me in my hospital room in the winter of 1954.

I did not think them strange because they had stepped from the past—a step which required no pass, no approval by the head nurse, not even a knock at my door—for those who doze in hospital beds with the aid of various medical devices are accustomed to enjoying frequent obliteration of those walls that separate the past from the present, that distinguish fantasy from fact and that divide the dreams of the unsleeping imagination from the realities of room 1032. Nor did I think my visitors strange because they were that very day the leading characters in books my wife was reading aloud at my bedside—for meditation upon a literary description could lead very easily in those drowsy days to the imagination of personal visits and intimate conversations. I did not even think it strange that they all shared a somewhat unique distinction—despite the differences in their ages, manners and styles of dress—they were, I realized, all United States Senators from Massachusetts.

I thought my visitors strange because I at first thought them untypical—because I found them singularly unwilling to declare—as I thought all United States Senators would declare—that the objective of their service in the Senate had been to represent the views of the State, the people and the political party who had elected them. I had been reading—rather, at that time, my wife had been reading to me—the biographies of previous Massachusetts Senators, searching for some common clue of greatness, hoping to find a wealth of material for a book on illustrious statesmen of the Commonwealth and their dedication to the people whom they had represented. I was certain that the greatness as well as the success of our greatest and most successful Senators lay in their mastery of the democratic system—that is, in their ability to represent faithfully the views of those who had sent them to Washington.

But my four visitors smashed beyond recognition every assumption in my hypothesis, switched to a completely opposite course the basic theme of my book and added to the fundamental political principles to which I had always subscribed a new set of startling doctrines from which I could not shake them.

But then they were men not accustomed to being shaken from their principles, however startling or unpopular.

The rest of the chapter, a typescript with handwritten corrections, presents the book's argument in the form of Kennedy's successive conversations with these ghostly senators. Their message to him is that he should retain his independent judgment and be prepared to one day defy the constituents of his state by voting his perception of the national good.

This version of the chapter was more than a passing whimsy. It appears in four revised drafts. Only in the fifth version do the opening dream narrative and subsequent conversational framework disappear. Much of the remaining material, including whole paragraphs, survives in the opening and closing chapters of the published book. On page 22 of the typescript appears the paragraph invoking Ernest Hemingway's phrase "grace under pressure" that would appear as the opening of the published book.[1] Shown the typescript over three decades later, Sorensen could summon no recollection of it. He nevertheless noted that the penciled corrections on the typescript were in his hand, and therefore offered that the draft might have been his "suggestion."[2]

The spectacle of Senator Kennedy paying serious attention to visits from ghosts, or from dream figures he had hallucinated with the "aid of medical devices," would have been a dubious contribution indeed to his political image. And, however tongue-in-cheek, the stock melodramatic form hardly worked to establish a mature tone. The personal narrative would not be the tactic finally chosen for opening the book. But it has survived in the president's personal papers to reveal an important fact about the history of the book's composition. This document offers us a look at the process of scripting a public character for the man about to burst upon the national political scene.

As Americans reflect today upon the seemingly impossible gap between the John F. Kennedy they knew as a popular hero in print and images and public performances, and the John F. Kennedy constructed from posthumous revelations and gossip, this passage offers information analogous to that which a discarded early idea for a novel offers a literary scholar. The discarded idea may be aesthetically inferior, but for that very reason may afford a more transparent, because less made-over, view of the relation between the work of art and the raw material and basic intention at its source.

3

This deleted passage exemplifies the reproduction of the flesh-and-blood Kennedy, a man with both ambitious political goals and a heroic but troubled (and potentially troubling) private history, as a popular hero. Here we can see John Kennedy's actual situation being worked through a mythological formula into an archetypal hero tale. During the last months of 1954 and the early months of 1955, when Kennedy was near death after the first of two operations on his back, his wife Jacqueline sat at his hospital bedside reading to him, exactly as she does in the dream passage.[3] She also sent him a "dream visitation": during a dinner party, she persuaded the Hollywood star Grace Kelly to help lift her husband's spirits by entering the hospital room dressed as a nurse. Kelly whispered in his ear "I'm the new night nurse" and began to feed him. But Kennedy was too ill to recognize her or to show any particular response, and Kelly left suggesting to others that she must be "losing it." The next morning, when told of the event, he is reported to have said that he thought he was dreaming.[4] In the deleted opening of *Profiles in Courage*, the voice of the wife who has been reading by the side of the narrator's bed also summons wondrous visitors.

In stories, as in dreams, images are generally fusions of disparate ideas and impulses. The wish fulfillment intended by sending into Kennedy's room an impossibly beautiful nurse from the realm of Hollywood reappears in the deleted opening to *Profiles in Courage* in a more direct manifestation of the masculine desire it was meant to catalyze. The invalided "hero" of the tale is visited by fantasy images of his desired self, an indisputably strong male. These figures of masculine autonomy and strength, who can break through the guard of the "Head Nurse" and who cannot be "shaken" from their principles, give the incapacitated narrator what the visit of the Hollywood-image-made-flesh Grace Kelly was unable to deliver to the actual Kennedy: a vision of his own possible reinvigoration. The "Kennedy" of the narrative is presented with a thesis for his book, the need for independence and autonomy, that makes over his "drowsy" situation into a wish-fulfilling fantasy of rescue from childlike passivity within the woman-dominated hospital room.

If the draft was indeed written by Kennedy's alter ego Sorensen, it appears to be based on his observation of Kennedy's situation and his knowledge of Kennedy's reaction to it. An alternative explanation is that Sorensen was working with an idea that Kennedy had dictated and sent to him. Whatever the precise circumstances of its writing, the deleted chapter is a backstage look at how the character of the future presidential candidate was being scripted from the actual man's situation.

While the passage uses Kennedy's intimate experience, it also demonstrates for us how ready Kennedy and Sorensen were to shape personal material according to a formula of myth. Kennedy's actual sickbed experience serves in the passage as the basis for a fictional episode that manifests the transcultural mythic archetype of the Young Hero receiving a visit from a protective figure who brings knowledge of magic or other special powers required for the hero's future mission. In his study of world myths, Joseph Campbell found that "For those who have not refused the call, the first encounter of the hero-journey is with a protective figure (often a little old crone or old man) who provides the adventurer with amulets against the dragon forces he is about to pass." In this case the young senator, isolated and powerless, is visited by dead men who are magically summoned by the feminine power of literature (identified with his wife's Muselike voice) to hand their successor a powerful guide for his future political action. Campbell further informs us that such supernatural visitors represent "the benign, protecting power of destiny" conferred upon the hero daring to leave the familiar:

The fantasy is a reassurance—a promise that the peace of Paradise, which was known first within the mother womb, is not to be lost; that it supports the present and stands in the future as well as in the past (is omega as well as alpha); that though omnipotence may seem to be endangered by the threshold passages and life awakenings, protective power is always and ever present within the sanctuary of the heart and even immanent within, or just behind, the unfamiliar features of the world.[5]

While the supernatural visitation would be banished from *Profiles in Courage*, its essential theme, a potential young hero's receiving powerful knowledge from visitors out of the past, was submerged into the controlling narrative of the book as a whole. The text of *Profiles in Courage* was framed with information on the jacket concerning its author's war heroism and his present service in the Senate, together with a photograph of his youthful face. These elements positioned the contemporary reader to ask on every page if the young politician who had written the book would carry into the present the knowledge afforded by the examples of past senators. Would the young hero answer the call to moral courage? Readers who identified with the narrative viewpoint of the book could also ask this question about themselves.

Trite in form and too intimate in content to finally survive editorial scrutiny, the passage deleted from *Profiles in Courage* is a striking example of how Kennedy and his collaborators were intent on making Kennedy the man over into a universal image, the transcultural figure of the young hero. They were attempting to distill Kennedy, and his actual struggles and fantasies, into an image and a story configured according to heroes and hero tales already known to the public. We will begin our biography of that designed object with a look at the young boy, called Jack, who in consuming books produced the core image—his own desired self-image—that would be both anterior and interior to his subsequently constructed public image.

CHAPTER ONE

How Kennedy Awoke: Jack's Reading and *Why England Slept*

The key elements of Kennedy's youth reappear years later in the deleted opening of *Profiles in Courage*: the weakened youth in the sickbed, the woman reading hero tales, and the ensuing restoration of masculine vigor through the heroes' visit. Making an excursion into the realm of Kennedy's early biography, we will seek to identify how these elements figured in the youthful Kennedy's interior projection of a self-image. Kennedy's character and personality can themselves be usefully approached as a text. Distinct and diverse voices left their traces upon him; Jack Kennedy was in part a product of family members, of schools, of books, and of the ideologies behind them all. But he ultimately made himself up by putting together his choices from among these often-conflicting messages. And it is in this creative self-making that we can locate the beginning of the production of Jack's second self, the popular hero.

At the age of two and a half, Jack Kennedy nearly died of scarlet fever. For the safety of the rest of his family, he was quarantined in the South Department of Boston City Hospital. The small boy spent nearly three months in a sterile room that doctors, nurses, and attendants could enter only after scrubbing thoroughly with disinfectant and donning disinfected gowns. His mother, recovering from a recent birth, did not visit. Surrounded by nurses, the child projected an appealing sweetness and vulnerability to win their approval. So powerful was his charm that the nurses found it difficult to let go of their patient after he left the hospital: two of them visited him at his home; one even wrote to his father with a request for Jack's picture. This was the first public manifestation of John Kennedy's power to win a special identification from others. It was also the beginning of the important part that nurses would play in his life.

His father, normally away for weeks and months at a time on business, visited repeatedly, sitting for long periods on the side of Jack's bed. In desperation, he promised God that he would give up half his growing fortune if Jack survived. Jack thus experienced the force of his father's concern for him precisely when he was most weakened and isolated, separated from the pressures and activity of the Kennedy family and kept under the guard of nurses.[1] The visiting father, able to stride past the guards and place his large masculine figure on the side of the boy's bed, strikingly foreshadows the visiting senatorial "ghosts" in the deleted opening episode of *Profiles in Courage*.

Born May 29, 1917, John Fitzgerald Kennedy was the second of nine children. His mother, the former Rose Fitzgerald, was the daughter of the mayor of Boston, John "Honey Fitz" Fitzgerald. The father, Joseph Kennedy, was the son of Patrick "P. J." Kennedy, a ward politician and saloon keeper. Both Joseph and Rose Kennedy were intensely interested in the upbringing of their children. They were also, like all parents, flawed human beings; their deficiencies, like their virtues, were in part magnifications of their Irish-Catholic culture and of the democratic, individualist, and capitalist society in which they lived.

Joe Kennedy was a Harvard graduate and a young businessman of extraordinary ability and even more extraordinary ambition. Seeing that money was the means to freedom and independence, and wounded by the rejection of Anglo-Protestant clubs at Harvard, Joe determined to penetrate each of the barriers that lay between his family's immigrant-Irish past and the opportunity promised by American society. He accumulated a fortune during successive involvements with several of the major institutions shaping the twentieth-century United States. Despite his long absences, Joe Kennedy maintained an intense interest in his children and demanded their vigorous pursuit of success. He impressed upon his children that when he was absent he was nevertheless always aware of them and ready to interrupt his affairs to attend to their accomplishments or problems. When he was home he devoted his full attention to his children. He would insist that they seek to win at sailing and any other endeavor they attempted, and if they

8

failed he took them aside for a supportive critique. If they didn't do their best, they were made to eat in the kitchen.[2] A close friend of the family once told a reporter: "Every single kid was raised to think, First, what shall I do about this problem? Second, what will Dad say about my solution of it?"[3]

At least as important in Jack's formation was a highly intelligent and energetic mother denied outlets beyond her family and church. The vivacious young Rose was compelled by her father, himself under pressure from the archbishop, to forego her plans to attend Wellesley College and to instead set an example, as the Catholic mayor's daughter, by going to the Convent of the Sacred Heart on Commonwealth Avenue in Boston. Bitterly disappointed, she had no choice but to submit to the father who had always treated her as his special delight and companion. Forced to come to terms with her new environment, Rose gradually came to identify completely with the order and idealism of the nuns. Individual ambition and curiosity were replaced by an absorption in an intellectual milieu of martyred saints and villainous pagans and heretics, of good and evil historical periods. Sent for a year to boarding school at the Convent of the Sacred Heart in Blumenthal, Prussia, she became entranced by the atmosphere of Old World spirituality.[4]

After marrying Joseph Kennedy—over her father's initial objections—Rose was dismayed to discover that her husband was determined to exclude her from the business affairs that consumed his time. Joe's insistence on a rigid division between work and home resulted from his dissatisfaction with the way his father, as a generous local official of a political machine, had allowed neighbors to intrude upon his family's daily life. Joe was determined to build a fortune while keeping his domestic life separate from business. Since he was absent for months at a time, Rose found herself left alone to manage the household and care for the children. She went back to her parents' home for a brief time, then returned to dedicate herself to bearing and raising children, striving to inculcate in them the ideals of service she had imbibed from the Catholic Church.

The acknowledged crown prince of Rose and Joe's family was the oldest son, Joe Jr. Brawny and extroverted, he enjoyed the approving gaze of his parents as he easily molded himself into their image of the model son. Only Jack was close enough in age to challenge him. Frail and impish, "elfin" in his mother's perception, Jack profoundly resented Joe's status as the ideal for the rest of the siblings to emulate. Their parents, believing this an effective strategy for raising a large family, consciously conferred this role upon the eldest.[5] While Joe Jr. was kind and protective toward his

9

other siblings, he bullied Jack relentlessly, hurling footballs at him at excessive velocity and giving him impromptu beatings.

Jack's childhood was darkened by the specters of loneliness, debilitation, and even death resulting from an astonishing array of illnesses and injuries. He furiously combatted both his overbearing older brother and his own body. Biographers have speculated as to whether Jack's illnesses were in part a neurotic response to his inability to compete successfully with the elder brother who seemed to effortlessly fulfill parental demands. He fought Joe Jr. in a hopeless but ongoing duel, rather than defer to him as surrogate for their generally absent father. The unequal battle was exemplified by the results of the headlong collision that occurred when the two raced on their bicycles in opposite directions around the house: Joe emerged unscathed, but Jack needed 28 stitches to his head.[6]

The connection between mind and body can only be a matter of speculation. Certainly injuries resulted from Jack's desperate attempts to overcome his frail body and physically powerful brother. But his efforts were futile; he could never best his older brother in physical competition nor in conforming to the image desired by their parents. When Jack tested as having a higher I.Q. than Joe Jr., his mother went to the school and suggested there must be a mistake.[7]

Rose Kennedy organized and supervised the large family with the institutional efficiency she had learned from the Ursuline nuns of Sacred Heart Academy. She insisted on strict adherence to domestic routines and an idealistic dedication to the doctrines of the Roman Catholic Church. Jack was the only one of the siblings to resist her orders and pronouncements. While Joe Jr. played the role of substitute father, Jack presented a different example to his many younger siblings—Rosemary, Kathleen, Eunice, Patricia, Robert, Jean, and Edward. In her memoir Rose repeatedly expresses her exasperation at the irreverent statements with which Jack deflated her instructions in piety, the imaginative games with which he diverted the younger children from her planned activities, and the irrepressible tardiness and messiness with which he disrupted her mealtimes and rules for neatness. The most informed and sympathetic toward Rose of the Kennedy chroniclers, Doris Kearns Goodwin, summarizes the inevitable comparisons that Jack's mother made:

For years, it seems, faced with an eldest son who answered a mother's dream, handsome, neat, studious, and self-possessed, and a second son who didn't, who remained sloppy, irritating and undisciplined, Rose had a hard time hiding her preference, and this only exacerbated the advantage of age that Joe already possessed.[8]

For a second son who found it difficult and in some ways undesirable to fit the parents' ideal, establishing a satisfactory identity was an unusually intense crisis. Physically weak, mentally inquisitive, and temperamentally skeptical and rebellious, Jack seems to have alternated between resisting his parents' attempts to mold his identity and struggling to win their approval. Jack increasingly responded to his mother and father's anointing Joe the model son and surrogate father to the rest of the children by projecting an opposing image.

His frustration of his mother's plans by his tardiness and messiness, compounded by his leading the younger children astray, had its intellectual parallel. Jack questioned his mother's devotion to family and sometimes resisted her religious teachings. Once, he refused her request on Good Friday that each of the children wish for a happy death. When three days later she was departing for one of her extended vacations from the demands of her large brood, he told her that she was a fine mother to be leaving all the time. He at first would cry when she left on these long trips, but when he discovered that his crying only caused her to withdraw further he learned to stop and appear outwardly detached. She remembered how he sometimes disrupted her religious lessons by asking impious questions. For example, when she told the story of Jesus' entrance into Jerusalem and his subsequent crucifixion, Jack demanded to know what happened to the donkey Jesus had ridden.

Jack's feelings toward his mother would remain ambivalent. Even to the writer of a biography timed to appear before his presidential campaign, he would describe her in terms that contained undercurrents of rage and pity: "'She was terribly religious,' Kennedy says. 'She was a little removed, and still is, which I think is the only way to survive when you have nine children. I thought she was a very model mother for a big family.'" In her memoir Rose confessed her worry in later years that Jack had felt neglected as she devoted a considerable amount of her time to her third child, the retarded Rosemary. His intimate friend Lem Billings said that Jack loved his mother but saw how she had been "beaten down" by his father. He once confided despairingly to a woman friend that "My mother is a nothing."[9]

Alone among the Kennedys, Jack was a reader. So often bedridden, he developed a love of books. His mother believed that Jack's repeated con-

11

finement probably encouraged what appeared to be his natural bent. Jack later acknowledged that "She was the one who did get me started and encouraged on books." His warmest moments with his mother were when she read to him for an hour at a time. He could see the approval in her eyes when of all the children he was the most attentive and asked the best questions about the story. In Rose's words, he "gobbled books." His childhood favorite was an illustrated series of children's books by Frances Trego Montgomery about a mischievous goat named Billy Whiskers. The trickster protagonist would instigate chaos in an ordered environment and then bemusedly watch the resulting crisis. When writing her memoir after her son's death, Rose was still emphatic in her disapproval of the Billy Whiskers books.[10]

In addition to filling up the hours of a sickly boy, books supplied Jack with a special identity within the family as well as a zone of refuge and a base for resistance. Yet his mother's idea of appropriate influences had an effect. As he grew older he read virtually all of the PTA- and library-approved books that Rose kept in the family library. In her memoir she supplies a list that shows that this youthful reading was virtually all British literature. The tales of King Arthur and his Knights of the Round Table and the novels of Sir Walter Scott and Rudyard Kipling offered Jack adventures in faraway settings of British history when illness denied him everyday outings and play. The Scott-influenced tales of the early American frontier by James Fenimore Cooper were among the rare exceptions to Jack's absorption in British literature. Approved classics, his mother's books provided fantasies of heroic adventure and achievement as alternatives to her lessons in approved sacrifice and self-denial. When he eventually concentrated on history and biography, he chose romantic works emphasizing the role of the heroic individual.[11]

Kennedy was finding in his self-chosen heroes guidelines for the formation and sustenance of an ideal self. Such heroes could compensate for the reader's present inadequacies. They also offered a model for a fantasy self that could resolve the opposing messages the Kennedy children were receiving from their father and mother. Romantic heroes from remote history offered a model of the individualistic, aggressive behavior epitomized by Joe Sr. while also embodying the service to higher ideals espoused by Rose.

Jack's reading thus suggests an escapist fulfillment of his frustrated aspirations to please his parents as well as a set of alternative scripts according to which he could shape his private self-concept. His sister Eunice remembered that "When we were reading *Lives of the Saints*, Jack was reading Carlyle." His mother identified in Jack's reading choices his "strong romantic and idealistic streak," and said that she "often had a feeling his mind was only half occupied with the subject at hand, such as doing his arithmetic homework or picking his clothes up off the floor, and the rest of his thoughts were far away weaving daydreams."[12]

The brief episode that was to have opened *Profiles in Courage* presents a symbolic paradigm of young Jack's recurring dilemma. A weak young boy was prevented by his debilitated body from fulfilling the socially prescribed idea of masculinity. He found comfort in the stories that came his way through the voice of a woman. In American culture, literature and art had traditionally been defined as a "feminine" realm of cultivated removal from the world of action. The gendering of the aesthetic realm was particularly acute in the Kennedy family, whose father had little use for poets and artists and among whom Jack alone was a "bookworm." This "feminine" realm of literature distracted him from the reality of his physical inadequacy while supplying him with "masculine" images of power and freedom with which to identify. He began to weave compensating dreams, fantasies in which he was in a sense visited by the heroes entering his imagination from books. It seems that his father's demand for masculine power, his mother's religious idealism, and his own skeptical rebelliousness were resolved through the images of lonely heroes, powerful but doomed individuals who sacrificed the immediate approval of friends and family to answer a higher call. The competitive masculine image demanded by the father and denied Jack by his debilitating body was available to him in the images that traveled upon his mother's voice, reading aloud. Romantic history offered heroes who were at once strongly masculine, idealists admired by the women they served, and rebellious individualists. The father figures of the deleted tale opening *Profiles in Courage* possess and transmit the power that Jack found in his childhood heroes.

While young Jack was struggling with his illnesses and becoming absorbed in literature, the senior Kennedy was being drawn to the power that he saw could be won through projecting fantasy images upon a screen. He had developed a prescient interest in the early movie industry that culminated in his work from 1926 to 1929 as a Hollywood producer. Joe and Jack were thrilled when their father brought home Tom Mix cowboy outfits. Hearing their reaction to the idea, he once cast real-life football star Red Grange in a leading role in a college football movie. Joseph took over Gloria Swanson's career, enhancing her stardom while making her his mistress. So deep was his involvement that he nearly abandoned his family for her when pressured by the Catholic hierarchy. But when he eventually returned from Hollywood, he brought a renewed commitment to the family as an extension of his ambitions and an insider's knowledge of the power involved in the manufacture of a star image. Eventually, Joe Kennedy's appreciation of that power and the pleasure his son Jack found in projecting himself as such an object of desire would brilliantly mesh.

Jack received his first intimations that his literary interests could win him some desperately needed recognition. At thirteen he wrote his father from the Catholic boarding school Canterbury that "We are reading *Ivanhoe* in English, and though I may not be able to remember material things such as tickets, gloves and so on I can remember things like *Ivanhoe* and the last time we had an exam on it I got a ninety eight."[13] Upon his move to the exclusive Episcopal preparatory school Choate, Jack's scholastic performance was often an occasion for more defensive letters home. But evidence of his literary ability continued to show. A schoolmate later recalled his surprise at hearing Jack, otherwise a mediocre student, told by their English teacher that he had a "definite flair for writing" and should consider it for a career.[14]

The second son of this intensely Irish-American family was thus finding his source of identity and potential through his reading of British literature. Jack had listened to the Irish lore of resistance to English oppression, especially in his youthful outings with his beloved grandfather "Honey Fitz." He and his family had personally experienced discrimination from the Boston brahmin class of Protestant descendants of the English. This background would hardly seem to have made Jack identify with the heroes of England. Ironically, the British culture that turned Ireland into the colonial nation within Europe offered Jack liberating fantasies of heroic adventure and mission that supported him in his rebellion against parental pressures.

Actually, British literature made such fantasies easily available. *Kim* was one of the books in the family library that his mother was sure Jack had read. The hero of Rudyard Kipling's novel is a blue-eyed boy, dressed in native garb in India, who is actually an Irish lad working in Intelligence in the service of the British Empire. And the heroes of *Ivanhoe* are the Saxon title character and the Saxon noble-turned-outlaw-rebel Robin Hood. These men struggle with an illegitimate Norman establishment while awaiting the return of the good king Richard (who, though Norman, is associated in Scott's telling with the "true" English values of the Saxons).[15]

The theme of the ethnic individual struggling to form a greater national identity could have a powerful appeal indeed for an Irish-American who was also an overshadowed but resourceful second son. Jack's love of English history soon led him to Winston Churchill, who would become his literary model. By adolescence Jack was absorbing Churchill's multivolume biography of his late-sixteenth- and early-seventeenth-century ancestor John Churchill, the Duke of Marlborough.[16]

At Choate Jack continued to be plagued by illness. In the hope of correctly diagnosing a mysterious stomach ailment, his parents sent him to the Mayo Clinic in Rochester, Minnesota. From there he wrote a series of letters to his Choate friend Lem Billings that mixed his developing adolescent interest in sex with his humiliated masculinity. In an adolescent reenactment of his infant experience winning the devotion of the Boston City Hospital nurses during his confinement with scarlet fever, Jack tried to turn his sickbed into a stage for his power to charm women.

Doctors forced him to endure a series of painful and humiliating tests. As he recounted the outrages against his person, he boasted of his successes at verbally turning the tables on the doctor-tormentors. He claimed, for instance, that when a doctor was anally penetrating him he won the laughter of the young nurses by assuring his tormentor that "you have a good motion." He similarly worried over the draining of vigor from his penis while attesting to his having become the "pet" of the hospital staff. He informed Billings of the insertion of a tube into his stomach through his nose, a violation immediately followed by his pleasure at being massaged "all over" by a beautiful young nurse, so that "I now have both a 'head-on' and a 'hard-on.' " Kennedy's sexual development in early adolescence was accompanied by assaults on his body, humiliations of his masculine identity that he attempted to counter by projecting an aggressive image of wit and sexual bravado.[17]

For all their ingenuity, the doctors were unable to determine the source of Jack's ailment. After returning to Choate, and after Joe Jr. had moved to Harvard, Jack formed the Muckers' Club, which he dedicated to precisely all actions and attitudes that the headmaster defined under the label "mucker"—a Protestant term for Irish laborers—as undesirable. Such behavior had already won Jack the considerable hostility of his mother and now nearly caused him to be expelled from school. It also made him the center of attention, drawing the admiration of his schoolmates as it once had that of his younger siblings and forcing authority to react to a situation that he had shaped. In the case of the Choate disturbances it even forced

15

a personal intervention by his father, who covertly complimented his son on his daring while making it clear that this self-destructive activity would have to stop.[18] Jack turned his mischief to a campaign that succeeded in having him elected by his class "most likely to succeed."

The strategy of rebellion, however, had a built-in trap. A psychologist's report at Choate following the Muckers incident documents Jack's cultivation of an opposing identity. Rather than compete and inevitably come in second, he proudly told the Columbia University psychologist that he had chosen to be the opposite, the thoughtless and careless antithesis of the orderly and efficient good son. The psychologist found that Jack actually saw himself as a "self-reliant, intelligent and courageous boy." When the psychologist asked Jack how he would carry his public persona into success in business, he found Jack stumped.[19]

At Harvard Jack first seemed to have little idea what to do about his dilemma. As at Choate, he succeeded in drawing a circle of male friends around him. He also resumed his duel with his brother Joe, now displaced into athletic competition but as hopeless and self-destructive as ever. He severely injured his back when he insisted on scrimmaging with the varsity football team over the warnings of his brother that he was too light in weight. He would struggle with this debilitation the rest of his life. While on the swim team he likewise refused to surrender to a case of jaundice. In a doomed quest for a varsity letter, which in its fanaticism suggests his near-hatred of a body that was a constant obstacle to his desired image, he had a friend smuggle milkshakes into the campus infirmary and sneak him out to practice in the pool.[20]

From his earliest years Kennedy's efforts to succeed had been blocked by a body and a disposition that were not adequate to the demands presented by his family. In compensation he had developed a private image of self-reliance, intelligence, and courage modeled on his British heroes. But he needed to defend both his failures and his private fantasies from the patronizing stares of those around him; consequently, he had projected the public image of a thoughtless wastrel. He had for some time cultivated the ability to live with a self-projected image that served his private needs.

A solution to his dilemma only appeared with his father's appointment in 1938 by Franklin Roosevelt to be the U.S. Ambassador to Great Britain. Joseph Sr. had long ago moved his family to New York when his financial success did not prevent his being blackballed from the clubs of Boston. His admission now to the Court of St. James was an outstanding success. But whereas the ambassador's opposition to American support of Great Britain in the confrontation with Nazi Germany would soon destroy his own political ambitions, Jack's response to this moment in British history would reveal something of his dreamed other self.

Testimony from all directions attests to the influence that the British experience had upon Jack. Indeed, the transformation became apparent immediately upon his return from his initial, summer months abroad. Jack applied to spend the second half of his junior year at Harvard working as a courier for his father in Great Britain. Perhaps motivated by anticipated resistance as well as stimulated by the exciting prospect of an extended stay in Europe as the threat of war increased, Jack began applying himself to his studies, bringing up the "gentleman's Cs" that had contented him his first two years. Once he arrived in Britain, he found himself welcomed by the same English families he knew from his reading. He admired the casual sophistication and elegance of the British aristocracy. As Rose Kennedy explained in an interview shortly after his death, Jack was delighted to find that in Britain his dual interest in literature and politics was shared by the young aristocrats into whose homes he was invited. The homes themselves were the settings of many of the works of history he had read. He could now enjoy the pleasurable sensation of entering the books he had so enjoyed in his youth, and of finding his fantasy heroes' living descendants as congenial as the lonely boy in bed might have fantasized the knights and merry men and band of brothers that had been his company in books.[21]

Kennedy's friends and biographers expand on Rose's testimony. In *A Thousand Days* Arthur Schlesinger emphasizes that Jack's time in London "speeded his intellectual awakening." Jack found the casual sophistication of such young Englishmen as David Ormsby-Gore, who would become a lifetime friend, more impressive than the manner of his Harvard classmates back home.[22] In his study *President Kennedy and Britain*, David Nunnerly, reporting on interviews with Jack's associates from this time, concludes that the experience in Britain, coming as he entered young manhood, helped Jack to overcome much of his tendency toward introversion and the anti-British biases of his family upbringing.[23]

But no matter how much he admired the British, his not being one of them could have posed a barrier, either to his identification with them or to his continuing identity as an American. Since Jack could never be British, he could have found himself feeling excluded or overshadowed. Or, his emulation of the British drawing him to other sources of value, he could have found himself unable to retain pride in being Irish and American.

The reason this was not the case may be found partly in the larger dynamic of British-American relations. If John Kennedy had in his imaginative life moved from within an Irish-American family and an Episcopal school to an absorption in British history, the United States had in the period immediately preceding his birth made a similar journey from a legacy of opposition to a recognition of shared heritage, values, and mission. The period of American movement onto the world scene—from isolationism, frontier expansion, and civil war and reconstruction to missionary movements and overseas empire-building—had been accompanied by a healing of the historical rift with the mother country. In *The Great Rapprochement: England and the United States, 1895–1914*, Bradford Perkins has made an extensive study of the movement of American political culture back toward identity with the history and "mission" of the country from which it began by declaring its independence:

The concept of duty, at least as old as imperial Rome, sprang forth again in the 1890s. Even those who opposed political imperialism believed superior races ought to lead the less successful. Newspapers, magazines, and speeches, both English and American, frequently referred to torches illuminating the wilderness, preachers of the Anglo-Saxon gospel converting the heathen, and so on. . . .

Rudyard Kipling, the crotchety little prophet of empire, a virtual recluse dominated by an American wife—Henry James gave away the bride when they were married—bestowed upon the concept its popular name with a poem, "The White Man's Burden," published in an American magazine, *McClure's*, in February 1899. . . . He considered the British and American people basically similar in their ideals and aspirations, and he welcomed the American decision, approved by the Senate the same month in which his poem appeared, to join England in a task beyond the resources of any single country. Thus Rudyard Kipling quite sincerely penned a plea to the Americans to:

"Take up the White Man's burden—
  Send forth the best ye breed—
Go bind your sons to exile
  To serve your captives' need;
To wait, in heavy harness,
  On fluttered folk and wild—
Your new-caught, sullen peoples,
  Half-devil and half-child."

This stern call to duty gave a moral tone to the imperialistic crusade. . . . By ser-vice, by a demonstration of vigor, by devotion to an ideal, it was hoped, a nation might justify its favored position in the world.[24]

This process began in the 1890s as a racial or ethnic ideology, but it quickly evolved into a more flexible cultural identity:

Individualism, political liberties, perhaps peace and Protestantism—these charac-teristics gave Anglo-Saxons their uniqueness, their superiority—and their bond. As acquired characteristics rather than genetic ones gained emphasis and the phrase "Anglo-Saxon" hardened into a biological mold, it gave way to a new one, "the English-speaking peoples," which admitted the nonbiological emphasis.[25]

Kennedy was born in 1917, precisely the year that this "great *rapproche-ment*" was confirmed by the United States' entry into a world war on the side of the British according to the Wilsonian rhetoric of "making the world safe for democracy" and fighting "the war to end all wars." He grew up in a cultural milieu in which an American was encouraged to imagine himself part of an English-speaking tradition of democratic and individu-alistic values that extended far beyond American history in both geography and time. Indeed, the second half of the 1930s, when Kennedy moved from adolescence toward his college sojourn in Britain, was a period in which Hollywood presented many episodes of British history through lenses sub-tly suggesting a version of Americans' own struggles. *Lives of a Bengal Lancer* (1935) and *The Charge of the Light Brigade* (1936) were initial suc-cesses followed by such imitations as *Wee Willie Winkie* (1937), *Drums* (1938), *Four Feathers, Beau Geste,* and *Gunga Din* (1939) and many other films. The Victorian period in particular provided epic struggles of the English-speaking carriers of individualistic and democratic virtues with both "savage" races and agents of authoritarian empires. Hollywood pro-vided particular identification figures for American audiences by scripting heroes who displayed the American native virtues of rough independence and rule-breaking.[26] Kennedy loved the movies, and we can be sure he saw a number of these assertions of the common heritage of the "English-speaking peoples."

If Kennedy felt, upon his arrival in the Great Britain of 1939, as if he had entered the British history that for him was a series of romantic books and movies, he also could feel that he was actually taking part in that history as

19

it now unfolded. On the eve of the war he traveled about Europe as the ambassador's personal courier, seeing for himself the countries moving toward conflagration and reporting his observations to his father. After hostilities commenced, he was sent by his father to interview American survivors of a ship sunk by the Germans.

He had wandered among heroes, about the stage where history was being performed, but Kennedy returned from Britain to find himself rejected by a woman in favor of a young writer. He seems to have been genuinely interested in marrying the beautiful, brilliant, and fabulously wealthy Frances Ann Cannon. Friends testify that she was an exception to his general view of women as objects of conquest, for she had a fine mind and was interested in literature and political issues. His Catholicism was a barrier, however, and her mother had forced a separation by taking Frances on a world tour. When Kennedy came back from his own trip to Britain, he was introduced by Frances to her fiancé, John Hersey, a recent Yale graduate.[27]

Soon after his first real defeat—losing his girl to a writer—Kennedy turned to writing to produce what would become his first real success. He decided to build on his British experience by writing a senior honors thesis on "Appeasement at Munich (The Inevitable Result of the Slowness of Conversion of the British Democracy to Change from a Disarmament Policy to a Rearmament Policy)." He had considerable help with the research from his father's staff in London, but he wrote the thesis himself, bringing his analytical talents to bear upon the question of how the Empire that so fascinated him had come so swiftly in the 1930s to its terrible predicament. Upon completion he proudly reported to his father the unprecedented effort he had put in:

Finished my thesis. It was only going to run about the average length, 70 pages, but finally ran to 150. . . . I'll be interested to see what you think of it, as it represents more work than I've ever done in my life.[28]

With the substantial accomplishment of this extended meditation upon the present dilemma of the country he so admired, Kennedy was graduated *cum laude*.

After completing the thesis Kennedy reluctantly attended the wedding of the woman he had hoped to marry. He noted that his successful rival had been the private secretary of the Nobel Prize-winning author Sinclair

Lewis and was already a writer for *Time*. In his response to receiving the wedding invitation, Kennedy expressed despair while displaying his determination to avoid playing a certain recognizable role. He wrote his friend Billings that "I would like to go, but I don't want to look like the tall slim figure who goes out and shoots himself in the greenhouse half-way through the ceremony."[29] Kennedy clearly felt an intense competition with John Hersey, whom Frances Cannon had deemed the better prospect.

His father's journalist friend Arthur Krock suggested turning the thesis into a book and calling it *Why England Slept*, as a contrast to Winston Churchill's recent book *While England Slept*. The ambassador was enthusiastic, and Krock aided Jack in making stylistic revisions. *Time-Life* publisher Henry Luce was persuaded to write an introduction, and with publication in 1940, the year of Dunkirk, the book became a best-selling success (partly due to Joe Kennedy's own mass purchases) and Jack a minor celebrity.

Why England Slept, little changed in substance from the original thesis, represents the self-making of the young man as well as the first moment of his being made over into a public image. As Nigel Hamilton has shown definitively, Kennedy wrote his thesis on his own, with no interference whatsoever from his father and without any guidance from the Harvard faculty.[30] It was written in an astonishingly short period, and represents his first application to a literary and historical pursuit of the determined will he had shown in his conflicts with his brother and with his own body in athletic contests. Here the compensatory love of reading and absorption in Great Britain brought him the triumph he had never found in physical struggle. *Why England Slept* is an expression of Kennedy's authentic ideas and psychology as well as his awakening from the shyness and confusion of his youth. Yet the publication of the book, edited and presented by friends of his father, is the first moment of Kennedy's doubling into a public image with additions and embellishments.

Why England Slept is the crucial first text in the production of John F. Kennedy, in terms of both Jack's projection of his own ideal image and his father's and others' collaborative presentation of that image as an idealized representation of its reader. The book is rooted in Kennedy's self-analysis; in the guise of a journalistic essay, it reveals his most private thoughts and feelings concerning his own character. At the same time, he allowed his father to bring in established talents—Arthur Krock and *Time-Life* publisher Henry Luce—who could, respectively, give the book a stylistic makeover and frame it for public acceptance.

Why England Slept takes a clinical approach. Kennedy presents Britain's failure to rearm in time to avoid the disastrous appeasement policies of the late 1930s as a psychological problem of the British people. In his judgment the British leaders had little choice but to buy time through appeasement because of military weakness, the result of the reluctance of the British people earlier in the decade to support armaments. The young author argues for the broader significance of his psychological study as a "test case" of democracy. In Kennedy's analysis, the British people were partly motivated by a pacifist reaction to the Great War. But he concludes that a deeper problem was the nature of democracy itself. While superior to a totalitarian system in the long run because of its respect for the individual as a reasonable being, democracy is weaker in the short run because individuals are free to pursue their various desires. It takes "violent shocks to change an entire nation's psychology."[31]

Kennedy's narrative is structured by a pattern of inertia and arousal. It is not difficult to see this analysis as itself an expression of the author's psychology. Kennedy places the Britain of the 1930s in a sickbed, languishing from the memory of its sufferings during the preceding war and finding it difficult to focus on the problem at hand. It must overcome internal weaknesses and desires in order to rise to the role history demands. The plot of Kennedy's book recapitulates, is perhaps driven by, Kennedy's knowledge that his writing the senior thesis and book is his own overcoming of internal weaknesses. Like his protagonist, the British people, he is at last rising to meet a challenge he has too long put off because of confusion and distraction.[32]

The book is Kennedy's first expression of the theme that would lie at the core of his personal and political vision throughout his subsequent career: the need to arouse diverse energies and focus them to meet a crisis. We find this theme again in the subtext of the discarded personal narrative of *Profiles in Courage* and in the Inaugural Address. This rhetorical idea would also be expressed by Kennedy again and again in action, from his intense campaign efforts to his crisis-oriented presidency. Its first active expression is the writing of *Why England Slept*: Kennedy articulated the theme of arousing diverse and dormant energies in a focused effort in his first successful act of doing precisely that. *Why England Slept* is secretly as much about "Why Kennedy Slept" as it is an inquiry into the somnolence of the country with which its author so identified.

Why England Slept is a psychological study of England and capitalist democracy that mirrors Kennedy's own self-analysis. Young authors typically pour out their autobiographical passions into their first books. This raw, if disguised, self-projection can be as true for a journalistic or scholarly writer as for a novelist. With an awareness of the author's personal situation while writing, the question and the exhortation with which young Kennedy introduces his book may be read as self-directed as well. The first sentence asks "Why was England so poorly prepared for war?"[33] As he concludes the introduction, Kennedy explains that he wishes "to trace the gradual change in the nation's psychology from the peaceful year of 1931 . . . to the events of the past May" (xxviii). Kennedy explicitly addresses the relevance of this subject to his own and his American readers' collective future: "We have the benefit of their experience. From their mistakes we should be able to learn a lesson that may prove invaluable to us in the future" (xxv). The last sentence of this introduction refers directly to the avoidance of pain: "In studying the reasons why England slept, let us try to profit by them and save ourselves her anguish" (xxviii).

The twenty-two-year-old man who presented this scheme drew on his research for its facts, but on his own psychology for its analysis. His construction of the British public as an "England" with a psyche that can be analyzed in the same way as the mind of an individual is a fiction, perhaps valid and useful, but a fiction nonetheless. It ignores the diverse complexities of a population in favor of a collective representation based on a generalized understanding of salient national characteristics and experiences. It should not be surprising that, in devising that fiction of a national psyche, the author should project his understanding of his own characteristics and experiences on it.

Writing this psychological analysis of "England," Kennedy inevitably drew on his own experience over the decade. The book is Kennedy's disguised autobiography of the "gradual change" in psychology from self-absorbed, lazy, and pleasure-pursuing boy during the 1930s to intensely diligent and energized author ready to meet the next decade. The question of why England was "so poorly prepared" for Hitler's challenge at Munich parallels the question the author-in-the-making must have been asking regarding his own immediate "anguish": Why had the "literary" member of the Kennedy family been so utterly lacking in credentials and accomplishments when competing with the writer John Hersey for a wife? England's response to Munich had been rapid preparation for war; Kennedy's response to Hersey's triumph had been a whirlwind pursuit of academic and literary credentials through the writing of the thesis/book.

23

In the first chapter, Kennedy says that "To be bothered as little as possible and to be allowed to go his peaceful way was all the average Englishman asked" at the outset of the 1930s, and thus "the Englishman had to be taught the need for armaments" (4). Throughout the book, Kennedy insistently repeats that "it takes time to change men's minds, and it takes violent shocks to change an entire nation's psychology" (5). He identifies two fundamental aspects of the English psychology, deeply held aspects of the Englishman's self-image, as underlying the initial complacency: the sense of island immunity and the sense of national superiority (21–23).

Clearly, Kennedy sees himself in the collective Englishman with whom he had identified so long in his reading and more recently in his visit. As an adolescent, Kennedy had also wanted to be "allowed to go" his own way and not be "bothered" by the pressures of his family and school headmasters. Like his partly observed, partly projected "Englishman," Kennedy had to be "taught the need for armaments," in his case the credentials and achievements needed for strength in society. His own change in psychology had come very gradually during his years at Choate and Harvard, culminating in the radical change following the "violent shock" of losing Frances Ann Cannon. And like his protagonist, "the average Englishman," Kennedy knew that his vulnerability came from his failure to realize before it was too late that his "island immunity" and "natural sense of superiority" were illusions in a changing world. As the psychologist had reported during Kennedy's time at Choate, the teenaged Kennedy had considered himself safe from the pressures of his parents as long as he kept an impassable gulf between them and his self-image as a superior person. Being replaced by John Hersey in the eyes and arms of Frances Ann Cannon had vividly impressed young Kennedy with the necessity of changing these assumptions about himself, whereas the blandishments and threats of his parents and headmasters had only gradually made their mark.

As Kennedy develops his argument in detail, his observations about England continue to correlate with his own experience viewed in retrospect. He observes that in the mid-1930s "a slow change was coming about" (107), but that England "was not to get that united effort until Munich had shocked the people into an awareness of their vulnerability" (118). Midway through his Harvard years Kennedy had begun to apply himself more seriously to his studies, but it was only after the unexpected loss of a woman that he had truly focused all of his energies on a single task. The explanation of Kennedy's sudden change of habits is in his analysis of England's reaction during the year following Munich:

Emotions move people far more strongly than facts. . . . [Fear of death from the air] resulted, while it lasted, in bringing the country to a sharp realization of its vulnerability more quickly than all the logic of Churchill's arguments over the preceding three years. (155)

As Kennedy brings his narrative to a climax, he describes how that shocking realization of vulnerability brought about the same focusing of energy that Kennedy was now demonstrating to himself by writing the book: "All of [England's] energies would have to be molded in one direction" (183). Again, in a statement strikingly applicable to his change in scholarly habits, he observes: "England had had a diplomatic defeat. . . . This was realized, and the energy with which England attacked the problem was in great contrast to her previous lackadaisical methods" (195).

As long as Kennedy analyzes the psychology of his subject, the tone of *Why England Slept* is clinical. Only at the transitions in his narrative does the author drop this detached mask and show his excitement about the story he is telling. He closes chapter 3 by breathlessly announcing, "But time is slipping by, the crucial years are coming: England must begin to awaken" (57). Later he declares, "For the tragedy was that England *did not start her armament* drive in this crucial year" (83). When he at last concludes his account of Britain's long sleep and ultimate awakening, it is with a paragraph in the exuberant tone of the romantic history he loved:

With this new spirit alive in England my story ends. England was now awake; it had taken a great shock to bring home a realization of the enormity of the task it was facing. All the latent energy stored up in England during the last seven years is being expended in a vigorous drive for victory. Industry and labor, the rich and the poor, are contributing to England's fight for survival, with the knowledge that this is a supreme test of democracy's ability to survive in this changing world.

Substitute "Jack" for England, and one might take this passage for Kennedy's triumphant mood upon the surprising outcome of his academic career.

The passage also shows that Kennedy had achieved an imaginative identification with England specifically and capitalist democracy in particular. Like Jack in his long struggles with his brother Joe, democracy was the underdog and, despite outward appearances, in the long run superior. But the triumph of both Jack and democracy depended on a willingness to make sacrifices and focus energy in an intense effort.

25

Why England Slept initiates the pattern of the production of John F. Kennedy as a public image. The personal psychology of Kennedy himself produces an image, which Kennedy's powerful father then persuades connections in the media to heighten into an idealized representation of the potential best self of the American audience. Arthur Krock's revisions improved the style of Kennedy's book, and his astute advice on the title boldly positioned its author as aspiring to speak in the same league as Churchill. Joe's purchases pushed the book into the best-seller status that would easily label it a success. Most important was the enlisting of Henry Luce to write the introduction. Kennedy's own text contains such words and phrases as "sacrifices," "energies," and "supreme test" that would echo all the way through Kennedy's rhetoric to his most famous presidential speeches. But it is Luce, in his introduction to *Why England Slept*, who names the role in which Kennedy would be cast in his first political campaign and then again in his run for the presidency:

In recent months there has been a certain amount of alarm concerning the "attitude" of the younger generation. If John Kennedy is characteristic of the younger generation—and I believe he is—many of us would be happy to have the destinies of this Republic handed over to his generation at once.

Indeed, Luce's final paragraph foreshadows the Inaugural Address Kennedy would author twenty years later, which would begin with evocations of "our ancient heritage," proceed to celebrate America's moment as the defender of liberty, offer a balanced vision of the need for Americans to be both dreamers and realists, and end with visions of going forth into a new era of peace and love. Luce foreshadows this vision:

We arm ourselves, in body and spirit, not to rescue some small paltry bankruptcy settlement out of the wreckage of the past. We go forward to win in actual achievement nothing less than the brave-in-heart have hoped for and striven for before us. We shall go forward with regiments of "realists," with whole divisions of determination. And let no one doubt that our united army shall also have squadrons of dreamers who alone are equipped to mount up as eagles to look beyond the ranges: behind us and ahead—seeing behind us the long way we have come from servitude, and seeing ahead of us the promised lands of Peace and Freedom. (xvi-xvii)

Kennedy's father was delighted with the published result of his son's literary and his own media-working efforts. In August he wrote Jack: "You would be surprised how a book that really makes the grade with high-class people stands you in good stead for years to come."[34] Four months later, the day after President Roosevelt's reelection to a third term, Joseph Sr. resigned as ambassador to London. The Kennedy patriarch's political career, which had included presidential ambitions, was ended by his defeatist stance toward Nazi Germany. Jack, the bookworm of the Kennedy family, had written himself the basis of a future political career. While neither fully understood this potential, Jack and his father had both found a rebirth in Jack's authorship and his father's media production of it.

Within a year of the publication of *Why England Slept*, the two books that would become Kennedy's lifelong favorites, David Cecil's *The Young Melbourne* (1939) and John Buchan's *Pilgrim's Way* (1940), were published. Both authors are British lords (Buchan was Lord Tweedsmuir), and Kennedy's love for these books, like his choice of a thesis topic, is part of his more general absorption in British literature and history and his recent visit to that country. Biographers have consistently been impressed by the interconnections among the friendships Jack and his sister Kathleen made among the ruling class of England, the admiration he formed for Winston Churchill's speeches and writings, and his love of *Pilgrim's Way* and *The Young Melbourne*.[35] Kennedy read the books not long after their publication, and many friends would remember the fervent admiration he expressed for them during the ensuing years.

After his graduation from Harvard and the publication of *Why England Slept*, Jack Kennedy seems to have marked time. Like many young men, he may have found it difficult to commit himself to a life course when the prospect of American involvement in a world war loomed. In addition, his health problems continued. A letter from his father to an associate indicates that Jack's tender stomach, perhaps resulting from ulcers, was a serious cause of concern. His back made it difficult for him to drive more than an hour without stopping and getting out of the car.[36] He was also troubled by painful urethritis resulting from gonorrhea.[37] In September 1940 he went to California, to Stanford University for a year. While he was ostensibly attending the Graduate School of Business, he seems to have been more interested in the sunny climate, the great number of beautiful young college women, and the political science courses conducted on the other side of the campus. He also made his first trips to Hollywood, where his father's connections and wealth allowed Jack to mingle with stars and *Why England Slept* gave him the status of a minor celebrity.

Kennedy's intellectual friend at Stanford, Henry Adams, told Kennedy's biographer Hamilton that Jack was very concerned with sleeping with young women to prove his masculinity. According to Adams, Jack's favorite saying was "Slam, bam, thank you ma'am." But Adams saw evidence that this first acting out of masculinity-as-super-heterosexuality masked elements that would be considered feminine:

I think Jack had far more of the feminine in him than he'd ever admit. He was not a real macho. He *pretended* to be. He worked hard at it. But his very frame as a light, thin person, his proneness to injury of all kinds, his back, his sicknesses, which he wouldn't ever talk about, you know—he was heartily *ashamed* of them, they were a mark of effeminacy, of weakness, which he wouldn't acknowledge. I think all that macho stuff was compensation—all that chasing after women—compensation for something that he hadn't got, which his brother Joe had. Jack was a woman's man *and* a man's man. He wasn't as simple as Joe in that respect—he was a prism through which a lot of things would filter, and different lights would come out. He was very narcissistic, which is very characteristic of a gay person—incredibly so. If you know any homosexuals, you'll know how they are constantly looking in mirrors at themselves. Appearance is *very* important to them—and it was to Jack. I'd say, "Jack, it's *ridiculous* for you to go out in the sun like that! You just can't wait to get down to Florida to get your tan in the quickest time so you can come back and look so handsome at these parties you go to." And he'd say, "Well, Henry, it's not only that I want to look that way, but it makes me feel that way. It gives me confidence, it makes me feel healthy. It makes me feel strong, healthy, attractive."[38]

Adams is pointing out the logical implications of being a "man's man." Kennedy was playing a character who reflected his audience's ideas about what a man was more than his own innermost feelings and inclinations. Home movies of the Kennedy siblings and friends from just before Jack's stay at Stanford confirm Adams's observations about Jack's "feminine" aspects. Playing in and around the pool, Kennedy can be seen using his laughing charm to deal with roughhousing from brawnier companions, and then displaying his delicate body, wrapped at the waist in a towel, with a bright-eyed playfulness. Kennedy's narcissistic "work" at his macho persona and appearance was an understandable behavior of someone whose

28

sense of masculine identity had been undermined. In Kennedy's case the distinction between his poor physique and his attractive appearance was especially marked, as was the gulf between his inner psychology and his ability to project a winning personality, which had become evident as early as Kennedy's stay at the age of two-and-a-half with the nurses of Boston Hospital. Flip Price, one of Kennedy's girlfriends at Stanford, recalled how he once stopped the car in town and got out to throw his arms around one of his nurses, whom he had not seen in ten years.[39]

Kennedy left Stanford after the fall quarter and returned to the East Coast. He was convinced that the United States would eventually have to fight and he used his father's help to join the Navy despite his obvious inability to pass the usual physical examination. He made another intellectual friend, Charles "Chuck" Spalding, a Yale student who traded visits with Kennedy during summers at Cape Cod. Spalding has recalled that during this period Kennedy thought about Lord Byron a great deal;[40] he was convinced that Jack's fascination flowed from his recognition of parallels between himself and the romantic poet and early-nineteenth-century celebrity:

He'd read everything about him and read most of the poetry too. There were a lot of similarities. Byron too had that conflict between irony and romanticism; he too wanted the world to be better than it was; he also had the disability—the club foot—and the conviction of an early death; and most of all he had the hunger for women and the realization that the hunger was displaced, which led to a fed-upness too. The whole thing was more philosophical than physical.[41]

In *Reckless Youth*, Nigel Hamilton even speculates that Kennedy was drawn to combat in the Second World War by "the wayward urge to cut a figure—and to be seen to do so—that would bind him to his latest hero, Lord Byron, the roguish star of David Cecil's *The Young Melbourne*."[42]

Those biographers who have commented on *The Young Melbourne* have more often assumed that Kennedy was drawn to the book by admiration for the title character William Lamb, who became Lord Melbourne, and the world from which he emerged, the eighteenth-century landed gentry, the Whigs. But Kennedy's fascination with Byron would logically seem to have been a large factor in his love for the book. The subtitle of *The Young Melbourne* is *And the Story of his Marriage to Lady Caroline Lamb*. That story, which dominates the middle of the book, is primarily about

29

Byron's affair with Melbourne's wife and her subsequent deterioration. Cecil's description of Byron echoes both Spalding's comparison of Byron to Kennedy and Adams's analysis of Kennedy's narcissistic "performance" of masculinity:

Indeed, Byron at twenty-four was, in almost every respect, the opposite of the version of himself he sought to impose on the world. By nature acutely sensitive to the opinion of others, his confidence had been early undermined by his lame leg, his bullying, drunken mother and the poverty-stricken and provincial circumstances of his childhood. . . . [He had] an obsessing desire to make an impression on anyone by any means. . . . Byron had a robust eighteenth-century mocking kind of outlook. But the romantic attitude, by the scope it gave for individual self-glorification, gratified his egotism; and he could not resist adopting it.[43]

Kennedy first read these words at virtually the exact age of the man in the portrait. It is not difficult to see how he found in Byron, across the pages of history and literature, a sharer of his own dilemma—and a solution to it. With his sense of worth, well-being, and masculinity undermined by his own body and by a mother who could not hide her hostility toward him, Kennedy had drawn upon his talents for self-projection to put forward an image that made him notorious to authorities but admired by many of his peers.

If Kennedy's identification with Byron is a key to understanding his love for *The Young Melbourne*, the attitude of its narrator toward the romantic *poseur* suggests that Kennedy's stance was somewhat complicated. As Cecil chronicles Byron's cuckolding of the title character, which extends even to winning the friendship of Melbourne's mother during the course of the affair, he is constantly disapproving. He makes it clear that he finds Byron's and Caroline's theatrical antics a base self-indulgence compared to which Melbourne's passive tolerance gains dignity. Throughout the affair, we are told, "Alone among those closely concerned, he [Melbourne] realized the essential unreality of the situation. It was long since he had believed in Caroline's grand passions."[44] Cecil has already portrayed the young Melbourne as an idealist, drawn to the mystical idea of Britain's majestic history, who from his earliest youth developed an opposing skepticism about the motivations behind the fine words that people used to justify their actions. Cecil assures us that since Melbourne was "himself genuinely well-bred, genuinely detached, genuinely disillusioned, he was not taken in by Byron's pretence of these qualities."[45] The narrator gives Byron himself the task of comparing the two men, quoting the poet's exclamation that compared to him "William Lamb is as Hyperion to a satyr."[46]

When Byron breaks off the affair, Caroline descends into a sequence of increasingly childish attempts at returning to the public theater they had shared. Attempting to win him back, she plays a series of public pranks, such as having herself served under a silver tray at a dinner party Byron attends. When she sees that she is regarded as ridiculous, she retreats into her own chambers to write a wildly self-indulgent romantic novel. This literary narcissism is followed by tawdry reenactments of the Byron affair with a series of lovers. She transforms her bedroom into a stage setting of romantic caprice, and finally dies, a dark example of romantic disintegration. With the earlier exit of Byron and the death of Caroline, Melbourne survives their narcissistic self-dramatizations to become once again the central interest of the narrative.

Cecil's portrait of Melbourne corresponds to Kennedy in a number of ways. Like Kennedy, Melbourne grew up a detached, bookish youth in a household that favored action. Also like Kennedy, Melbourne is a second son who knows that the elder brother is the presumed future political leader. Therefore he has lived an indolent, detached early life of reading and observing while considering eventual literary pursuits.

If we compare the characters and events of *The Young Melbourne* and Kennedy's own situation during the early 1940s, the correspondences become yet more pronounced. In 1941, while serving in Naval Intelligence in Washington, D.C., Kennedy met Inga Arvad, a former Danish beauty queen who, while working as a journalist, had won the admiration of Hitler and other top Nazis. She had been Hitler's guest at the 1936 Olympic Games in Berlin. This sensuous, sophisticated, and alluring woman was several years Kennedy's senior, and was working on a Washington newspaper with Kennedy's sister Kathleen. Once introduced, she and Jack quickly became involved in an affair. It seems to have been the one truly passionate love affair of Kennedy's life, but it was dangerous and tumultuous. Because of Arvad's Nazi associations, the FBI regarded her with suspicion. Her involvement with an intelligence officer hardly allayed their concerns, and agents secretly tape-recorded Kennedy and Arvad's bedroom conversations. Kennedy's father became determined to break up the affair. Although the couple were discussing marriage, when confronted by his father Jack reverted to his macho stance, calling Arvad "something I picked up on the road."[47]

The evidence indicates that Jack's eventual breakup with "Inga-Binga," as he called her, came despite his addiction to her maternal solicitude and sexually experienced love. To her he even confided his secret dream of climbing to the White House, an idea she encouraged.[48] His father's demands and his own strong skepticism about romance and idealism appear to have caused Jack to withstand Arvad's allure and to let the affair diminish by failing to make a commitment.

This crucial experience in Kennedy's life mirrors his identification with the two male protagonists of *The Young Melbourne*. Both Byron and Melbourne distrust romance. Kennedy could see himself reenacting Byron's stance, pursuing romance's delights while refusing to give himself over to it completely. For both, the attitude and its accompanying escapades must be a pose. And while Kennedy was obviously drawn to Byron's talents for self-projection, he was pulled in the opposite direction by the desire to prove himself a man of action. Similarly, Melbourne had been bookish, but the death of his older brother shortly before the Byron affair unexpectedly gives him political prospects.

With the publication of *Why England Slept*, Jack Kennedy had not replaced Joe Jr. as the focus of his family's political ambitions. Nevertheless, the growing appreciation of Joe Sr. for his second son's talents, and the acclaim of reviewers and other influential elders, had given Jack reason to believe his interest in government might not be impossible to pursue. When in 1944 his older brother Joe died in a fiery explosion over the English Channel, the similarity between the young Lord Melbourne's situation at the end of the book and Kennedy's own must have seemed truly eerie. Both were second sons, bookish and detached, who found fate turning them into heirs apparent with political prospects. Both had survived dangerous affairs. Kennedy identified as strongly with the cuckolder as with the cuckolded in this respect, and like Byron would go on to feed his narcissistic needs with countless romantic intrigues. But his other half, the Melbourne half, would serve a political philosophy, marked by a conservative respect for tradition and order, that emphasized the need for progressive adaptation to change. In *The Young Melbourne* we can read a mirror image of the deeper workings of Kennedy's conflicted psyche, seeing a Byron and a Melbourne offering solutions within his mind to the alluring urge toward rebellious attention-getting, represented by Caroline.

When in 1943 Kennedy transferred to PT boats and was on his way to the South Pacific, he recommended his other favorite book to his fellow young

32

officers. One of them, James Reed, recalled how much Kennedy talked about John Buchan's *Pilgrim's Way* and about one of the book's heroes. Reed tells us that Kennedy greatly admired Raymond Asquith, a prime minister's son who died in the Great War.[49] In *A Thousand Days*, Arthur Schlesinger notes that Kennedy included two quotations describing Asquith's death in a looseleaf notebook he kept in 1945. One of them was from *Pilgrim's Way*:

He loved his youth, and his youth has become eternal. Debonair and brilliant and brave, he is now part of that immortal England which knows not age or weariness or defeat.[50]

In *A Hero for Our Time*, Ralph Martin reports further evidence of Kennedy's fascination with Asquith. Chuck Spalding, who was so impressed by Kennedy's fascination with Byron, also "never forgot how often Jack Kennedy talked about Raymond Asquith, quoted him, described him, discussed him." David Ormsby-Gore was convinced that "Whether Jack realized it or not, I think he paralleled himself after Asquith all the way, I really do."[51]

Buchan's description of Asquith takes up only several pages of *Pilgrim's Way*. It is perhaps the most memorable portrait in a virtual album of brilliant young men whom Buchan elegizes. All are young aristocrats who served the British Empire at various outposts or on the Western Front and who met premature deaths. One of them is T. E. Lawrence, or "Lawrence of Arabia," whom Buchan tells us was surprisingly diminutive in appearance but, "as boxers say, he stripped well."[52] We know that in the early 1940s Kennedy also read Lawrence's *Seven Pillars of Wisdom*.[53]

Throughout his life Kennedy had been afflicted with illnesses and debilitation. Since prep school he had especially suffered from a mysterious wasting disease that doctors were at a loss to diagnose. Acutely concerned with his appearance and his masculine image, Kennedy had compensated for his lack of athletic prowess with sexual conquests. Suffering as well from his strained relationship with his mother, he had been reluctant, perhaps even unable, to give himself wholly to a love relationship with a woman. He had instead surrounded himself with young male friends, most of whom were athletic or in other respects strongly masculine. Their comradeship reinforced his own sense of masculinity, provided him with companionship that did not threaten his autonomy, and acted as a counterbalance to the influence of his father and family.

33

In Buchan's portraits of wonderful young men dying in the service of the British Empire, Kennedy was presented with a fused image of his peculiar experience of physical violation, sexual need, and masculine aspiration. Buchan's elegiac prose echoes British poetry of the Great War. In the work of Rupert Brooke, Siegfried Sassoon, Wilfrid Owen, and Robert Graves, as Adrian Caesar has observed, "an ideal is made of beautiful male youth self-sacrificed in battle."[54] This ideal, an expression of an ideology formed in the Victorian and Edwardian ages, parallels the ideologies of Christianity, imperialism, and Romanticism, each of which promotes self-sacrifice and pain as necessary to the achievement of a "true," which is to say chaste, love. Christianity holds up a young man crucified as its image of the highest love, and urges the martyrdom of the flesh; each man must take up his cross. Romanticism turns art and love into a religion, idealizing the artist who suffers for his art and for a Platonic, or nearly Platonic, love affair. During the Victorian period the British Empire transformed this ethic into an ideal of service in the far-flung regions of the earth.

In each of these overlaid ideologies, sexual repression is paramount. The English public schools segregated young men and women while also denigrating effeminacy and homosexuality. In place of what today we would consider a healthy sexuality, "the idealism inculcated by the English public schools, which had its basis in Christianity, gave rise to a code of 'manliness' immediately before the First World War which actively encouraged and rejoiced in pain."[55] Caesar concludes that the idealization of sadomasochism held especially strong appeal for anyone who felt compelled by his society to hate his sexual preference.

Caesar is speaking of homosexuals, but the same logic would apply to someone as conflicted over his body and its desires as John Kennedy. He had received strongly contradictory signals on sexuality from his family. His father told him there was sex and there was marriage, and made a point of degrading women to him; Kennedy once came home from school to find that his father had laid out pornographic magazines over his bed, open to pictures of women's genitalia. His mother, speaking for the Church, had early stressed the sacrifice of Jesus and the Saints. The young Kennedy's intimate friends inferred that he knew that his skirt-chasing was "displaced," a futile attempt to satisfy the longing for warmth and intimacy withheld by his mother and to prove the manhood that his body failed to realize on the athletic field. His body had from the earliest age been the site of humiliation by other males (his older brother most of all), but also of female devotion. The bed became a setting for humiliation and compensation, especially during his prep school years when he was subjected to the procedures performed by doctors and nurses.

In the early deaths of war heroes in *Pilgrim's Way*, Kennedy could see male beauty preserved by death, a narcissistic, admired masculine image ennobled by self-sacrifice for a great cause. On his way to the South Pacific, Kennedy was in a somewhat different situation from most of the men around him. While he enjoyed enormous advantages of wealth, he journeyed toward war with considerable reason to believe that an early death, or perhaps a debilitated life, awaited him if he survived to return home. Kennedy was hardly suicidal in his intent, but his recommendations of *Pilgrim's Way* to his fellow officers reflected his love of a book that depicted suffering and death in war in achingly beautiful, even homoerotic, terms—as an achievement of a masculine nobility that could never be lost.

John Kennedy would always carry with him the insecurities that developed from the clash between his inadequate body and a demanding family. He would also carry his solution, in both its destructive and creative forms, with him into his political career. He would pursue sexual intrigue and conquest in private, while adopting a public pose that reflected fantasies adopted in compensation for his inadequacies more than his perception of his innermost self. Both in bed and on the podium, Kennedy would be a performer. This Byronic need to play the hero and celebrity would be countered by his Melbourne-like profound skepticism and sincere idealism. His identification with the heroes of British history would be translated into his vision of America as the legitimate successor to the Empire as defender of freedom in the world.

Buchan acknowledged the imminent passing of the torch to America in a late chapter of *Pilgrim's Way*. He had unknowingly prepared the young man who would be his most significant reader for that conclusion through his nearly homoerotic portraits of beautiful young men dying. Coming into manhood as America headed toward world war at Britain's side, Kennedy could pleasurably see his ideal self in these spectral forms. His own suffering in sickbeds, from his earliest childhood to his subjection to humiliating "tests" seeking to uncover his fundamental weakness, was mirrored by the destruction of youth in the Great War. His attempts to feel worthwhile by looking strong and healthy were reflected in Buchan's aesthetically rendered images of heroes.

Kennedy nearly did die in the South Pacific. But he would live to tell

35

his tale to someone who would tell it again, placing Jack Kennedy within a text where fact, literature, and myth intermingled. The image of Kennedy as a young man narrowly escaping death in war would prove as resonant for readers of Kennedy-as-hero as his British heroes had for Kennedy himself.

CHAPTER TWO

John Hersey's "Survival": A Literary Experiment and Its Political Adaptation

In the South Pacific, at about 2:30 a.m. on August 2, 1943, the PT boat commanded by John F. Kennedy was cut in half by a Japanese destroyer. The exact circumstances of this disaster have never been satisfactorily explained, and the incident constituted the only loss of a PT boat to the enemy during the Second World War. But Kennedy's feats of endurance and daring in the aftermath helped save a crewmate and kept alive hope until the crew was rescued.

In 1944 John Hersey wrote an account of Kennedy's climactic war experience that was published in *The New Yorker* as "Survival." Shortly thereafter a condensation appeared in *Reader's Digest*. *Why England Slept* had positioned Kennedy in the public eye as a capable young scholar whose seriousness was perhaps representative of the younger generation's response to the world crisis. But "Survival" authored Kennedy as a hero. Hersey's article was the literary work that would be adapted into the script for Kennedy's first campaign for Congress in 1946, and it would be similarly used in his campaign for the Senate in 1952. Subsequent writers' accounts of Kennedy's war experience and character would most often be based on "Survival." Hersey's article would continue to be essential as Kennedy and his collaborators developed his image on the journey toward the White House.

In 1975 Joan and Clay Blair documented how the article came to be written and evaluated it according to their own subsequent research of Kennedy's war record. While excerpting from or summarizing Hersey's writing in "Survival," Kennedy biographers have occasionally noted its high literary quality, but no one has ever examined the text as a journalistic and literary experiment.[1] Yet the merger of literary and journalistic effects in "Survival," combined with its transformation by Kennedy's father into an artifact of mass culture, is the true beginning of the production of John F. Kennedy as a popular hero. In his first campaign for Congress, Kennedy would merge with the "Kennedy" of Hersey's text to become a popular myth.

"Survival" is an early experiment with a genre, later to become highly influential, in which a writer presents factual material through methods developed by fiction writers. *The New Yorker*, which published "Survival," would become a major venue for this movement, publishing other famous examples by Hersey as well as by Lillian Ross and Truman Capote. Such techniques as manipulation of point of view, presentation of setting, and development of theme are practiced, ostensibly without any inventive or imaginative additions by the author. These techniques offered writers such as Hersey the possibility of conveying actual human experience in a more powerful and meaningful way than the formulas of conventional journalism, as practiced in the mid-twentieth-century United States, allowed. In the 1960s this journalistic practice would broaden into the genre known as the Nonfiction Novel or New Journalism.

The first importance of Hersey's text in the creation of the Kennedy hero is that reading it means identifying with its protagonist, a literary character through whom the reader can share the experiences described in the narrative. This identification results from the fictionlike construction of the text as a self-contained experience occurring in the reader's head as the text is read. But at the same time the reader understands the text to be journalism. Therefore the reader knows the character "Kennedy"'s experiences — more precisely, Hersey's verbal and narrative construct representing Kennedy's own report of his responses and actions — as the subjective experiences of an actual person outside the text. The writer can thus produce a feeling of intimacy between a reader and the actual person who is the subject of the narrative.[2]

Inviting this identification, "Survival" presents Kennedy in the mode of a familiar mythic figure. In the course of the narrative, "Kennedy," and with him the reader, undergoes a transcultural pattern of initiation and transformation analogous to rituals by which cultures bring members through a passage to new identities within the world. In the production of John F. Kennedy, "Survival" is a narrative experience made possible by the vehicle of a mythic hero, not a simple celebration of a "war hero." In Hersey's text Kennedy is the means by which the reader undergoes a set of literary operations creating an experience of deeply mythic resonance. In 1946 readers in Kennedy's congressional district in Boston would bring this experience, felt internally but perceived as that of the man before them, to Kennedy's performances as candidate.

The Blairs have fully demonstrated the role of celebrity in the early fanfare in the press surrounding the crew's rescue. The newsworthiness of a son of the ex-ambassador led the senior officers of the PT base at Rendova to contact an Associated Press reporter and a United Press reporter, both of whom rushed to the scene of the rescue and made Kennedy's role the lead. The rescue of the crew of PT 109 would not have been a front-page story in the *New York Times* if the ex-ambassador's son had not been a "minicelebrity" already. Certainly the newspaper would not have proclaimed him a "hero" in the headline.[3]

When he had been notified that Jack was "missing in action," Joe Kennedy had kept the wire in his pocket, not informing Rose or the other children. When four days later the news came on the car radio that Jack was rescued, Joe nearly ran off the road. Proceeding home, he was greeted by Rose, who had heard the news of the rescue without ever having known her son was missing, and they fell into each other's arms.[4] Soon after the exhilaration of learning that Jack had been rescued, Joe Kennedy became determined to exploit the event. He attempted to interest *Reader's Digest* in his son's experience, apparently sharing a long letter from Jack with an editor.[5]

Returned to the United States, Kennedy went to the theater on a double date with John Hersey and Hersey's wife, Kennedy's former girlfriend Frances. After his arrival in the South Pacific the year before, Kennedy had written to his sister Kathleen about how impressed he was by a *Life* article Hersey had written about PT boats, which he found far superior to the "Wild West" stuff of *They Were Expendable*, the book that had glamorized the small, speedy crafts. In the next breath, he ruefully compared himself to the man who had won the beautiful and intelligent young woman he had wanted to marry: "Speaking of John Hersey, I see his new book 'Into the Valley' is doing well. He's sitting on top of the hill at this point—a best seller—my girl, two kids—big man on *Time*—while I'm the one that's down in the God damned valley."[6]

At the time of the theater performance and the group's drinks at the Stork Club afterward, Kennedy's erstwhile rival was indeed an established writer who had already emerged from work as a *Time-Life* writer to produce two books of war reportage, *Men on Bataan* (1942) and *Into the Valley* (1943). That same week, his first novel, *A Bell for Adano* (1944), had been published (the following year it would be awarded the Pulitzer Prize). Kennedy related some of the PT boat misadventure to Hersey. Intrigued, Hersey asked if he could write an account of it for *Life* magazine. After consulting with his father, Kennedy agreed the next day, on the condition that Hersey first talk to members of Kennedy's crew. When Hersey reported back to Kennedy that the crew thought highly of him, Jack consented to the project.

His stomach ulcers and deteriorating spine forced Kennedy to go to New England Baptist Hospital for a month-long series of tests to determine if a major operation would be needed. In February Hersey visited him in his room. Since their initial talk Kennedy had experienced the contrast between war stories told by civilians and his own knowledge of the reality of war. He had as a result become more enthusiastic about Hersey's interest in a war story that would be a tale of human survival rather than a celebration of killing. According to Hersey's recollection, the interview proceeded over a long afternoon and evening, with Kennedy drawing maps of the area and of the route of his nighttime swim in search of help.

By the first week of March, Hersey had completed the story and submitted it to *Life*.[7] The magazine rejected it, probably because it was quite long and because the subject was no longer timely. Soon after, however, *The New Yorker* accepted it. The story would be Hersey's first publication in the prestigious magazine, but he found Kennedy disappointed and assumed it was because *Life* would have "been a better vehicle for him." Kennedy's father was in fact dismayed at the loss of a mass-market publication. Hersey's lengthy account of Kennedy's and his crew's ordeal appeared under the title "Survival" in the June 17th issue of *The New Yorker*, in the department labeled "A Reporter at Large."[8]

40

"Survival" is an experiment in the application of methods of representation associated with fiction to strictly journalistic subject matter. It was Hersey's rehearsal for the task he would take on two years later in *Hiroshima* (1946), his classic account of six survivors of the first use of the atomic bomb. Hersey himself has testified that his interest in this experiment inspired his writing of "Survival." Interviewed thirty years later by Joan and Clay Blair, Hersey summed up his motivations in writing the piece by stating that "I was then interested in using novelistic techniques in journalism."[9] The experimental form of "Survival," Hersey speculated, might have been one of the reasons that *Life* rejected the story.[10]

In an interview in the *Paris Review*, Hersey would elaborate on the positive value he saw in using devices appropriated from fiction, as long as the journalistic promise not to invent was kept. His primary emphasis was that with these devices he and other journalists in the 1940s had begun "making it more possible for readers to identify with the figures and the events about which they were writing. The fictional mode made it easier for the reader to imagine that these events were happening to him." Stating that he had felt dissatisfied as a conventional journalist because "the writer is always mediating between the material and the reader," Hersey explained that "my hope was, by using the tricks and the ways of fiction, to be able to eliminate that mediation and have the reader directly confronted by the characters. In this case, my hope was that the reader would be able to become the characters enough to suffer some of the pain, some of the disaster, and therefore realize it."

When asked what some of the "tricks" he employed were, Hersey emphasized first the presentation of characters through a depiction of their point of view. He described how *Hiroshima* "enters each survivor's state of mind without representing his thoughts—it's all done in terms of action, of what happened to them, what they saw, heard, and did. The reader looks at what is happening through the eyes of each of these characters, as he would through a point of view in fiction."[11]

Besides the opportunity to apply novelistic techniques to journalism, Hersey was drawn to Kennedy's narrated experience by its correlation with a story he already carried around in his own head. "Survival" looks forward to the theme of human survival of disaster that pervades *Hiroshima*. Many years later Hersey would include "Survival" in a retrospective collection of his work he called *Here to Stay* (1963). Hersey saw in Kennedy's oral narrative a means for refracting a theme that he had written about before and would write about again.

A central fascination of Hersey's throughout his literary career was how and why humans survive. This is the great theme of both Hersey's journalistic and fictional work, and he explicitly stated to the Blairs that it was what drew him to write the story:

41

What appealed to me about the Kennedy story was the night in the water, his account of floating in the current, being brought back to the same point from which he'd drifted off. It was the kind of theme that has fascinated me always about human survival, as manifested in the title of the piece. It was really that aspect of it that interested me, rather than his heroics. The aspect of fate that threw him into a current and brought him back again. And that sort of dream-like quality. His account of it is very strange. A nightmarish thing altogether.[12]

Hersey's interest in Kennedy's "nightmarish" experience adrift in the water clearly resulted from personal preoccupations. His focus on that experience in "Survival" is part of the process by which Hersey infuses Kennedy's original experience with his own feelings and ideas.

At a later point in the *Paris Review* interview, Hersey emphasized the crucial role of the writer's own memory in the success of the fiction he is writing: "The things that have worked best for me have been the things that really mattered in some deep way to me." He elaborated on how the narrative material must elicit from the author a deeper pattern in his own experience:

I don't mean by that that the substance of the book has to come from what the author remembers; but it seems to me important that the fiction should have the kind of relationship to the writer's memory that dreams may have. The dream material doesn't often seem to have any direct source in the person's life, but it must have been constructed from what the writer remembers. So I think a measure of the power of a work lies in the depth of the memory that is drawn on to fabricate the surface of the work.[13]

This role of the writer's deeper memory is another, perhaps the most important, of the "tricks" of fiction Hersey and other literary journalists employ.

Kennedy's own telling of his experience to Hersey, with the inevitably selective details and emotions of retrospective memory, would also necessarily have transformed the original experience. For that matter, the childhood and adolescent experiences Jack brought forward to events chronicled in "Survival" would themselves have affected his thoughts, feelings, and perceptions. "Survival" is logically a compound of Kennedy's deeper memory and Hersey's, as much as of the facts of the experience. The text is what it is because each man found in the experience a story that elicited deeper stories already resonating in his consciousness.

The same is true for those readers—voters—who apparently found "Survival" a text that could both delight and instruct. In part this effect was calculated by both Kennedy as storyteller and Hersey as writer, since both would have reasons to censor and shape the material presented to the reader. Transforming material into a story with an eye on the reader means making sure the story conforms to others that already exist in the culture and comprise the boundaries of its ideology. For Kennedy this would keep his "character" safe from being scorned or rejected by a reader. For Hersey it would lessen the odds of his text being similarly treated.

The "Kennedy" of "Survival" is an entity, actually an experience, formed by the triangle of subject, writer, and reader. John F. Kennedy emerges as a hero in the point of intersection where his memory meets Hersey's and then the product of that meeting encounters the memory of each reader.

Subsequent authors, especially the Blairs, have subjected Hersey's text to intense scrutiny concerning its factual accuracy. The main attack mounted by the Blairs focuses on selection. They complain that Hersey tells of Kennedy's survival of a disaster, rather than of his undistinguished record leading to the disaster. They also object that he tells Kennedy's story rather than any of a great number of others from the war in the South Pacific that they feel were objectively more interesting and dramatic. And finally, the Blairs note that Hersey suggests that the crew were given up for dead by the base back at Rendova, when in fact reasonable efforts were being made to watch for any survivors. But it is precisely through such selection and focus that Hersey's text combines the materials of Kennedy's experience into a more universal experience of passage and transformation, thus offering the reader a story that correlates with a deep cultural memory. And this story begins the construction of John F. Kennedy as a public image of fictionlike, even mythic, resonance.

In *The Ritual Process: Structure and Anti-Structure*, anthropologist Victor Turner focuses on what he calls the "liminal phase." Any rite of passage involves three phases: separation, margin (or *limen*, signifying "threshold"), and aggregation. During the liminal period, the "passenger" journeys through a cultural realm lacking most aspects of either the past or the future state. The person in this liminal state is typically made to endure certain conditions—nakedness or near-nakedness, a passive acceptance of pain and suffering as one is "reduced or ground down" in obedience to an instructor or instructors—all in preparation for being "fashioned anew." The fundamental significance Turner finds in this crosscultural process is

43

that traces of the "transient humility" of the experience carry over to temper the pride of the officeholder who emerges from this phase. Turner points out that his readers will recognize this ritualistic process in their own culture in rites of religious initiation.

Hersey's transformation of Kennedy's actual experience into a literary experience of liminality for the reader in no way precludes the actual experience's having been liminal for Kennedy himself. We will return to the issue of the actual Kennedy's experience (which is a matter of his perception as much as of his actions). But the liminality of the reading experience depends on Hersey's construction of his narrative (and, in the end, on the reader's perception of it).

The crucial fact that biographers and other commentators on Kennedy have overlooked in discussing Hersey's text as a contribution to Kennedy's political career is that "Survival" is not a tale of stock heroism. Hersey himself called it "a case of trying to tell a story that had some reverberations beyond just a hero handling himself well."[14] Kennedy is certainly the hero of the tale in the literary sense, the protagonist. That has more subtle, though in the end more profound, implications for Kennedy's significance as a political "hero" outside the text. It is the transforming experience that the protagonist Kennedy, and with him the reader, undergoes in the text that is significant to the image of the Kennedy outside it.

That the text of "Survival" is the author's dreamlike imagining of a story told to him is suggested in the first sentence of the narrative proper. Hersey reports: "It seems that Kennedy's PT, the 109, was out one night with a squadron patrolling Blackett Strait, in mid-Solomons." The opening "It seems" is a convention by which a storyteller claims to be retelling a tale that he or she has been told by another person. The phrase also suggests that there will be a quality of wonder to the tale, warranting a suspension of one's normal parameters of experience. Most literally, "seems" is a synonym for "appears." With the vague setting in time of the phrase "one night," which echoes the fairy-tale opening "once upon a time," the introductory sentence takes on the quality of fable. The opening suggests that the text is created by someone retelling a tale he has heard, and therefore is not unlike a fairy tale, in which a long process of retelling has distilled the universal level of significance from a wondrous adventure.

The story that Hersey proceeds to narrate resembles, and is perhaps consciously modeled upon, such canonical tales of American literature as Edgar Allan Poe's "A Descent into the Maelstrom" and Stephen Crane's

"The Open Boat." Like those stories, "Survival" is a tale of disaster and survival at sea. That essential narrative enables Hersey to explore human behavior under extreme pressure, examining the nature of nature, of humanity's position in it, and of what emerges as of true value after such a primal confrontation with annihilation. In the opening sentence of his journalistic frame tale, Hersey has already told the reader that "our men in the South Pacific fight nature, when they are pitted against her, with a greater fierceness than they could ever expend on a human enemy." He has thus informed the reader that the specific characters and events of the story should be read as signifiers of a universal struggle that he is figuring according to the cultural script of an ideology that sees humanity as "men" and nature as "her." The story he presents is indeed about a struggle to resist the force of an overwhelming and capricious nature that threatens to emasculate, repossess, and annihilate a young man desperate both to survive and to help his crew survive.

The narrative begins with a devastating experience of the overwhelming power of nature. PT 109 and the other boats of their squadron "had entered Blackett Strait, as was their habit." The word "habit" suggests an assertion of willful pattern, a certain human arrogance. Hersey emphasizes the ominous blankness that the PT boats have brashly entered, reinforcing the name "Blackett" with his description of a "night that was a starless black." Aware that Japanese destroyers are in this seeming void, PT 109 is "leading three boats on a sweep for a target." But a destroyer emerges from the darkness and cuts PT 109 in half. Hersey narrates this disaster in terms emphasizing the crew's experience of complete helplessness before an overpowering force. Kennedy "was thrown hard to the left in the cockpit, and he thought, 'This is how it feels to be killed.' In a moment he found himself on his back on the deck, looking up at the destroyer as it passed through his boat." The engineer McMahon, down below the deck, "was just reaching forward to slam the starboard engine into gear when a ship came into his engine room." This engineer is "lifted" by the force of the invading machine and lands "in a sitting position." When a fiery explosion comes toward him, he "put his hands over his face, drew his legs up tight, and waited to die." Water hits McMahon after the fire, sucking him downward with his half of the boat, and he struggles up through the sea holding his breath, "so his lungs were tight and they hurt." Johnston, an engineer asleep on deck, is lifted and dropped over the side: "Then a huge propeller pounded by near him and the awful turbulence of the destroyer's wake took him down, turned him over and over, held him down, shook him, and

45

drubbed on his ribs." In the aftermath of this chaos "The destroyer rushed off into the dark."

The experiences of Kennedy, McMahon, and Johnston—narrated in rapid succession—register in the reader's "depth of memory" as a nightmarish reenactment of the birth experience. Each character is unable to resist a powerful force that has suddenly ripped him from his complacency: Kennedy can only watch the destroyer's "inverted-Y stack" in a "brilliant light"; McMahon places himself in a fetal position, closes his eyes, and holds his breath; and Johnston is turned upside down and "drubbed" violently. These experiences of gazing up at a strange new world, of waiting out a violent passage, and of undergoing a shocking blow collectively reenact the reader's deepest, if wholly unconscious, memory—that of being taken from the mother to life. By so figuring the crash, Hersey establishes imagery with which he constructs the story in the pattern of a "fight" between "our men" and a "nature" that is their mother. With the violence of their original separation from nature, the men are now separated from "us," the society that is logically their father, a "he" who organized them into a crew and within a machine that sought to reenter nature in a controlling move. Instead, the result is a terrifying return to the helplessness of infancy.

In the immediate aftermath of the crash, Kennedy and other members of the crew save the seriously injured among them, cling to the floating half of the wreck, and await their rescue by the squadron. But Hersey, in his narrative omniscience, informs the reader that "the other boats had no idea of coming back." Believing that PT 109 and her crew have been utterly destroyed, they have "turned away." Back at the base, according to Hersey, "the squadron held services for the souls of the thirteen men, and one of the officers wrote his mother, 'George Ross lost his life for a cause that he believed in stronger than any one of us, because he was an idealist in the purest sense. Jack Kennedy, the Ambassador's son, was on the same boat and also lost his life. The man that said the cream of a nation is lost in war can never be accused of making an overstatement of a very cruel fact. . . .'"

Literally dead to the world, the crew look around the next day to find themselves adrift amid islands where they know "Japanese swarmed" and upon a wrecked hulk that they realize is gradually sinking. After ordering the men to stay as low as possible, Kennedy asks if they want to fight or surrender in the event that the Japanese come out for them. Told that he is the boss, he replies: "There's nothing in the book about a situation like this. Seems to me we're not a military organization any more. Let's just talk this over." Kennedy thus asserts that the men are now outside the "book," the law or structure of their culture (the military).

Kennedy's first instinct is to give up command in favor of a conversation out of which a *communitas* of equal individuals can form a collective judgment. But "pretty soon they argued, and Kennedy could see that they would never survive in anarchy." Kennedy retakes command when he sees that human nature, like the external nature in which they are afloat, is characterized by conflicting patterns and impulses rather than any clear purpose. He has no choice but to bring back the military structure. Determining that they must leave the listing hulk for an island that appears uninhabited by the Japanese, Kennedy organizes a three-mile swim. Pulling the badly burned McMahon by means of a life-jacket strap in his teeth, Kennedy swims breaststroke for five hours, regularly swallowing salt water.

By the time they reach land, they have spent fifteen and a half hours in the water. But Kennedy calculates that their best chance for rescue is for him to swim back out into Ferguson Passage, where the PT boats have been ordered for several consecutive nights and, he assumes, will be again. But his effort to return to the larger structure of his military squadron instead continues the pattern of a reverse birth journey in which the crash has been figured. Kennedy first strips nude, leaving on only a pair of shoes and a rubber life belt. He then hangs a .38 pistol around his neck on a lanyard and picks up the ship's lantern, instructing his men that he will use it to signal them if he finds a PT boat. Kennedy thus enters the water wearing only the most necessary tools, stripped down to the barest form of culture.

The journey is a passage through pain and fear. Kennedy begins in early evening, and after a half hour of swimming reaches the reef of a neighboring island. Stumbling along in four feet of water, he sees "the shape of a very big fish." He frightens it away with his lantern and hard splashes upon the water: "Kennedy remembered what one of his men had said a few days before, 'These barracuda will come up under a swimming man and eat his testicles.' He had many occasions to think of that remark in the next few hours." This frightening return to mother nature thus includes a most literal threat of emasculation. Hersey's use of Hemingwayesque understatement not only conveys the unimaginable weight of Kennedy's fear but evokes comparisons between this experience and the theme of overcoming threats to one's masculinity characteristic of the famous author's stories.

Hersey's account emphasizes Kennedy's increasing lack of control over his body: "Now it was dark. Kennedy blundered along the uneven reef in water up to his waist. Sometimes he would reach forward with his leg and

47

cut one of his shins or ankles on sharp coral. Other times he would step forward onto emptiness. He made his way like a slow-motion drunk, hugging the lantern." After determining that the boats have apparently taken another route, Kennedy starts back. Exhausted, and in a current now running fast, he is unable to make the shore and futilely flashes his lantern at the crew. At this point he has an experience that in Hersey's narration is reminiscent of that of the fisherman-protagonist of Poe's "A Descent into the Maelstrom," drawn into a whirling vortex in the ocean:

Kennedy had drifted right by the little island. He thought he had never known such deep trouble, but something he did shows that unconsciously he had not given up hope. He dropped his shoes, but he held onto the heavy lantern, his symbol of contact with his fellows. He stopped trying to swim. He seemed to stop caring. His body drifted through the wet hours, and he was very cold. His mind was a jumble. A few hours before he had wanted desperately to get to the base at Rendova. Now he only wanted to get back to the little island he had left that night, but he didn't try to get there; he just wanted to. His mind seemed to float away from his body. Darkness and time took the place of a mind in his skull. For a long time he slept, or was crazy, or floated in a chill trance.

This passage completes Kennedy's experience of being drawn by an irresistible nature into the annihilating unity of death. His heroic efforts to restore his original connection to the community have failed, and he is inexorably pulled into a larger pattern defined by nature. Only his embrace of the lantern shows that he resists that pattern when all his conscious will is gone. At this point the lantern is arguably the least useful of his tools, but it proves that there is a community with which to communicate, that he retains a tie beyond the annihilating current. For Poe's protagonist, the key to survival is the retention of a ratiocinative power of observation enabling him to calculate a means for survival (he sees that a log that goes with the whirling pattern is eventually sent back up to the surface, and thus recognizes a strategy for himself). But Hersey sees in Kennedy's experience that ultimately the chance for survival comes from the sense of a tie to the community established with others. Kennedy is sustained only by his sense of a link to his wrecked crew. Hersey's treatment of this scene, while it evokes Poe's story in the terms with which it figures the crisis, moves toward the vision of Crane's "The Open Boat," which posits human community in opposition to an indifferent, capricious universe:

The currents of the Solomon Islands are queer. The tide shoves and sucks through the islands and makes the currents curl in odd patterns. It was a fateful pattern into which Jack Kennedy drifted. He drifted in it all night. His mind was blank, but his fist was tightly clenched on the kapok around the lantern. The current moved in a huge circle—west past Gizo, then north and east past Kolombangara, then south into Ferguson Passage. Early in the morning the sky turned from black to gray, and so did Kennedy's mind. Light came to both at about six. Kennedy looked around and saw that he was exactly where he had been the night before when he saw the flares beyond Gizo. For a second time, he started home. He thought for a while that he had lost his mind and that he only imagined that he was repeating his attempt to reach the island. But the chill of the water was real enough, the lantern was real, his progress was measurable.

Kennedy thus returns to the "rational" perception, itself no more real than the mystical one he had in the night, that the universe is separate from him, an entity in which time and distance are "measurable." Vomiting on shore when his crewmates reach him, he tells his second-in-command, "Ross, you try it tonight," before passing out.

Hersey's portrayal of Ross, in its rugged credibility, functions as a foil for Kennedy. The reader has learned earlier that Ross is perceived by the letter writer as a pure idealist. Here, seeing Kennedy so sick, Ross is a realist who has little desire to follow Kennedy's example. He makes a halfhearted attempt that night—which Hersey summarizes in a few sentences—but only after a lengthier and more pungent account of Ross's attempt to fortify himself with food. When the men are too tired to climb the trees for coconuts, one of them finds a snail on the beach: "He said, 'If we were desperate, we could eat these.' Ross said, 'Desperate, hell. Give me that. I'll eat that.' He took it in his hand and looked at it. The snail put its head out and looked at him. Ross was startled, but he shelled the snail and ate it, making faces because it was bitter." Hersey's description replaces the revulsion of Ross, a civilized human being, at the prospect of eating a raw snail with the underlying repulsiveness of a human being exchanging a face-to-face look with another living creature, however low in the chain of being, and then eating it. But the "idealist" overcomes his "startled" confrontation and matter-of-factly devours the low life form, complaining only that it is "bitter." The man and snail reverse the earlier confrontation of barracuda and man during Kennedy's night-sea journey, ironically suggesting that nature is a creature-eat-creature realm in which the only "good" is the ability to survive.

49

This grim vision is elaborated on in the next section of the story, which opens with the announcement that "the next morning everyone felt wretched" and narrates the third day of the aftermath of the crash, describing a state of increasing desperation. The men hide from overflying planes because they see that the planes are fighting, and thus some are Japanese. Some of the men pray, eliciting the anger of Johnston because they were previously indifferent to religion. Kennedy leads them to another island, again towing McMahon with a strap in his teeth, because it appears to have more coconut trees and is nearer Ferguson Passage. The swim takes three hours, and Kennedy finds walking on the island to meet the other members of the crew even worse than the swim because his wounds from the cuts on the coral have festered. But all of the men's efforts seem mocked by nature. Suffering most from thirst, Kennedy and McMahon avidly drink coconut milk and become sick. The heavens seem actually perverse. When it rains in the night, the men crawl into the trees to lick water off the leaves, but they become separated in the dark and frightened that each other's shape might actually be a Japanese. In the morning they discover that the leaves were covered not only with rain but also with bird droppings; "Bitterly, they named the place Bird Island." The purpose of the section is to suggest a power indifferently showering life-giving water and poisoning waste.

In the next section, narrating the fourth day, we are told that the men "were low" and that Johnston "had changed his mind about praying," encouraging the Catholic McGuire to use the rosary hanging around his neck. But Kennedy is "still unwilling to admit that things were hopeless." He proposes to Ross that they swim to an island called Nauru, which is yet closer to Ferguson Passage and the possibility of rescue. There they see two men by a Japanese barge. The men apparently see Kennedy and Ross, and hurriedly paddle away from the island in a dugout canoe. After hiding from imagined Japanese all day, Kennedy leaves Ross to return to the crew with some Japanese provisions he and Ross have found. There he learns that the two men were natives, who had paddled to Bird Island and told the crew that there were Japanese on Nauru. When before dawn Kennedy goes back in a canoe to rejoin Ross, his boat is swamped and he is rescued from drowning by more natives who appear "from nowhere." Kennedy carves a message on a coconut and tells them "Rendova, Rendova."

Feeling exhausted and ill, Kennedy and Ross lie on the island for the rest of the day until, "When it got dark, conscience took hold of Kennedy and he persuaded Ross to go out into Ferguson Passage with him in the two-man canoe." Ross argues against the idea, and goes only on Kennedy's insistence. On the water, they struggle for two hours with a tide threatening to carry them out into the ocean. When rain begins pouring down, their situation becomes extremely perilous and Kennedy shouts apologetically to Ross, "Sorry I got you out here, Barney!" The canoe swamps, and they hang on as the wind and waves carry them toward the reef. Allegorical tales of spiritual transformation often require that the experience be marked by the number three—three days in the tomb, three wishes—and Kennedy undergoes his third "death":

When they were near the reef, a wave broke Kennedy's hold, ripped him away from the canoe, turned him head over heels, and spun him in a violent rush. His ears roared and his eyes pinwheeled, and for the third time since the collision he thought he was dying. Somehow he was not thrown against the coral but floated into a kind of eddy. Suddenly he felt the reef under his feet. Steadying himself so that he would not be swept off it, he shouted, "Barney!" There was no reply. Kennedy thought of how he had insisted on going out in the canoe, and he screamed, "Barney!" This time Ross answered. He, too, had been thrown on the reef. He had not been as lucky as Kennedy; his right arm and shoulder had been cruelly lacerated by the coral, and his feet, which were already infected from earlier wounds, were cut some more.

The walk over the reef to the beach is so agonizing for Ross that Kennedy has to place a paddle from the canoe ahead of Ross for him to step on, then the other paddle for the next step. Finally, they fall asleep on the beach. Hersey begins the next section with Kennedy and Ross awakening the following day to find "four husky natives" standing over them. They have brought a message of rescue from a commander of New Zealand infantry. By so quickly effecting their rescue after the furious near-disaster of the previous section, Hersey makes Kennedy's compulsive insistence on taking action, his subsequent apology to Ross, and finally his horror at the possibility that he has perhaps caused Ross to drown the climax of the story. The action motivated by his "conscience" has been revealed not only as unwise, but also as having woeful consequences for his comrade. Kennedy's pain at this realization is the culminating moment of his tenacious battle against nature, and represents in that context his discovery of the limits of "conscience."

The protagonist of the story is thus not a hero in the military or legendary sense, but rather a hero in the literary sense of a protagonist, the

51

character with whom the reader identifies ("becomes," as Hersey repeatedly termed it in the interview)[15] and with whom the reader undergoes the defining experience of the story. As a literary character, Kennedy is an existential hero, a fallible human being whose tenacious efforts enable his and his crew's survival only in the sense that they seem to be hope-in-action, answered at last by grace. Indeed, Kennedy nearly renders that "grace" futile when that same tenacity almost kills him and his closest comrade after rescue has, unknown to him, been effected.

Hersey ends the story with a brief scene of the crew being picked up by a PT boat. Kennedy verbally expresses his bitterness about his navy peers not having come sooner, but is last seen in the story reentering the community: "Kennedy jumped onto [the PT] and hugged the men aboard — his friends." The story then ends with the lyrics of a song that Johnston sings on the way back with two "roly-poly, mission-trained natives":

Jesus loves me, this I know,
For the Bible tells me so;
Little ones to him belong,
They are weak, but He is strong.
Yes, Jesus loves me; yes, Jesus loves me . . .

A close reading of "Survival" reveals that it has little in common with the stock heroics of either conventional "war stories" or political press relations. It is true that such elements would make up the medal citation Kennedy would receive from the navy as well as much later recountings of the episode, ranging from a segment of the television show *Navy Log* to books by Robert Donovan and Richard Tregaskis to a Hollywood film. As a result, PT 109 has for some time been thought of in the same way as such earlier compounds of fact, legend, and press agentry as the Alamo and the ride up San Juan Hill. But Hersey's "Survival," the text that formed Kennedy's initial "character" as a public figure, is of a completely different order.

52 Beyond the issue of the narrative's accuracy as an account of the actual events lies the issue of its accuracy regarding Kennedy himself. Traces of the emotions and ideas Kennedy brought to the experience are discernible. As noted by such critics as the Blairs, his repeated forays into the water seeking help are marked more by daring than by wisdom. In that regard

they follow Kennedy's pattern of documented reckless driving, ignoring physical inadequacies and illnesses in pursuit of sporting activities, and even his having his father pull strings to get him assigned to a combat unit despite his debilitating back. What fascinated Kennedy about the young men of *Pilgrim's Way*, who found their apotheosis in their sacrifice in war, perhaps drove him on repeated lonely journeys into the sea.

The central passage of Hersey's text, the swim around the island at night, was inspired by what Hersey found to be Kennedy's "very strange" and "nightmarish" account to him. That passage replicates not only the events but also the young Kennedy's repeated experiences of having to survive an overpowering situation. The lacerating coral and the fear of castrating barracuda are surely reminiscent of the torments of doctors' "tests" in the hospital. Kennedy's floating in the water, with virtually no power but the capacity to retain hope, is strikingly similar to his endurance of possibly fatal illnesses. Like the scarlet fever and the mysterious wasting disease for which the doctors could not yet find a convincing name, the currents of the channel straits allow Kennedy no response other than to hold on to his own relentless desire to return to his fellow human beings.

Traces of Kennedy's actual experience, and more directly his account of them, are powerfully present in the text along with Hersey's own "depth of memory" and interpretive consciousness. But ultimately the only person undergoing the experiences in "Survival," the only person *in* the text, is the reader. Only the reader follows the traces of Kennedy's and Hersey's narratives to construct a literary experience by reading the text. Kennedy may have experienced the change implicit in the story, Hersey may have experienced the change while contemplating and writing about the events, but only the reader experiences the change as it takes place—as he or she activates the story by reading it.

Kennedy was one of those readers. When in March he read the first draft of the story, he both praised and criticized it. He admired a narrative that could turn its ostensible subject into an enthralled reader: "Needless to say you did a great job with the story—even I was left wondering how it all would end." Nevertheless, while agreeing with Hersey that "as you say, everyone sees the same thing differently," he also pointed out how the narrative created that suspense through a selective focus that necessarily misrepresented the full events: "I understand, of course, that in an article of this length—in order to keep the story's continuity and to prevent over-flow with detail—you have to limit the story to a few central themes." With this acknowledgment, Kennedy proceeded to list changes he felt should be

53

made. These included giving more credit to the executive officer Lennie Thom, obtaining naval clearance on the handling of issues of specific operations, adding credit to Ross, and above all deleting the portrayal of one of the crew who was subsequently killed. Kennedy successfully persuaded Hersey that the "ironic and dramatic" aspects of this character's role did not justify tarnishing the man's memory.[16]

More than any other reader, Kennedy was in a position to recognize that the text could not be the experience itself. Just as he understood, as shown by the above observations, the transformative aspects of devices of suspense and irony, he no doubt saw, in the thoughts and feelings he enacted in reading the "Kennedy" of Hersey's linguistic construction, an experience that was not and could not be precisely the same experience he had in the South Pacific waters. Art is not life, even when art is journalism, for it inevitably confers or at least emphasizes a simpler pattern. That pattern is Hersey's contribution to the experience conveyed by the text; it may seem as valuable to the reader who is also the ostensible subject of the text as it does to any other.

Another example of this process of selection is provided by the testimony of a wartime girlfriend of Kennedy's. He told her that on the swim out to Ferguson Passage, when he was frightened by the thought of barracuda eating his testicles, he "swam a lot of backstroke" and "never prayed so much in my life."[17] Nowhere in Hersey's text may Kennedy be found either joking or praying in response to his desperate situation. Those responses are left to others in the crew. Hersey chooses to emphasize only Kennedy's tenacious determination to exert his will to the full limits of his bodily and mental powers, so that he becomes a figure of what Hersey calls hope—a metaphor for the aspect of Hersey's and the reader's minds that will not quit even when there appears virtually no point in going on. The ironies of the specific relations between Kennedy's actions and their results in no way undercut—indeed, they reinforce—Kennedy's signification of this virtue.

Thus Kennedy was in one respect like any reader in his congressional district holding one of the reprints of the *Reader's Digest* version of "Survival" with which his father blanketed the district during the 1946 campaign. In reading the text, Kennedy potentially underwent the experience crafted by Hersey; Hersey's text should have done something *in* Kennedy's mind, and thus *to* his mind. That experience is of psychic death and rebirth figured as a movement into extreme bitterness and isolation, a spiritual death saved only by the retention of hope—symbolized by the lantern—that depends on the longing for a tie to others, to a community.

54

In Hersey's text, Kennedy, as much as any reader, could see that "Kennedy's" actions did not clearly lead to the rescue of himself and his men at the end, any more than efforts of his own had earlier in the story brought him back from helplessly floating in the current. Indeed, his climactic action nearly led to his and Ross's death. But the persistence of those actions sustained him and his crew while a pattern of fate outside their control determined whether or not they would eventually be saved. Therefore, Hersey's text is not so much about individual autonomy and power as it is about initiation into some profound lesson concerning oneself, one's relation to nature, and one's relation to the community.

In his prefatory note to the reprint of "Survival" in the *Here to Stay* collection, Hersey presented the reader with a new framing of the tale:

It is a tale of a young man's discovery of his inner funds of resourcefulness, optimism, and stamina, and it exemplifies, better than any other story in this book, the courage-giving force of a sense of community. Here the community was a small crew, Kennedy's own; as commanding officer of a Patrol Torpedo boat, he was responsible for the ten of his twelve who survived the precipitating accident, and the extent to which he grasped his duty toward them—so that his thoughts and anxieties and actions were all turned outward from himself—may well have been what saved both him and them.[18]

Hersey's retrospective interpretation, explicitly emphasizing Kennedy's turning "outward from himself," suggests the religious or spiritual dimension of the text. Whether Hersey's statement reveals his intentions as author in 1944 or his response as a reader of the text in 1963, it gives evidence of a category of experience that the text constitutes for a reader.

The reader of "Survival" undergoes with its protagonist an extended experience of Turner's liminal phase. After opening with a violent separation, the text takes Kennedy and the reader through the stripping, terrifying, and crushing experiences that should render them humble in the recognition of their ultimate helplessness as autonomous individuals. When the phase at last ends as abruptly as it began, the conclusion of the narrative with the song asserting knowledge of Jesus' love because "the Lord has told me so" strikes precisely the note of achieved humility Turner points out in cultural rites of passage.

Along with the psychological, unconscious memory of the birth experience, this cultural experience—or at least, this felt need for such a reenactment of birth in cultural experience—constitutes the "depth of memory" that Hersey's readers could collectively bring to the text. As a literary character in "Survival," Kennedy thus functions as a figure of the liminal phase, moving from one state to another while proceeding in life as a member of a community. Turner asserts the necessity of this phase in the constant dialectic between what he calls community, or structure, and *communitas*, or the relation of individuals as whole beings to other whole beings within that structure. As he puts it, "There is a dialectic here, for the immediacy of communitas gives way to mediacy of structure, while, in *rites de passage*, men are released from structure into communitas only to return to structure released by their experience of communitas."[19]

Kennedy's father, still determined to get his son into *Reader's Digest*, subsequently prevailed over the editorial policy of *The New Yorker*, which prohibited condensed reprints of its publications. He apparently persuaded the magazine to grant this "right" through such pressures as grandly promising to commit all proceeds to charity for servicemen's widows.[20]

Though he had relentlessly competed with his brother Joe for their parents' approval, Jack had nevertheless welcomed the measure of protection that the model son provided him from the intense pressures to conform. After Joe Jr., serving in Britain as a naval aviator, disappeared in a spectacular explosion over the English Channel in 1944 while on a voluntary mission to bomb Hitler's V-1 rocket-launching pad, Jack suddenly found himself "terribly exposed and vulnerable" to the scrutiny of his parents and siblings. In the months after Joe Jr.'s death, as his inconsolable father remained locked in his study, Kennedy complained to his close friend Lem Billings that he was now locked in competition with a Joe that had become an idealized image: "I'm shadowboxing in a match the shadow is always going to win."[21] He at first took the lead in praising that shadow, editing and assembling the reminiscences of family and friends in a book. In the privately printed *As We Remember Joe*, Kennedy wrote of "a completeness to Joe's life, and that is the completeness of perfection. His life as he lived and finally, as he died, could hardly have been improved upon."[22]

Kennedy was in a complex situation. He had since his teens been fascinated by government and had secretly harbored dreams of a political career. To enter politics meant following his true inclinations, yet at the same time giving himself over to the role his father had planned for his elder brother Joe. Whatever he did, he told his navy buddy Paul Fay, "I can feel Pappy's eyes on the back of my neck."[23]

In planning Jack's nascent political career, Joseph Kennedy drew upon his Hollywood experience. At the end of the war Charles Spalding, the Yale graduate who was the most intellectual of Jack's friends during the 1940s, was working in Hollywood as assistant to Gary Cooper. Spalding has reported that when Jack visited him in Hollywood and rubbed shoulders with movie stars, he was obsessed with the question of how one acquired "the binding magnetism these screen personalities had."[24] Spalding found Jack's pursuit of women, his reading about Byron, and his observation of Hollywood stars to all be connected by his growing awareness of the power of image:

He had a short attention span, you could see, if you were looking back at it, which was kind of Byronic, in a way, and Byron is somebody he spent some time thinking about. He began at that time, and girls were a part of it, to consider this business of image. It wasn't even called image then but the very first person to understand about public relations in politics was Mr. Kennedy. I mean he was the first person I ever knew who really understood that what you did was to merchandize a conception and he had enough experience in radio and motion pictures to grope around in that whole thing which has become a common practice. . . . But at that time, he began thinking about it so that Jack would go out to California and notice the parallels between people out there—like personalities drawing crowds. Why did Cooper draw a crowd? We'd spend hours talking about it. His magnetism, did he have it or didn't he? And the whole thing. And other people he met out there. Spencer Tracy and Gable and other people who were floating through that world. So that *self* conscious as he was in this way, he was always interested in seeing whether he had it or didn't have it. As I think lots of politicians are. So that I think that sort of challenge is frequently, if you're a male, thrown up against a woman. To me that's always accounted for a lot of the numbers, if you will. You know, does he have it or doesn't he have it?[25]

Once Jack agreed to run for Congress in 1946, his father began making over Jack's public image according to the methods of the Hollywood star system. Joe Kennedy supervised family and aides in providing the press with photo opportunities, themes, and "facts" that enabled them to present his son within appealing formulas. Perceiving the voting power of returned veterans, he accepted the slogan "a new generation offers a leader" suggested by a senior politician named Joe Kane, who was inspired by *Time-Life* editor Henry Luce's foreword to *Why England Slept*. Kennedy's father set about casting his son in that role. When private polls found that voters were more interested in his son's wartime heroism than in his views on issues, Joe Sr. insisted that Jack's standard campaign speech should evoke his PT 109 fame through references to the men under his command. Joe manipulated the media to produce timely articles in both local and national publications, and he ordered 100,000 offprints of the *Reader's Digest* condensation of the PT 109 story to be distributed throughout the congressional district.[26]

Like a novice actor contracted by a film studio, Kennedy cooperated in the image-making while gradually discovering aspects of his appearance and personality he could use to perform the role that had, in effect, been adapted by his father from Hersey's literary work into the script for the campaign. Kennedy's efforts at presenting a strong masculine profile could not hide his stiff back posture, alarming changes in skin color, and sudden drops in weight. Fictively explained as originating from wartime injury and malaria, these visible weaknesses, coupled with his clear refusal to give in to them, only strengthened his heroic persona while adding an appealing vulnerability. The professionally written speeches and elocution lessons made available by his father could not prevent Jack's sometimes stumbling over his words, but since childhood he had possessed an ingenuous charm, and he soon discovered that audiences responded warmly to the determination, self-deprecating humor, and embarrassed sincerity with which he struggled to overcome his shyness. As he came to know the responses of his audiences, he increasingly resisted speeches and actions with which he did not feel comfortable. From his father's calculations, his own disposition and physique, and his audience's responses, he gradually developed a public persona that fit.

When Hersey wrote and published "Survival," and still in 1946, when it was being read throughout Kennedy's congressional district as he ran for office, Americans had every reason to see themselves, both as individuals and collectively, as going through a rite of passage. Long accustomed to isolationism and to an understanding of themselves as separate from the violent quarrels of nations across the seas, they now knew that they had irrevocably left behind that physical and psychological safety. Hersey's "Joe Is Home Now," a *Life* article distilled from the experiences of 43 discharged soldiers, is itself one testament of the concern during the climactic years of the war that the veteran must go through a difficult and dangerous period.[27] And by the time of Kennedy's campaign for Congress, it had become apparent that the United States was passing through an uncertain new phase in its history, leaving a state of war but not returning to the old peace. The Kennedy in "Survival" mirrored the experience of liminality, of enduring a trial from which one surely emerges transformed, with some profound knowledge, ready to "take office."

In the 1946 campaign, knowing that his listeners had been given Hersey's text, Kennedy avoided referring directly to his own actions. Far more effectively, he evoked their knowledge of "Survival" by opening with a detailed account of the sinking of PT 109 and then focusing on the bravery of another man he had known in the South Pacific.[28] He would then draw analogies to the situation of all the soldiers now veterans at home.

A speech that Kennedy delivered to various veterans' groups during the campaign provides a compelling illustration of how "Survival" was brought together with the political candidate and the electorate. The theme of the speech is that of Hersey's text: the experience of an existential loneliness and with it the temptation of bitterness and alienation from community, with the offered solution the discovery of necessary interdependence. Kennedy begins by describing McMahon's terrible burning when the Japanese destroyer wrecked PT 109. Kennedy only refers to himself once, as McMahon's commanding officer. Instead of recounting how he towed McMahon to safety or any of the other events in "Survival," he tells how McMahon turned down a medical discharge and stayed in the South Pacific to keep repairing PT-boat engines with his painfully burned hands:

I felt that his courage was the result of his loyalty to the men around him. Most of the courage in the war came from men's understanding of their interdependence on each other. Men were saving other men's lives at the risk of their own simply because they realized that perhaps the next day their lives would be saved in turn. And so there was built up during the war a great feeling of comradeship and fellowship and loyalty.

Now McMahon and the others are coming home. They miss the close comradeship, the feeling of interdependence, that sense of working together for a common cause. In civilian life, they feel alone, they feel that they have only themselves to depend on. They miss their wartime friends, and the understanding of their wartime friendships. One veteran told me that when he brought one of his Army friends to his home, his wife said, "What can you possibly see in O'Brien?" The veteran remembered O'Brien in Italy, walking with him from Sicily to the Po Valley, every bloody mile of the way. He knew what he could see in O'Brien.

We forget that dependence on other people is with us in civilian life just as it was in the war. We are dependent on other people nearly every minute of our lives.

59

In a larger sense, each one of us is dependent on all the other people in this country—on their obedience to our laws, for their rejection of the siren calls of ambitious demagogues. In fact, if we only realized it, we are in time of peace as inter-
dependent as the soldiers were in the time of war.[29]

Having read "Survival," or perhaps reading it afterward, the veterans
spoken of in—male listeners to—this speech could see in the young man
standing on the podium the experience that as readers they themselves
went through in the text. Kennedy the politician thus incorporated into his
image Kennedy the literary character, an entity that was the product of a
triangular encounter of dreams, the site where the deep psychological
experiences of Kennedy, Hersey, and the reader met. In each case the
dreams concerned the self and the community, alienation and longing,
love and death. Kennedy, flesh and blood, was now also a dreamlike image
to be viewed, collectively, as other and yet as interior to each self. The
emergence of John F. Kennedy as a political figure of liminality—of transition and potential—was complete.

As a literary-journalistic experiment, Hersey's story positioned its readers to
identify with Kennedy as a fictionlike hero—a true-life literary protagonist
through whom they could imaginatively undergo a defining experience.
That merging of the world of literary narrative, which readers generally
experienced in works of fiction, with the world of fact became the basis for
the production of Kennedy as a new kind of politician within the literary-
cinematic format afforded by the post-World War II communications network.

"World of literary narrative" and "world of fact" do not refer to an opposition between falsehood and truth. Readers were accustomed to finding in
journalism only the satisfaction of being informed about a completed experience located in the recent yet definite past. Hersey had brought them a
realm of experience that they were used to finding only in stories marked
"fiction." Within textual frames marking the story as journalism, readers of
"Survival" found themselves identifying with a hero as he or she was undergoing an experience in the fictional present.

Kennedy's father used his wealth and connections in the media to move
Hersey's literary text from an elite venue to a popular audience. Kennedy
himself would soon take that move even further, turning the political
podium into a setting for such "fiction"—that is, a narrative experience

eliciting identification by the reader, who was also a citizen, with the protagonist, who was a politician.

Hersey's "Survival" produces John F. Kennedy as a hero, but not in the sense of a model person seen as performing great exploits; the hero of Hersey's narrative is rather a youth who has enormous bravery and energy but who is transformed by chastening experience. More complexly, the production of Kennedy as hero begins in his transformation into the narrative sense of that term, the protagonist or main character of the story with whom the reader is positioned to identify. As a true-life "character," Kennedy then walks off the page into the text of a political production in the media age.

Far from a one-dimensional matter of public relations and legend-making, Kennedy's public self was a complex intersection of journalistic, literary, and political interests. The text of "Survival" is the product of a series of mediators. Kennedy-as-hero emerged in this text first of all from a reporter's desire in World War II to bring to the home front the news of soldiers' life-and-death experiences. He emerged from the prism of Kennedy's reflections on the experience, which shaped the story he gave Hersey. Kennedy-as-hero emerged from Joe Kennedy's efforts to market Hersey's text to a mass audience, and he emerged from the narrative forms and ideological codes available to Hersey. Ultimately, Kennedy-as-hero took form in the minds of that reporter-turned-fiction-writer's audience. As voters, they brought their own experiences of the text and its protagonist to their perceptions of the candidate's meaning.

Top: The Kennedy children in 1925. Jack stands between his three younger sisters and his elder brother, Joe Jr. Resenting the status their parents conferred upon Joe as the model for the rest of the siblings to emulate, Jack diverted the younger children from his mother Rose's pious stories and planned activities. The bookworm of the family, he upset his mother with his love for a series of children's books by Frances Trego Montgomery about a mischievous goat named Billy Whiskers, who would instigate chaos in a domestic environment and then bemusedly watch the resulting crisis. *JOHN F. KENNEDY LIBRARY*

Bottom: During a collapse at the end of summer 1937, Jack lies in a London hotel. Books not only filled up the hours of a sickly youth, but also served as private models for the shaping of a fantasy self. The novels of Sir Walter Scott and biographies of Marlborough and Byron offered Jack adventures in faraway settings of British history. *JOHN F. KENNEDY LIBRARY*

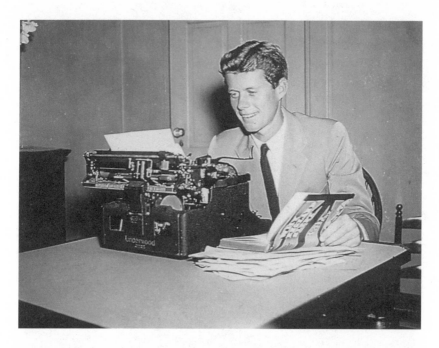

ABOVE: While his father was U.S. Ambassador to Great Britain, Jack enjoyed entering the settings of the books he had so enjoyed in his youth. In a surprising conclusion to an undistinguished academic career, Jack returned to Harvard to work hard on a senior honors thesis dealing with Britain's failed appeasement policies of the 1930s. With its publication as *Why England Slept* in 1940, Jack emerged as both an author and a minor celebrity. *ARCHIVE PHOTOS*

RIGHT: Kennedy's involvement with literature and history took a new turn after his PT boat was sunk in 1943 in the South Pacific. John Hersey's account in *The New Yorker* turned Kennedy into a literary protagonist with whom wartime readers could experience feelings of uncertainty and transformative suffering. *JOHN F. KENNEDY LIBRARY*

Top: Jack appears before a veterans' group in 1945 as he prepares to run for Congress. Joe Kennedy had 100,000 offprints of the *Reader's Digest* condensation of Hersey's PT 109 story distributed throughout the district. *JOHN F. KENNEDY LIBRARY*

Bottom: Kennedy stands between his parents on the night of his election victory. Joe Kennedy had successfully brought his experience in Hollywood to a political production of the media age. *JOHN F. KENNEDY LIBRARY*

Top: As a young congressman plagued by illness, Jack struggled with his father's attempts to direct his views and career. Jack's favorite movie in those years was the 1948 *Red River,* a western in which a slender young Montgomery Clift confronts an overbearing stepfather, played by John Wayne, for control of a cattle drive. *MUSEUM OF MODERN ART/FILM STILLS ARCHIVE*

Bottom: After his election to the Senate in 1952, Kennedy hired the brilliant young Theodore Sorensen as a speechwriter and adviser. Kennedy's father remained a powerful presence, but Jack's collaboration with his alter ego Sorensen would increasingly shape the young senator's image. *JOHN F. KENNEDY LIBRARY*

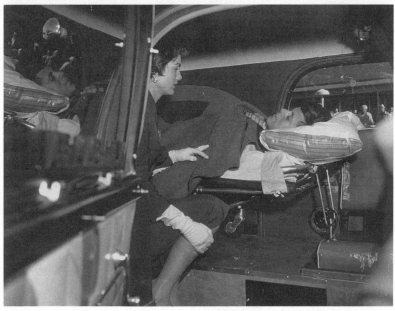

Left, top: Kennedy's associations in Hollywood merged life with the movies. At a late–1954 dinner party, Kennedy's wife Jacqueline persuaded Grace Kelly, star of that year's hit film *Rear Window,* to go with her to the hospital room where Jack was groggy with medication from spinal surgery and introduce herself as "the new night nurse."
MUSEUM OF MODERN ART/FILM STILLS ARCHIVE

Left, bottom: Jacqueline accompanies her husband by ambulance to spend the Christmas holidays at his father's Palm Beach residence. During his hospitalization and convalescence in 1954–55, Jacqueline helped Kennedy with the book he was writing on political courage by reading history and biographies aloud at his bedside. In an episode of *Profiles in Courage* discarded before publication, her reading catalyzes a dream visit to Kennedy's hospital room by the ghosts of four dead senators. *UPI/CORBIS-BETTMANN*

Above: Ernest Hemingway on African safari in 1954. In *Profiles in Courage* Kennedy invoked the famous author's definition of courage as "grace under pressure." During the domestic Eisenhower era, popular magazines presented Hemingway as a cultural sage keeping alive American frontier virtues of individualism, risk-taking, and vigorous masculinity.
JOHN F. KENNEDY LIBRARY

LEFT, TOP: The Pulitzer Prize that Kennedy was awarded in 1956 for *Profiles in Courage* added to his political image an aura of moral seriousness and high aspiration. *JOHN F. KENNEDY LIBRARY*

LEFT, BOTTOM: As the 1960 presidential campaign approached, Joe Kennedy boasted to interviewers that his son had more "universal appeal" than either Cary Grant or Jimmy Stewart, major film stars seen here together in the 1940 *Philadelphia Story*. John F. Kennedy combined their opposed images of suave sophistication and bashful sincerity.
MUSEUM OF MODERN ART/FILM STILLS ARCHIVE

ABOVE: At the dinner honoring the Nobel laureates, President Kennedy escorts the widows of Ernest Hemingway and General George Marshall to a reading by Fredric March of Hemingway's "The Sea Chase." Whereas previous presidents had been father figures, the handsome young Kennedy offered himself to the public as a romantic hero daring to fill the shoes of past American great men. His New Frontier answered contemporary yearnings for adventure and greatness.
JOHN F. KENNEDY LIBRARY

LEFT, TOP: January 1961: the youngest man ever elected president welcomes former-president Harry S. Truman back to the White House. The previous July, the elder statesman had attempted to stop Kennedy's nomination; Kennedy faced him down in a dramatic television appearance. JFK's crisis politics shaped problems into dramatic narratives in which Kennedy performed the role of heroic protagonist. *JOHN F. KENNEDY LIBRARY*

LEFT, BOTTOM: In Oliver Stone's 1991 *JFK,* New Orleans District Attorney Jim Garrison (Kevin Costner) directs attention to a model of Dealey Plaza in Dallas as he spins out his story of what "really" happened, and what it means. *MUSEUM OF MODERN ART/FILM STILLS ARCHIVE*

ABOVE: After the assassination in Dallas on November 22, 1963, Kennedy's widow asked that an "eternal flame" burn at the grave. As American political life deteriorated into Vietnam, rebellion, Watergate, and revelations about Kennedy's private life, the sad reality seemed the result of Kennedy's absence. *JOHN F. KENNEDY LIBRARY*

Democratic National Convention, 1960.

CHAPTER THREE

The Old Man and the Boy: Papa Hemingway
and *Profiles in Courage*

In the Kennedy Library, filed among the *Profiles in Courage* manuscripts in Kennedy's personal papers, are two separate versions of the opening chapter, both of which were discarded and neither of which has ever been published or, until now, publicly described. One of these versions is the dream sequence, set in Kennedy's hospital room, discussed in the prologue of this book. The other is an epistolary narrative. In each of these overtly literary devices "Kennedy" engages in dialogue with a father figure or figures, older men who offer him their acquired wisdom.

In the epistolary narrative, letters from "John Kennedy" are exchanged with letters from a "Senator Oldtimer" (in a subsequent draft "John Kennedy" becomes "Edward Youngfellow," a name that emphasizes the opposition of age while apparently making an in-family jest about Kennedy's youngest sibling). In this satirical (and flatly repetitive) debate, Kennedy gradually works out his case for a legislator's following his conscience against Oldtimer's blustering exhortations to follow the will of the constituents. At the close of the narrative, Kennedy acknowledges that "Oldtimer" is a fictional character:

Author's Note: There is, of course, no Senator Oldtimer. If a reference is needed, it might be said that he represents the mistaken concept of a Senator almost universally portrayed by Hollywood, Broadway and fiction writers; or that he is based upon that delightful character in Dickens' *Nicholas Nickleby*, Member of Parliament Gregsbury—"a thick-headed gentleman, with a loud voice, a pompous manner, a tolerable command of sentences with no meaning in them, and, in short, every requisite for a good Member."[1]

Not acknowledged is that the "Kennedy" portrayed as writing to "Old-timer" is a fictional character as well. He is a representation of the character that Kennedy defines for himself as opposed to a fictional stereotype of a bad role model or, in effect, father.

Instead of using either of these fictional dialogues with his political father figures, Kennedy opened the published version of *Profiles in Courage* with a paragraph that invoked Ernest Hemingway's famous definition of courage as "grace under pressure" and then stated that the stories of senators Kennedy would be narrating would chronicle the "grace" with which they suffered certain political "pressures."[2] Thus Kennedy substituted Hemingway, the famous writer and adventurer, for the fictional father figures of the two discarded drafts, the dead senators who come to "Kennedy's" bedside to hand him the thesis for his book and the composite Senator (Oldtimer) of popular culture. Instead of either listening to great senators from the past or arguing with a popular stereotype, the "Kennedy" of *Profiles in Courage* introduces himself as a maturing youth who is paying attention to the teachings of the older American author who is a popular sage and symbol.

By this simple stroke, the author of *Profiles in Courage* replaced the heavy-handed dialogue between a stripling and a succession of authority figures with a conventional invocation of a cultural authority. Hemingway's image as major author and celebrity had recently been enhanced by the Nobel Prize, which he was awarded following his phenomenally successful novella *The Old Man and the Sea* (1952). Calling upon Hemingway to open his own book was a seemingly offhand literary tactic, but in doing so Kennedy furthered his larger strategy for redefining his own public image.

Profiles in Courage was conceived and written to reposition readers' perceptions of its author in the larger cultural "text" represented by the picture magazines. In the 1950s *Life*, the most popular general-interest magazine in the country, enjoyed a readership of more than five million. Its closest rivals—*Saturday Evening Post*, *Colliers*, and *Look*—all imitated its emphasis on the photo-essay. Since television news programs did not make a major effort to gather pictorial news until the next decade, for most Americans in the 1950s these magazines were the primary media for visual images of actual people and events. These texts were perhaps more effective because readers did not even think of them as texts. The picture magazine was certainly not thought of as a place inhabited by "characters" constructed in ways and for purposes analogous to those of fictional characters in novels and films. But in the pages of the picture magazines, certain white, middle-class families were used to represent a nationalized norm of American life as simply "America" and were juxtaposed with figures of American value, "celebrities."[3]

The advantages accruing to Kennedy from his decision to invoke Hemingway were not necessarily all consciously thought out. Kennedy's decision made sense because he personally was fascinated with the author and because, as he was aware, a large proportion of the electorate shared that fascination. At the time *Profiles in Courage* was published, Hemingway and Kennedy had each been playing a distinct role in the picture magazines. With *Profiles in Courage*, the boyish Kennedy brought himself into a close juxtaposition with the values represented by "Papa" Hemingway. In doing so, he made a decisive stride forward in developing his public image from that of immature senator to that of prospective Democratic Party challenger to President Dwight Eisenhower, who presided over the 1950s as a father who truly knew best. Kennedy implied that he would be the legitimate successor not to Eisenhower but to Hemingway, the other great American father figure of the era. For Hemingway was represented in the picture magazines as the aging embodiment of an alternative set of traditional American values.

Perhaps as important for Kennedy was that his opening focus on the Hemingway father figure unobtrusively implied that he looked elsewhere for guidance than to his own powerful and controversial father, Joseph Kennedy. Given that the book represented Jack Kennedy's move to take control of his image by following his own lifelong interest in literature and history, the invocation of a famous author may well have had such private implications.

In the mid-1950s "Papa" Hemingway functioned in the picture magazines as a father figure providing an alternative to President Dwight Eisenhower. The majority of Americans had proclaimed in 1952, "I Like Ike," and emulated the constellation of domestic values suggested by Eisenhower's well-publicized devotion to the golf course. But opinion makers and cultural commentators expressed unease with the Eisenhower *ethos*.[4] It became a commonplace that amid the complacency and detachment of this milieu, heroes were hard to find. Social pundits observed a preference for conformity and security over the traditional American virtues of individualism and self-reliance. David Riesman's *The Lonely Crowd* (1950) supplied the much-invoked concept of the "outer-directed" versus the "inner-directed" man, referring to the growing dominance of the social ethic over the Protestant work ethic, to suggest that a new mass society was fundamentally altering the character of Americans.

Argument with this dominant *ethos* continued throughout the decade. Perceiving the uneasy feeling that something vital had been lost, critics on the Right lamented the loss of the heroic individual. On the Left there was a converse perspective, a criticism of the lack of social commitment that had bred a "Silent Generation" unwilling to risk dissent. If the new world of bureaucracy, domesticity, and caution had Eisenhower as its preeminent exemplar, the traditional heroic values of individualism, exploration, and achievement continued to be held up as models to the public by opinion shapers and cultural spokespersons of various political persuasions. Hemingway, as famous for his adventurous life as for his literature, became a vehicle for the celebration of these values.

As early as 1949 *Life* had published a major feature by Malcolm Cowley entitled "A Portrait of Mister Papa" that emphasized the heroic aura of Hemingway's world, pointing out that most of Hemingway's chosen friends had achieved "excellence," taken "risks," and demonstrated "physical or moral courage combined with the habit of being dependable in a crisis."[5] These would be the characteristic themes of Kennedy's presidential-campaign rhetoric eleven years later as he campaigned against the complacency of the Eisenhower years. As early as 1950 Hemingway expressed his contempt for the soldier-politician whose influence Kennedy would at the end of the decade seek to overturn. In his novel *Across the River and into the Trees* (1950), Hemingway's protagonist, Colonel Cantwell, a transparent surrogate for the author, attacks Eisenhower as "some politician in uniform who has never killed in his life, except with his mouth over the telephone, or on paper, nor ever has been hit. Figure him as our next President if you want him. Figure him any way you like."[6] This denigration of Eisenhower placed the author's image in direct opposition to that of the man who would preside over the 1950s.

Across the River and into the Trees was a best-seller but was scorned by critics, many of whom gleefully claimed that the writer was washed up.

The same year, commentators had expressed ridicule and contempt for the Hemingway in Lillian Ross's *New Yorker* profile "How Do You Like It Now, Gentlemen?" Hemingway's stature was severely threatened by his enemies in the literary world.

In 1952 *Life* printed a Hemingway cover issue that included the full text of his new work *The Old Man and the Sea*. In an editorial entitled "A Great American Storyteller," the magazine carefully positioned its readers to admire both the text and the author as exemplifying superior values. Observing that "Hemingway has always been preoccupied by courage or the lack of it," and has written about men who "have led dangerous lives," *Life* asserted that "Being a great writer is also dangerous and needs courage." The magazine illustrated Hemingway's courage by offering its own allegorical interpretation in which the old Cuban fisherman was the author, the great fish his literary work, and the sharks the critics. *Life* further celebrated Hemingway as an embodiment of a classical vision missing in the literature of the new generation: "Hemingway's work may be disaster-haunted, but his heroes face up to disaster nobly. If he has influenced any of the twisted young men now writing fiction, he hasn't influenced them enough in this respect."[7] The reference to "twisted young men now writing fiction" probably explains the readiness of the Luce publication, despite Hemingway's associations in the 1930s with the Left, to prop up the wounded author. If a notorious individualist and hedonist could be celebrated as an exemplar of traditional American values of work and achievement, he could serve as a credible counter to younger writers, such as Norman Mailer, peddling radical political and social critiques. Thus Hemingway was enlisted by *Life* to function as an authoritative representative of "mainstream" ideology.

The Old Man and the Sea was a huge critical and popular success. Within two days the September 1 issue of *Life* solely devoted to the novella sold 5,300,000 copies. As a Book-of-the-Month-Club edition the novella sold 153,000 copies in its first printing, and the Scribner's edition was at the top of the best-seller lists for a year. Overall, the early reviewers found the book to be the finest Hemingway had produced. Regarded as both a masterpiece and a triumphant comeback, it remade Hemingway's identity during the fifties as embattled but undefeated old hero and sage.[8] Seemingly a "timeless tale," the novella in fact addressed major cultural concerns of the time in a way that worked to reconstruct Hemingway's public image. The text of *The Old Man and the Sea* implicitly called upon the 1950s reader to reject the tendencies of his or her contemporary society and choose the values deemed traditionally American. Hemingway biographer Kenneth Lynn has explained the extraordinary reception accorded this simple tale of an old fisherman's noble defeat by the context of the opposite destinies that were revealed that same autumn for Eisenhower and the flamboyant Douglas MacArthur. These two generals had led the United States to victory over Germany and Japan, respectively. But the frustrating Korean War, in which MacArthur commanded the forces of the American-led United Nations, had demonstrated that the atomic bomb and other realities of the new world in which the United States found itself after World War II would prevent the cold war from being settled so decisively. In the fall of 1952, when MacArthur was fired by President Truman because of MacArthur's public insistence on unconditional victory, the public poured forth unprecedented accolades upon the old soldier.

Yet the same public spurned MacArthur's presidential aspirations, allowing him to, as he had offered, "just fade away." The subsequent election of Eisenhower thus represented the triumph of the bureaucrat and politician over the warrior. Lynn argues that the phenomenal success of *The Old Man and the Sea*, published that autumn, can best be explained by the resonance the public found in a tale of the heroic virtues of an old man who insists on struggling in a situation in which those virtues no longer seem to result in victory.[9]

Thus Hemingway's image did more than represent the fantasy of the heroic life as an alternative to both Eisenhower's complacency and younger radicals' critiques. Like a religious icon, it could enable its viewer to imaginatively inhabit a sacred space within society yet separate from its fragmenting categories and false drives. Hemingway had long since adopted the appellation "Papa" with those close to him, but now this identity was extended by the media to a culturewide role as old hero and sage.

In November 1954 it was announced that the Nobel Prize for Literature had been awarded to Hemingway, with special note made of *The Old Man and the Sea*. In its article on the award, *Life* used the title "The Old Man Lands Biggest Catch," conflating Hemingway with Santiago, the fisherman-protagonist of the novella. The article itself further developed this identification of the author with his protagonist, emphasizing that after a violent life of great achievement, Hemingway had survived the near-fatal plane crashes of his recent African safari to win the highest honor accorded an author.[10] Thus, the "old man" author had at last brought home the noble (Nobel) fish of which the "old man" protagonist had watched himself robbed by sharks.

The Old Man and the Sea, clearly possessing the "positive" values required by the instructions of Alfred Nobel, had enabled the Nobel committee to award the Prize to Hemingway after passing him over during previous decisions. For the same reason, the book allowed the American press to elevate Hemingway from the image of macho womanizer and man of action he had established during the 1930s and 1940s into something like an official status as America's sage.

Magazines ranging from the celebrity-gossiping *Focus* to the outdoor-sports-oriented *True* featured Hemingway's activities. Above all, *Life*, probably the single most important source of information for the mass of Americans during the decade, continued to celebrate the author. As John Raeburn concludes in his study of Hemingway's public persona, during the 1950s Hemingway "embodied values cherished by the society, ones related to what were believed to be frontier virtues—a taste for adventure, intrepidity, and a hearty, vigorous masculinity—and which were generally assumed to be collateral to any great accomplishment."[11] In Hemingway's image the "timeless" values of American culture could be perceived amid the disturbing flux of a society threatened by both its own materialism and alien ideologies.

Kennedy's decision to open *Profiles in Courage* by invoking Hemingway must be seen within the context of this public celebration of the writer during the months of Kennedy's near-fatal back operations and subsequent convalescence, a grim experience from which Kennedy would triumphantly emerge with his own book. When the announcement of Hemingway's Nobel Prize came over the news, Senator John F. Kennedy was in the New York Hospital for Special Surgery, faced with the possibility that death or debilitation would frustrate his ambitions. The previous month Kennedy had undergone a dangerous double-fusion operation on his back and nearly died. In less than two months, pain would compel a second operation, which would also nearly kill him and which would require a long convalescence.[12] But, like Hemingway in the well-publicized plane crash in Africa earlier in 1954, the young man cheated death. And just as Hemingway's writing *The Old Man and the Sea* led to his literary triumph with the Nobel Prize, Kennedy was working to produce from his brush with death a book that would similarly enhance his public image.

According to his friend and biographer Arthur Schlesinger Jr., Kennedy did not generally read fiction but, "at some point in his life, had read most of Hemingway," and "obviously" felt some kind of affinity for the writer.[13]

An invocation of Hemingway in the opening sentences of *Profiles in Courage* would thus appear to have been an easy suggestion for Kennedy to accept. Like Hemingway, Kennedy had suffered injuries and other debilitations that had made death, and consequently courage, a lifelong preoccupation. Kennedy could find in the fiction and legend of Hemingway the threat of violence in war that he himself had encountered in the South Pacific. Indeed, Hersey's terse portrayal of a stoic Kennedy enduring calamity had been after the famed Hemingway style. Kennedy may well have recognized that Hersey had portrayed him in the image of the characteristic Hemingway hero.

He could conceivably have recognized deeper correspondences. Both Hemingway and Kennedy felt at one time rejected or neglected by their mothers, and both had experienced a tense competition with an elder sibling (in Hemingway's case, a sister). The sexual thoughts about his nurses that Kennedy had entertained as early as his adolescent hospitalization while attending Choate were mirrored in the sexual fantasy that Hemingway had made in *A Farewell to Arms* (1929) out of his hospital romance with a nurse in Italy during World War I. Finally, both men had long since lived with images of themselves in the media that simultaneously compensated for and threatened their private self-images.

Kennedy might well have recognized that a negative aspect of his public image could be downplayed by aligning his image with that of the famous author. If Hemingway was now firmly identified in the media as the Old Man, or Papa, the senator from Massachusetts had for some time been consistently portrayed as the Boy. In the first half of the 1950s, the media repeatedly cast Kennedy as an all-American youth rather prematurely entering the world of men. The press may have been inspired by Hersey's portrayal of Kennedy's earnestness in "Survival." Perhaps they responded as well to the slogan "The New Generation Offers a Leader" that was devised for his first campaign for Congress in 1946. Perhaps they took their cue from Kennedy's assertion in a *Look* article during the 1946 campaign that "I have an obligation as a rich man's son to people who are having a hard time of it."[14] They may also have been simply recording Kennedy's callow, if earnest, appearance and the skepticism expressed by his elders in Congress.[15]

Recurring illnesses, leading to the private diagnosis of Addison's disease, had at first blocked him from entertaining serious ambition beyond pleasing his father. During his first term in Congress he worked hard at educating himself in foreign policy, labor, communism, and other major issues of the day. He also struggled with his father's attempts to make him an instrument of his own views. Kay Halle heard Jack respond to his father's overbearing admonitions at a cocktail party by saying: "Now, look here, Dad, you have your political views and I have mine. I'm going to vote exactly the way I feel I must vote on this. I've got great respect for you but when it comes to voting, I'm voting my way."[16]

But as his health problems continued during his next two terms, Jack Kennedy projected a poor image within the House.[17] Paying no attention to his dress or posture, he showed little interest in political ideas or problems. Complete collapses punctuated extended periods of fatigue and weakness. This physical debilitation, a love of pleasure, and an intellectual disposition that did not mesh comfortably with either his duties or his colleagues each contributed to absenteeism that the excellent aides provided by his father were able to screen from the public's perception. Kennedy devoted himself to pursuing a diverse array of women ranging from secretaries to movie stars, winning them and then moving on before any could become serious figures in his life. He confided to a friend that "the doctors say I've got a sort of slow-motion leukemia, but they tell me I'll probably last until I'm forty-five."[18]

Yet heroic aspirations continued to haunt him. Kennedy was gripped by a Walter Mitty-like fantasy of being a great quarterback in professional football, a fantasy he enacted in touch-football games with friends and associates.[19] And beneath his activities as playboy and fantasist lay deeper aspirations and beliefs that seemed unattainable as he was stalked by sickness and death. He continued to reread and recommend to others Buchan's *Pilgrim's Way*.[20]

Doris Goodwin has located Jack's mid-1950s emergence from diffidence toward politics in a confluence of factors regarding his relations with his family. The accidental death in 1949 of his close sister Kathleen, who had defied both her mother and her Church to seek fulfillment with a man she profoundly loved, catalyzed Jack into thinking about the contrasting way he himself was allowing his life to be used to fulfill his father's wishes. With the discovery a year later that his Addison's could be controlled with oral doses of cortisone, he was suddenly released from his sense of doom. And that same year, he was deeply moved by the outpouring of sympathy at the funeral of the daughter of a former Boston mayor, as well as by his long talk that night with another legendary former mayor—his grandfather, John "Honey Fitz" Fitzgerald. He began to consider the possibility that politics might after all afford a compelling, emotionally rewarding,

71

and meaningful life.[21] In 1952, when he challenged the popular Henry Cabot Lodge for the Senate, the *Reader's Digest* text served him once again as his father saw to it that offprints were distributed throughout the state.

After his upset victory, Kennedy began his term as senator by hiring Theodore Sorensen. This was a move by Kennedy toward making politics answer to his own yearnings. Sorensen had been informed by insiders that Kennedy would not hire anyone without his father's permission, but that proved incorrect as Kennedy broadened his perspective and image.[22] Kennedy was able to begin taking over the crafting of his own role by using the words that Sorensen could help him write to script that role. He could, in the image projected by words, photographs, and television, be the potential self hidden by his body. His power would be the power of storytelling and self-dramatization. When they were close friends as freshmen congressmen in 1946, Kennedy had told George Smathers that "he didn't like being a politician. He wanted to be a writer. He admired writers."[23] Kennedy's struggle for control over his own image climaxed in the hiring of Sorensen, a midwestern liberal and conscientious objector with whom Kennedy quickly felt a kinship: the two men shared the cerebral and literary tendencies that had set Jack apart from his family.

Along with the choice of Sorensen, who soon became the chief draftsman of his speeches and writings, Kennedy's selection of the former Jacqueline Bouvier as his wife expressed and enhanced his instinctive tendency toward literature and art within his self-crafting as a politician. In 1953 he had been forced to explain to his fiancée that announcement of their engagement must be postponed until after the publication of an article profiling him in the *Saturday Evening Post* as "The Gay Young Bachelor of the Senate." But it was precisely his dissatisfaction with the emphasis placed on his boyishness in such articles that led him to work hard at developing a compelling story of his own that writers would be happy to repeat.[24]

The theme of the June 1953 seven-page feature in the *Saturday Evening Post* was the unmarried Kennedy's boyish promise. The opening paragraph called him a "walking fountain of youth" who combined a "lean, straight, hard physique" with the "innocently respectful face of an altar boy." The basic judgment of the article was summed up in a description of Kennedy suggesting a yet-unresolved struggle between an impulse for adventure and a recognition of responsibility:

A surface impression of Kennedy is that instead of being in the Senate he ought to be making one of those transoceanic voyages in his own sailboat—something he probably would not be at all averse to. But Kennedy's diffidence is deceptive. Basically a mature and responsible fellow, he possesses an inner fire which has enabled him to rise gallantly to the occasion whenever it was required.[25]

Kennedy's engagement was a response to pressures from his father to move his image forward from that of a "gay bachelor"; Kennedy often joked that his father feared that the voters would begin suspecting that he was a "fairy."[26] Impressed with Jackie's old family manners and feisty spirit, and aware that she lacked the complete independence conferred by family wealth, Joe Sr. pressured Jack to marry her soon. Jackie worked as a freelance "inquiring" reporter; upon reading her articles in the *Times-Herald* on the coronation of Queen Elizabeth, Kennedy proposed to her in a transatlantic telephone call. After she accepted, Kennedy deferred to his father's insistence on a glitzy wedding that could work to political advantage.[27] Even before the wedding Jackie discovered that the Kennedys were determined to use her in projecting Jack's image. She arrived for a stay at Hyannis Port to find herself and Jack accompanied by a *Life* photographer. Only one month after the appearance of the *Saturday Evening Post* story on the "gay bachelor," *Life* published a cover story entitled "*Life* Goes Courting with a U.S. Senator." It described Kennedy as acting like "any young man in love." The four photographs, documenting Kennedy's weekend with his fiancée, Jacqueline Bouvier, began with a view of Kennedy's skipping stones along the water, which the caption described in an appropriate tone of light bemusement as his showing "manly skill in Atlantic surf on private beach at family's summer home."[28]

Jack and Jacqueline were married in virtually royal style on September 12, 1953 in Newport, Rhode Island. One month later, on an October show of his popular television program *Person to Person*, Edward R. Murrow began his introduction of Kennedy, sitting next to his new bride, with the words, "I am told that all little boys have dreams."[29] In an April 1954 feature in *Life* on the reputations of certain senators among their colleagues, readers were shown a photograph of Kennedy captioned "The Boy." It was accompanied by a text emphasizing that "despite his eight years in Congress he still looks like an under-graduate" and "is called 'Jack' even by clerks who have trouble remembering that he is 36 and has an honorary degree from Notre Dame."[30]

Kennedy knew that if he were to be taken seriously in the near future as a national candidate, he needed to find a way to cue the media to move his characterization forward from the role of immature boy. Kennedy conceived of writing an essay on political courage. His young wife played an important role in Jack's following his literary inclinations. Jacqueline shared her husband's interest in reading. During their courtship they had exchanged gifts of favorite books, including on Kennedy's part *Pilgrim's Way*, and had read Shakespeare's *Coriolanus* aloud to each other.[31] Her social manners and old family background, her knowledge of French, and her refined beauty potentially fit in with Kennedy's vision of how American politics could become more glamorous. Kennedy felt that European history was more interesting than American history because Europe had a leisure class. In handwritten notes he would make in late 1955 by the side of the pool at his father's home in Palm Beach, Florida, while re-reading David Cecil's *Melbourne*, Kennedy would ruminate over the lack of a Lady Melbourne or Mary, Queen of Scots in American history. Americans, he noted, had been Puritans struggling under the imperative of survival. He lamented that women were "either prostitutes or housewives," playing little role in the "cultural or intellectual life" of the nation.[32] While uninterested in politics, Jacqueline had in the spring of 1954, at Jack's suggestion, taken a course in history in order to enter more strongly into his professional world. When Jack became serious about expanding his idea for an essay on courage in politics into a book on senators who had demonstrated such courage, she suggested that her professor, Jules Davids, be brought into the project.[33] Jacqueline did not enjoy Jack's political associates, but she could encourage his projection of the literary world they shared into the political one that she only tolerated. Though she suffered bitterly over his infidelities, the couple had begun the partnership that would eventually impress the world with a new American elegance and charm.

But first Kennedy had to undergo an extended return to the sickbed familiar since childhood. While his Addison's was now manageable, by May 1954 his weak back had reduced him to constant dependence on crutches, and he was told that he would probably live out his life in a wheelchair. Despite the even odds that he would not survive the trauma, he determined over his father's objections to have an operation that held out some hope of renewed physical autonomy. He entered the hospital on October 10. In their extensively researched, if gossipy, *The Kennedys: An American Drama*, Peter Collier and David Horowitz quote an anonymous "friend" who recalled the regressive atmosphere of his room. A poster of Marilyn Monroe with her legs spread hung upside down on the wall, a Howdy Doody doll lay on the bed next to his, and young women were constantly in and out. The operation was performed on October 21, and when

Kennedy failed to improve he was forced in February to undergo a second operation. On two occasions his family was called to his bedside and he received the last rites of the Roman Catholic Church.

He spent weeks in a dark room, often asleep, forcibly awakened every half hour, unable to act on his own behalf; even for the consolation he had always found in books, he was dependent on his wife, who sat beside him reading aloud. When he did finally begin to recover after the second operation he still had to endure a lengthy period of isolation while convalescing at his father's home in Palm Springs.[34] Lem Billings, his close friend from school days, recalled the demoralizing month leading to that operation: "It was a terrible time. He was bitter and low. We came close to losing him. I don't just mean losing his life. I mean losing him *as a person.*"[35]

When Kennedy began to improve after the second operation, he turned his thoughts back to the idea that had first begun germinating in his mind in 1954. He used his extended convalescence to read, take notes, and dictate drafts.[36] By the accounts of close observers, the labor on what would become *Profiles in Courage* (1956) was as much a process of revising his self-image as it was of reworking the face he showed the public. Hugh Fraser, a friend since Kennedy's days as the son of the ambassador to Great Britain, suspected that the hospitalized Jack Kennedy's need to "think profoundly about profound things, final things" and the "amount of reading he did" for the book project were "something tremendous" that transformed the Kennedy of 1950 into the Kennedy of 1960.[37]

In 1960 his campaign biographer, James MacGregor Burns, was impressed by Kennedy's refusal, when pressed concerning his emotions during the worst days of his hospital stay, to say any more than "I was just darned sick."[38] In *Profiles in Courage* we can see Kennedy's resolution of those emotions. While composing the book he directed his energies toward the propagation of an image calculated to win the presidency. In pursuit of that goal, Kennedy needed to project a political image that could engage his own longings as well as those of the public.

Kennedy's decision to produce a book on political courage was a brilliant stroke. The book would reinforce his brave image in "Survival," only now this young man of authenticated physical courage would be seen contemplating moral courage. The more subtle, positive aspect of his boyish image was his association, through his precocious authoring of *Why England Slept* and through Hersey's text, with the quality of liminal potential. Presenting himself as the narrator of a text in which he admiringly and thoughtfully told the stories of great heroes of the American democratic tradition, Kennedy could implicitly continue the theme of his own liminal potential. Now he would stand on the threshold of a moral transformation for himself and the society.

Since Herbert Parmet's account of the book's composition in *Jack: The Struggles of John F. Kennedy*, it has been well known that Jules Davids, Jacqueline's professor at Georgetown University, and Kennedy's aide Theodore Sorensen did the bulk of the research and drafting for *Profiles in Courage*. While the idea for the book seems to have originated with Kennedy, and there is substantial evidence of his engagement at every stage of its production, there can now be little doubt that it was a group project that he sponsored and directed. Kennedy kept up with the research, was a source of ideas and material, and in the end decided what would and would not go into the book bearing his name as author. Parmet concluded that the effect upon Kennedy's image was "as deceptive as installing a Chevrolet engine in a Cadillac."[39] Parmet's findings have elicited further charges regarding Kennedy's ethics in accepting the Pulitzer Prize for biography. Garry Wills has judged that Kennedy may properly be called the "author" of the book in the sense that he "authorized" it, but that since it was a product of many hands, of which Sorensen's seems to have been the busiest, Kennedy should not have accepted a "writer's" award.[40]

Kennedy never denied that he had considerable help with the book, but at the same time it reflected his authentic engagement with the material and his own ultimate decisions. In the preface to *Profiles in Courage*, Kennedy points out that "I am not a professional historian; and, although all errors of fact and judgment are exclusively my own, I should like to acknowledge with sincere gratitude those who assisted me in the preparation of this volume." Among these acknowledgments, he proceeds to admit that Davids "assisted materially in the preparation of several chapters," and that "The greatest debt is owed to my research associate, Theodore C. Sorensen, for his invaluable assistance in the assembly and preparation of the material upon which this book is based." Sorensen himself, on the eve of the 1960 presidential campaign, told interviewers, "The way Jack worked was to take all the material, mine and his, pencil it, dictate the fresh copy in his own words, pencil it again, dictate it again—he never used a typewriter."[41]

My inquiry starts with the recognition that, no matter how great the contributions of others, the "Kennedy" narrating the book is in the end Kennedy's calculated self-representation. As a reader, Kennedy had observed how Hersey had remade him in "Survival" into a literary character. Kennedy's father had demonstrated in Jack's first campaign for Congress that the devices of Hollywood could be put to work in politics. Contemplating the lesson, Jack had considered the possibility that he could eventually be both an author and a hero in the romantic history that had been his private vision since his youthful reading of *Marlborough* and *Melbourne*. As a candidate in 1946 he had taken Hersey's literary character "Kennedy" before the public, playing it as a dramatic role to which his viewers brought the compelling narrative experience they had found as readers of Hersey's text. From his first experience of being "madeover" and "cast," Jack seems to have been interested in the potential of his image-self as the means for the self-expression and power that he had not found through his body or under the gaze of his parents.

In *Profiles in Courage*, as in Hersey's "Survival," Kennedy is a liminal self caught "betwixt and between," though now he is not the desperate protagonist struggling amid the waves of the Pacific Ocean but rather a thoughtful storyteller meditating upon the actions of past heroes in relation to a disappointing contemporary society. The narrator Kennedy, a young senator of proven physical courage, stands upon a new threshold, seeking through his immersion in stories of moral courage the determination to attempt a passage to his potential self. He becomes for the reader the protagonist of a story that *Profiles in Courage* implies should be enacted beyond the borders of its text. "Kennedy" is situated as a liminal figure passing from a barren contemporary society to a potential world of heroic individuals in a true community.

Since at the time of the publication of *Profiles in Courage* Hemingway presided on the covers of magazines as the white-bearded representative of masculine courage, Kennedy's simple quotation of this figure invests the young senator with the same frustrated aspirations toward heroic individualism. Kennedy places himself out in front of other politicians with the implicit yet bold assertion that he aspires to perform acts of moral courage that were difficult to find in the Eisenhower *ethos* but have been preserved by the figure of Hemingway in the specially demarcated zone of "literature."

The positive image of Kennedy's physical courage in war is reinforced by the invocation of the war correspondent and author of *For Whom the Bell Tolls*. At the same time, the negative image of a boyish stripling who is taken more seriously by the young secretaries in the Capitol than by his Senate colleagues is reconfigured into that of a serious young observer of moral heroism: "This is a book about that most admirable of human virtues—courage. 'Grace under pressure,' Ernest Hemingway defined it."

Indeed, Kennedy indicates that Hemingway is supplying him with the plot that he will present in each of the successive narratives of his book:

And these are the stories of the pressures experienced by eight United States Senators and the grace with which they endured them—the risks to their careers, the unpopularity of their courses, the defamation of their characters, and sometimes, but sadly only sometimes, the vindication of their reputations and their principles.

The fundamental plot of *Profiles in Courage* does in fact correlate with that of the Hemingway work that captured the public's imagination in the 1950s and inaugurated the aging writer's role as cultural authority.

The Old Man and the Sea is carefully abstracted from the contemporary social and cultural context and patterned according to "classic" patterns of epic tragedy. Hemingway's novella is set in a remote world of a single village and a great sea; centers upon the three universal characters of an old man, a boy, and a fish; and consists of a heroic struggle climaxing in suffering and loss. *The Old Man and the Sea* unfolds as a "timeless" statement of religious, or at least spiritual, import. The narrative structure develops with a ritual-like inevitability and sense of acceptance. The old man endures a purgative trial, and performs a sacrifice in which the fish and the fisherman achieve a transcendent communion eliciting tragic emotions in both the boy and the reader.

The narrative is framed by the story of the relationship between the old man and the boy. When the text begins, Santiago has not caught a fish in 84 days, and as a result the practical father of the boy Manolin insists that his son stop fishing with an old man who has become unlucky. The old man is clearly pained by the loss of the boy for whom he had functioned as a mentor and, in effect, surrogate parent. *The Old Man and the Sea* begins in a world that has become unaccountably barren, where the hero is failing and thus losing his authority over his disciple. This loss in turn presents the threat that the old values will be lost to merely commercial pressures.

Santiago determines to go out beyond the familiar boundaries respected by the fishermen. After he captures an eighteen-foot marlin through a nearly superhuman effort, he suffers the purgatorial loss of his fish, bit by bit, in a doomed struggle with sharks. Santiago, utterly exhausted, returns to the village with only the skeleton. In an obvious evocation of Christ's path to the cross, Hemingway has the old man fall several times as he carries the mast of his boat on his shoulders up to his hut.

Yet Santiago emerges from this ritualistic enactment of aspiration, effort, and loss a winner. The extraordinary skeleton that he brings back testifies to the profound dimensions of his struggle. His spiritual authority in the village is reaffirmed, and with it the old man regains his cultural authority. The boy Manolin, who always loved him, now feels justified in refusing to follow his father's wish and returning to the old man. The novella ends with the old man and the boy happily restored to each other: "Up the road in his shack, the old man was sleeping again. He was still sleeping on his face and the boy was sitting by him watching him. The old man was dreaming about the lions."[42]

By invoking Hemingway as the authority to whom he looks for his values, the young narrator of *Profiles in Courage* configures himself as the "boy" looking to "Papa," a perfect analogue to the boy at the end of *The Old Man and the Sea* gazing upon the old man. On the final page of the novella, Hemingway focuses attention on the inability of American tourists to be a proper audience for Santiago's courage and sacrifice. To them the marlin skeleton appears as no more than garbage amid the empty beer cans and dead barracuda. On the first page of *Profiles in Courage*, immediately upon identifying Hemingway with the past senators whom he intends to profile, Kennedy laments that "a nation which has forgotten the quality of courage which in the past has been brought to public life is not as likely to insist upon or reward that quality in its chosen leaders today—and in fact we have forgotten." Referring to the sacrifices of John Quincy Adams and Daniel Webster, he concludes this second paragraph of the book with "We do not remember—and possibly we do not care."[43] At the conclusion of *The Old Man and the Sea* Manolin and Santiago exist outside the ignorance of the tourists; at the opening of *Profiles in Courage* Kennedy and Hemingway stand outside a society indifferent to their timeless values. Like the reader of *The Old Man and the Sea*, the reader of *Profiles in Courage* is faced with a choice: either identify with the *communitas* formed by the mutual regard of an aspiring youth and a heroic old man, or remain with a society of isolated members ruled by self-interest.

Indeed, just as in the opening of Hemingway's novella Manolin feels compelled to go along with his father's wish that he abandon the old man for the practical success of a more conventional fisherman, Kennedy describes how he was pressured by a bad "parent" in Congress to follow a conventional route: " 'The way to get along,' I was told when I entered Congress, 'is to go along' " (in the deleted "letters" version of the first chapter, this admonition is delivered by "Senator Oldtimer"). In contrast to this

79

advice from an elder to conform, Kennedy celebrates the exhortation of one of the heroes from the past whom he will profile, Daniel Webster, " 'to push [his] skiff from the shore alone' into a hostile and turbulent sea."[44]

This quotation strikingly evokes the central image of Hemingway's recent novella. In fact, that is true of each of the eight profiles of past senators that make up the subsequent chapters of the book. Each chapter repeats the same plot, the story of a man who separates himself from his fellows by daring to take a stand that leaves him out alone, far beyond any political support, "in a sea of popular rule."[45] While in each case the senator performs the heroic deed, that achievement in some cases is futile (such as Sam Houston's defiance of Texans' determination to secede from the union) and inevitably ends in his political defeat. What saves the senator and his values from ultimate futility is posterity, the succeeding generations who from a distance can recognize the superiority of the individual's moral courage to the demands of his constituency.

Kennedy makes it clear that this posterity is an external image of the internal gaze that the senator in each story insists is more important than the gaze of the body politic:

It was not because they "loved the public better than themselves." On the contrary it was precisely because they did *love themselves*—because each one's need to maintain his own respect for himself was more important to him than his popularity with others—because his desire to win or maintain a reputation for integrity and courage was stronger than his desire to maintain his office—because his conscience, his personal standard of ethics, his integrity or morality, call it what you will—was stronger than the pressures of public disapproval—because his faith that *his* course was the best one, and would ultimately be vindicated, outweighed his fear of public reprisal.

Although the public good was the indirect beneficiary of his sacrifice, it was not that vague and general concept, but one or a combination of these pressures of self-love that pushed him along the course of action that resulted in the slings and arrows previously described.[46]

In *The Old Man and the Sea*, what saves Santiago amid the indifference of the village is his self-regard, his brave adherence to the hard-earned values of a lifetime, mirrored by the ability of one boy to recognize and desire to emulate those virtues. In *Profiles in Courage*, that mirror of the hero's love of his own highest potential is Kennedy, who thus fills the role of Manolin.

Like Hemingway's aspiring boy, "Kennedy" is the next generation who can assure the old heroes that their sacrifices will achieve a continuation of the values they embody.

This effect is emphasized by the repetitive quality of the stories making up the book. The "profiles" progress chronologically through American history, establishing a historical legacy that the reader can either take up or let die. They also comprise a judicious selection from among the regions and political identities of the country, further projecting Kennedy's desired image as a politician with a broad national vision. But neither the historical progression nor the regional and political variety alter the essential repetitiveness of the stories. As Kennedy constructs them, they always follow the same pattern: a seriously flawed but in some way extraordinary protagonist has a perspective on an issue that is sure to bring him ruin; he accepts the ruin, and he is vindicated either later in his career or in the eyes of posterity.

The reader moving from the fates of Adams and Webster and Houston through those of the following five heroes "chooses" to undergo the inevitable repetition of this experience of sacrificial doom. The reader generated by this textual experience thus willingly participates in a ritual of heroic defiance of the crowd that preserves the transcendent values of the culture. In *The Old Man and the Sea* Hemingway uses allusions to the Christ story to associate his fisherman with the concept of ritualistic sacrifice. Both Hemingway and Kennedy attempt to bring the reader from the conformist and materialistic 1950s United States into a shared preservation of an otherwise dismissed value from the past. The inevitability of their heroes' fates becomes both numbing and oddly reassuring.

The "Kennedy" of *Profiles in Courage* celebrates the lonely but strong male heroes who choose self-love over the love of an external body politic. Each hero indeed makes the culmination of his life the act of turning away from the demanding gaze of that capricious body. This pattern can easily be related to Kennedy's childhood conflicts with his mother and subsequent struggles with his father. His father's isolationist convictions as Ambassador to Great Britain early in World War II earned him precisely the vilification and political ruin suffered by the "profiled heroes" of his son's book. Yet Kennedy himself, in his determination to follow his own views, had struggled less with the demands of the public than with those of his father. To emulate the independence of his father, Kennedy had to be independent of his father.

The private themes of Kennedy's book, obviously unacceptable if presented directly, could be expressed in the disguised form of the profiled heroes because they were echoed by a broader ideological discourse. In the 1950s, when so many cultural spokespersons were expressing fears about the feminization of society, *The Old Man and the Sea* and *Profiles in Courage* pointed the culture away from "feminine" values of domesticity and community toward "masculine" risk-taking and autonomy. In the portrayal of autonomous men who prove themselves against the pressures of a feminine "sea" or "body politic," we may discern a metaphor for the struggle of capitalist ideology with the conflict between the traditional producer ethic from before the war and the newly ascendant consumer ethic.

Both Hemingway's Santiago and Kennedy's heroic senators court disaster, and their authors celebrate that impulse, with a relentlessness that suggests guilt. The poor fisherman might seem an unlikely signifier of such an impulse, but his inability to resolve his feelings about the exploitation of the fish by the customers at the market (after concluding that the buyers of sliced fillets are not worthy to eat a fish of such great "behavior" and "dignity," he decides that he does "not understand these things")[47] demonstrates his conflict over his participation in a system that violates his own ethical understanding of his proper relation to the fish ("his brother") and nature. The fisherman of *The Old Man and the Sea* and the senators of *Profiles in Courage* must suffer profoundly so that their respective authors and readers might purge the conflict they feel over the ultimate point of the system they serve. Ennobled by sacrifice, these heroes seem at the end of the ritual to be, in themselves, what is truly worthy in American culture. The contradictions felt by American society in the 1950s are glimpsed in these texts only to be illogically resolved through their heroes', and vicariously their readers', paradoxical experiences of apotheosis through destruction.

The reception of *Profiles in Courage* accomplished everything Kennedy could have hoped. It became a best-seller and was widely lauded in the press. Most important, it cued journalists and editors to move their characterization of Jack Kennedy forward from an energetic boy into a maturing young man. With the awarding of the Pulitzer Prize for biography, Kennedy's new image as a thoughtful student of history and democratic theory was further enhanced. He became the unofficial historian of the Senate, placed in charge of an effort to name five outstanding senators from history. He was selected as the "perfect man" to narrate a film on the history of the Democratic party to be televised at the 1956 Democratic convention.[48]

In *Profiles* Kennedy thus found a means to engage the public world of politics through the private world of his innermost inclinations. His father had appropriated Hersey's literary experiment and had employed speech-writers and publicists to construct a political image for his son; that son, who at the time would have preferred to be a writer, now drew on his literary instincts to produce a book that would rewrite that image. An associate recalled that Kennedy had proudly responded to the news that he was going to be awarded the Pulitzer Prize by suggesting that this success would indicate to people "another factor or facet in his overall personality and achievements, that he was a very capable and able individual, well-rounded in many ways."[49] As master of the production of a book acclaimed by the media, Kennedy gained control of his image and won a sense of personal power. He thereafter approached politics as a powerful *auteur*. Kennedy's image was the work that he was truly authoring, and his medium was the apparatus of post-World War II mass communications.

After *Profiles in Courage* became a massive best-seller and was awarded the 1957 Pulitzer Prize for biography, Kennedy's office was inundated with requests for further work from the senator. Kennedy responded by directing Sorensen in a huge production of articles appearing in periodicals ranging from *Foreign Affairs* to *McCall's*. The idealistic yet thoughtful and pragmatic voice of "Kennedy" speaking in these articles projected to readers across the land. The closest study of their production appears in Herbert Parmet's *Jack: The Struggles of John F. Kennedy*. Parmet calls it a "literary campaign" that "jibed with [Kennedy's] own instincts and political perceptions" and will probably not be seen again in the age of television.[50]

These are easily documented results of the book. But the 1950s reader's experience of *Profiles in Courage* as a narrative constructed within the context of the decade, and especially of Hemingway's significance to it, is at least as important. John Hersey's "Survival" transformed Kennedy into a literary character, which is to say a function of a text that produces a self-contained experience. Readers of that text thereafter brought the experience to Kennedy's image, so that the politician became an object of their imaginations. *Profiles in Courage* continued that process, quietly extending the production of Kennedy as literary protagonist by having that character narrate a book about other heroes. The narrator was the true subject of the text, and with his readers participated in enacting the ritualistic sacrifice performed by the successive heroes.

The ritualistic nature of the book constituted the experience of Kennedy not only as a literary character, a figure of aesthetic dimensions, but also as a figure of vaguely spiritual significance. Readers of *Profiles in Courage* could reexperience the narrative as they contemplated the image of its narrator gazing out from photographs in magazines. The character and icon "Kennedy" in the picture magazines was now seen in relation to the character-icon "Hemingway." Kennedy had joined Hemingway as a figure emblematizing the traditional American virtues that many saw as threatened. But whereas Hemingway was viewed as the sage who sent back his wise observations from a lifetime of struggle and achievement, Kennedy was the young hero who, having read those messages carefully, would soon set out into the future on his mission.

In 1960 Kennedy accepted a suggestion that he name his aspiration for the country the New Frontier, a vision of American life as an endless going out into "unknown opportunities and perils."[51] The vision of *The Old Man and the Sea* — in which a solitary hero "went out too far" — was one of the precedents for this concept. The New Frontier was, in part, Kennedy's appropriation of the world of Hemingway for politics, a creative excursion by a politician into literature — made possible by their shared status in the mass media as celebrity images.

How did Hemingway react to Kennedy's positioning himself as Boy to his Old Man? Hemingway was among the writers and artists invited to Kennedy's inauguration, but the doctors at the Mayo Clinic, where he was being treated for severe depression, would not allow him to go. His friend A. E. Hotchner has written that Hemingway "was pleased and moved by the invitation, and we spent some time composing a proper reply of declination."[52] In a letter to his wartime friend General "Buck" Lanham, Hemingway expressed his delight at the invitation and his bitter annoyance at a newspaper report that he had replied only "No comment" to an inquiry about whether he would attend.[53] He also indicated to artist William Walton how proud he was to have Walton as a mutual friend of the president.[54]

A Washington hostess and longtime friend of the Kennedy family asked Hemingway to write his thoughts about the inauguration for a volume of tributes to be given to the president. In emphasizing the tale of Hemingway's decline during those last months of his life, the better to explain his subsequent suicide, biographers have taken their cue from the widow's memoir and focused on Hemingway's difficulty in writing a mere four-line tribute.[55] Perhaps Hemingway's excitement over the power he saw in Kennedy to keep alive the values he himself had embodied was as much a factor as his own felt loss of power. Hemingway understandably had mixed

responses to younger writers who sought to succeed him, but he could welcome this Boy as his son, because as a president who read and quoted the
Nobel Prize-winning writer, Kennedy offered not to overthrow Hemingway's status but to enhance and fulfill it. And the words Hemingway finally
sent to Kennedy were a compelling expression of the approval a father
might give a son:

Watching the inauguration from Rochester there was the happiness and the hope
and the pride and how beautiful we thought Mrs. Kennedy was and then how
deeply moving the inaugural address was. Watching on the screen I was sure our
President would stand any of the heat to come as he had taken the cold of that
day. Each day since I have renewed my faith and tried to understand the practical
difficulties of governing he must face as they arise and admire the true courage
he brings to them. It is a good thing to have a brave man as our President in times
as these are for our country and the world.[56]

When, the following July, Kennedy learned of Hemingway's suicide, he
mourned the author in a statement observing that "Few Americans had a
greater impact on the emotions and attitudes of the American people than
Ernest Hemingway."[57] He helped Hemingway's widow, despite the ban on
American citizens traveling to Cuba, to go to Castro's island and negotiate
the removal of her husband's manuscripts.

In the spring of 1962, Kennedy honored Hemingway at the White
House dinner he held for American winners of the Nobel Prize. A performance in the East Room intended to represent the best in the nation
included a reading by actor Frederic March from Hemingway's yet-unpub-
lished *Islands in the Stream*. The president directed that, during the dinner and performance, the widow of George Marshall, architect of NATO
and namesake of the Marshall Plan, should sit on his right. On his left he
placed Mary Hemingway.[58]

By presenting himself to the camera as the escort of Hemingway's
widow, Kennedy signified to the public that he had completed his passage
from Boy of American politics to successor to the Old Man. *The Old Man
and the Sea* had become *Profiles in Courage* had become the New Frontier. After Kennedy's assassination, the widows of Hemingway and
Kennedy agreed that Hemingway's manuscripts would be housed in a
Hemingway Room of the Kennedy Library.

CHAPTER FOUR

The Hollywood Screen and Kennedy's Televised Showdown with Truman

After the overwhelming defeat of Adlai Stevenson in the 1956 presidential election, Kennedy unofficially began his campaign for the Democratic nomination in 1960. His health problems were at last under control. Though he wore an eight-inch-wide brace to support his back and his face was puffed out by the cortisone he took for Addison's disease, he had projected a vigorous and telegenic appearance at the Democratic convention. Despite Kennedy's failure to win the vice-presidential nomination, in an exciting last-minute contest with Senator Estes Kefauver when Stevenson left the choice to the convention delegates, the *New York Times* declared him a television "star."

Having set his sights on winning the presidency in 1960, Kennedy had to first convince the state party bosses that if nominated he could be elected. He knew that their two chief points of skepticism were his religion and his age. No Catholic had ever been elected president; and Kennedy, at forty-three, would also be attempting to become the youngest man ever elected. On the positive side, his proven strengths were the heroic aura conferred by the telling and retelling of his PT 109 adventures, the prestige of his best-selling and Pulitzer Prize-winning book, and the glamor that he and his wife projected on television. Kennedy's work on the Senate Labor

87

Subcommittee in 1957 and 1958, while his brother Bobby confronted a defiant Jimmy Hoffa in his pursuit of corruption in the Teamsters Union, added to this image of maturing seriousness, a tough-guy readiness to oppose injustice. Through the many articles that appeared under his byline and his countless appearances around the country, Kennedy attempted to build on these strengths.

As 1960 approached Kennedy became convinced that the only way to persuade the Democratic bosses that he was a winner was to enter the primaries. States selecting delegates according to their voters' preferences were a small minority, but Kennedy saw in them an opportunity to prove his power to capture votes outside his native Massachusetts, where he had been emphatically reelected to the Senate in 1958. His major rivals for the nomination—Senator Stuart Symington of Missouri, Senate majority leader Lyndon Johnson of Texas, and possibly Stevenson—would not enter the primaries. But the liberal Senator Hubert Humphrey of Minnesota would, and their contests in Wisconsin and, climactically, in overwhelmingly Protestant and poor West Virginia helped Kennedy prove that his combination of a powerful organization and a compelling image could overcome his seeming drawbacks as a candidate.

The strategy of the primaries worked for Kennedy in another way. His carefully produced image had presented him as a liminal figure, a youth undergoing a series of passages, from his contemplation of the mistakes made by his English heroes as they confronted Hitler, to his life-threatening initiation in fundamental truths of human and extrahuman nature in the South Pacific, to his hospitalization and meditations upon ultimate purposes and the place of heroism in contemporary democratic society. Readers—potential voters—had encountered Kennedy as a character in texts made up of words and photographs on pages in magazines or books. Now, with the novelty of the televised primaries, Kennedy had the opportunity to present himself as a real-life protagonist on a pilgrimage unfolding before viewers' eyes. Once again, he could be cast in the role of heroic protagonist moving through a transition, and the reader—now also viewer—could vicariously experience that movement as his or her own experience.

88 Strikingly, the construction of Kennedy's political image had been a matter of drawing on sources of energy outside politics. The initial image had been produced from a merger of journalism with literature, creating a "Kennedy" who was in fact a literary representation through whom the reader underwent a narrative experience. With *Profiles in Courage*,

Kennedy had gone deeper into the realm of encoded cultural energy demarcated as literature. Positioning himself in relation to older heroes, most immediately Hemingway, he had moved from merely allowing himself to be the basis for a character devised by others toward being the author of that character and of the roles he would play. Now he calculated the experience he wanted the reader to have in identifying with him.

In 1960 Kennedy would have to perform "live," taking this image before the television cameras. Whereas he had profited from the narrative devices and energies of literature in Hersey's "Survival" and his own *Profiles in Courage*, in moving before the television cameras he began to draw chiefly on the visual resources available in film. The discourses of post–World War II Hollywood became his chief point of reference, the language of faces and stories within which he constructed his meanings.

This chapter will first examine the many-featured apparatus of mass communications available to a candidate who in 1960 had the prescience and ability to use it, then move to a close study of one "text," Kennedy's televised response to an attack from the titular head of his party on the eve of the Democratic convention. In analyzing that text as both a social drama and a media performance, we will reconstruct its meaning, for both Kennedy and his viewers, within the cultural context that the performer shared with his audience.

Kennedy's pursuit of the presidency through a politics of image took place in a brief era that almost perfectly served it. While the American film industry had become the central source of mass entertainment in America as early as the 1920s, the 1940s and 1950s—the two decades leading up to Kennedy's New Frontier—were the great era of Hollywood in which "the movies" constituted a fully rendered, self-contained *world*. As Michael Wood points out in *America in the Movies*, only at the close of the 1930s did Hollywood develop production values that enabled it to make films more than just the magical effects of manipulated shadows. Using depth of focus, which allowed all planes on the screen to appear to be in sharp focus, the movies could project a world as fully rendered and detailed as the world the viewer saw outside the theater. The screen could now provide a more truly dreamlike illusion, a "licensed zone of unreality." This zone was a world that seemed to duplicate—and also improve upon—the reality of the viewer's social world.[1]

With the introduction of television at the end of the 1940s, Hollywood increasingly relied on this ability to provide a heightened reality to draw

89

people from their homes. As the small box in the living room inexorably replaced the movies as the major provider of cheap entertainment, Hollywood countered with magnificent on-location settings, dazzling Technicolor, and the breathtaking wide-screen processes of Panavision and Vistavision. Under pressure from television, Hollywood also concentrated on stories for its core audience. Discontinuing the occasional experiments of the 1940s with social realism and idiosyncratic tales, the film industry in the 1950s stuck to the more dependable strategy of casting major stars in such proven genres as the western, the musical, the comic romance, and the crime story.[2]

Thus, even more than the films of the forties, those of the fifties constituted a world of interchangeable, familiar stories with familiar faces in familiar settings. The Hollywood screen mirrored the actual world of its viewers back to them with a style and glamor that transformed it into myth. As Wood points out, "The movies *are* a world, a country of familiar faces, a mythology made up of a limited number of stories" possessing "a relation of wish, echo, transposition, displacement, inversion, compensation, reinforcement, example, warning. . . . What remains constant is an oblique but unbroken connection to the historical world."[3]

As 1960 approached, this mythology was coming to an end. The expansion of television into virtually every household in America had undermined the Hollywood studios. While major pictures still drew huge audiences, overall movie attendance had steadily declined from 90 million in 1951 to 43 million by the end of the decade.[4] Kennedy arrived at a unique moment of transition in the media: the film screen was being superseded by the sheer immediacy and accessibility of a home television screen, but Hollywood nevertheless provided a mythological world of immense cultural power. In addition, the glossy, large-format weekly magazines combining photojournalism with text still boasted huge circulations. *Life*, *Look*, and the *Saturday Evening Post* were losing not their readers but rather their advertisers to television. In this way television would ultimately undermine them more fundamentally than it would the movies. But at this point the picture magazines still complemented television with artful, full-color constructions of "reality" that entered homes across the land.

Kennedy brought to television news and photojournalism the components most prevalent in the world of film: star quality and mythic story. With his telegenic looks, skills at self-presentation, heroic fantasies, and creative intelligence, Kennedy was brilliantly prepared to project a major screen persona. He appropriated the discourses of mass culture, especially of Hollywood, and transferred them to the news. By this strategy he made the news like dreams and like the movies—a realm in which images played out scenarios that accorded with the viewer's deepest yearnings. As David Bordwell has demonstrated, the classical Hollywood film style centers on a character whose personal or psychological motivations drive a plot aimed at his (or, less often, her) overcoming obstacles and achieving goals.[5]

The news possessed the added power of being understood as pure fact. Kennedy played himself, and the viewer watched him not in a darkened fantasy domain but in a well-lit living room where television functioned as part of the actual environment. As a vivid storyteller and actor, Kennedy made the news a compelling site for his enactments of desire. Never appearing in an actual film, but rather turning the television apparatus into his screen, he became the greatest movie star of the twentieth century.

Kennedy's aestheticizing of the news was hardly a violation of an objective reportage formerly untainted by fiction. Despite its claims of representing "the way it is" with a mirror to the world, the news actually disguises a biased perspective behind the authority of a presumed objectivity. That perspective is easily hidden, because it is the public ideology of American democratic capitalism. As the given of the culture, it appears to emanate from common sense. The journalist's stance of objectivity—the claim that news representations and enunciations are the simple truth—is an assumed authority by which that subjective ideology may more powerfully draw new personages and events into the constructions of its world.[6] Like the networks and photomagazines—like John Hersey in his 1944 presentation of John Kennedy in the New Yorker article "Survival"—Kennedy built the facts into a story. What made Kennedy unique was the skill and compelling force with which he and his collaborators had learned to use the news apparatus to project a narrative of their own devising that gave television networks a star and story of such box-office power that they were eager to screen it.

Kennedy and his collaborators were engaged in this project at a time when the public still thought of the news as existing in a distinctly separate realm from that of fictive entertainment. That credibility was disturbed in 1959 by the Quiz Show scandal, which revealed that contestants who had competed for huge sums of cash had been actors playing roles cast for them by producers. The most successful of these real-life actors was Charles Van Doren. Under the intense pressure displayed on *Twenty One*, Van Doren charmed viewers with his ability to project an appealing sincerity and humility while producing the winning answers. As a young assistant professor at Columbia University coming on the show to face the unpopular but seemingly invincible current champion, Van Doren became a popular hero across the nation. NBC-TV even gave him the role of summer replacement for host David Garroway on the morning show *Today*. When the scandal broke, Van Doren finally had to confess that he had reluctantly followed scripts provided by his producers.[7]

Kennedy clearly understood that this disturbance of credibility could lead to public skepticism about the role and plot he was preparing to enact before the television cameras. A couple of months before the January 1960 announcement of his candidacy, Kennedy frankly discussed image-making in an article in *TV Guide*. Granting that "political shows, like quiz shows, can be fixed," Kennedy acknowledged the artifice of television images by emphasizing the importance of a contemporary politician's "creating a television image people like and (most difficult of all) remember." Kennedy even took the opportunity to assert that youth was a great advantage in constructing such a successful image. But he also claimed that, in his experience, the images of famous politicians such as Stevenson and Eisenhower most often had an "uncannily correct" mimetic relation to the person represented.[8]

By thus sharing with the audience of *TV Guide* his self-aware projection of an image, Kennedy was perhaps attempting to reassure the public by letting them in on the private strategy that by implication Kennedy himself had devised to prevent his own self-delusion. At the very least, his sophisticated discussion of television images complimented the viewers' intelligence. By holding the image up for their mutual contemplation as an artful representation of his authentic self, Kennedy sought a deeper bond with his reader/viewer. He even added to his image by making a part of that image his visibly ironic relation to it, taking the self-regarding creative stance of a character who acknowledges that he is also his author. The author and his viewer were both constructed as insider/outsiders, sophisticated participants in a world in which performance could mean both display and accomplishment.

As the campaign approached, his father also frankly discussed Jack's star image. In an interview, Joseph Sr. argued that his son's image could in effect "sell" the Democratic Party to the voters in the same way that images of major Hollywood stars sold movies or magazines to consumers:

Jack is the greatest attraction in the country today. I'll tell you how to sell more copies of a book. Put his picture on the cover. Why is it that when his picture is on the cover of *Life* or *Redbook* they sell a record number of copies? You advertise the fact that he will be at a dinner and you will break all records for attendance. He can draw more people to a fundraising dinner than Cary Grant or Jimmy Stewart. Why is that? He has more universal appeal.[9]

Joseph Sr.'s assertion of his son's "universal appeal" deserves examination. Exactly how was Jack more appealing than either of these actors? Grant and Stewart were preeminent stars of the 1940s and 1950s who defined strikingly opposite images. Grant's image was marked by his grace, his wit, his detached and amused sophistication—he was a man of the upper class able to manipulate others in a world of manners. The dark side of that image was the constant potential for insincerity and inauthenticity. By almost exact contrast, Stewart conveyed awkwardness, honesty, an innocent sincerity—marks of a man of the small town and working class whose feelings are expressed in action; the dark side of his image was the potential for naïveté and hysteria. George Cukor brilliantly contrasted Stewart and Grant in their competition for Katherine Hepburn in *The Philadelphia Story* (1940), and Alfred Hitchcock made his greatest films of the 1940s and 1950s as alternating meditations upon these two screen images, which culminated in the masterful *Vertigo* (1958) and hugely popular *North by Northwest* (1959).

Stewart's screen characters must consistently overcome weaknesses, often signified by such physical or psychological disabilities as the deaf ear in Frank Capra's *It's a Wonderful Life* (1946), the broken leg in Hitchcock's *Rear Window* (1954), or the acrophobia in *Vertigo*. These weaknesses are either acquired or discovered while the Stewart character performs an earnest deed in the world of "manly" action. In general, Stewart portrays a man who must wrestle with external threats while overcoming his human frailties on his way to achieving maturity.[10] With his love of the movies, Jack Kennedy must have encountered Stewart's popular screen persona many times. At the beginning of his political career, Kennedy had actually met Stewart at a Hollywood party while visiting with his friend Chuck Spalding.[11] Coming of age in the 1940s and still making his image in the 1950s, Kennedy may well have observed in Stewart's image a model for his own public presentation of his bad back, his shyness, and his seemingly callow youth among older politicians.

Stewart's screen persona belonged to a broad category that included such other major stars as Gary Cooper and Henry Fonda—a type that has been called the bashful hero. These characters shared self-effacing expressions of conviction, coupled with an ability to convey empathy. In movies such as *Young Mr. Lincoln* (1939) and *Mr. Roberts* (1955), Fonda consistently played ordinary heroes possessing mature authority drawn from their combination of professionalism, compassion, and integrity. Cooper did the same in such films as the 1940 adaptation of Hemingway's *For Whom the Bell Tolls* and the story of baseball star Lou Gehrig in *The Pride of the Yankees* (1942). In writing about this star type, a critic has observed: "In his natural state, it is hard to distance ourselves from him. Although he is an idealized character, he is an idealized character of us as we *naturally* are."[12] Stars in the mode of Stewart succeeded in mirroring the viewer's perception of her or his natural instincts toward right behavior.

As opposed to the Stewart type, Grant more typically struggles with his own elusiveness, a Brahmin remoteness and handsome glibness that make it difficult for him to commit himself or to be taken at face value. In such films as *The Philadelphia Story, Suspicion* (1941), and *North by Northwest*, he must overcome this detachment and superficiality to achieve substance and earn the trust of the woman he courts.[13] Kennedy, with his inherited wealth, cultivated charm, and adaptation of the style of British aristocrats, could see in Grant a model for making his advantages attractive and finally irresistible to those suspicious of being seduced. His fascination with the movie star was such that after Kennedy reached the White House he would sometimes call Grant "just to hear that impeccable voice."[14]

Kennedy fused the aristocratic traits of Grant and the democratic traits of Stewart. In Kennedy's image, manipulative charm and cool wit combined with disarmingly urgent idealism and vulnerability. The combination might make some suspicious, but for many more it offered a complementary assurance of authentic feeling and sophisticated command. A considerable degree of Kennedy's "more universal appeal" derived from his success at emulating aspects of both of these film actors' personae. By the end of the 1950s, he had combined them into a seamless persona of his own that his father could argue surpassed either of its models. This was a star who mirrored both the aspiration and the fantasy of the viewer.

Kennedy's televised image also drew on a set of film stars perhaps less easy for his father to evoke. As Kennedy's political image-making moved along with the popular culture of the 1950s, his long and unruly hair, his restless gestures, and his flashes of barely controlled fury all linked him to the young rebels who in the 1950s became heroes of the new youth subculture. In such films as *Red River* (1948), *The Wild One* (1954), and *The Left-Handed Gun* (1958), the new generation of actors represented by Montgomery Clift, Marlon Brando, and Paul Newman portrayed sensitive young men in conflict with their elders. They signified a comprehensive yet vague dissatisfaction, a mysterious anger emblematized in *The Wild One* by Brando's famed answer "What have you got?" to the question of what he was rebelling against. James Dean epitomized this rebellious young man in *East of Eden* (1955) and *Rebel Without a Cause* (1955). It was Dean's suggestion of vulnerability contained by a heavy-lidded cool that Kennedy most adapted to the public style he brought to presidential politics. In a 1957 *McCall's* article entitled "The Senator Is in a Hurry," Kennedy implicitly, if inadvertently, linked himself to Dean's image, and by that time Elvis Presley's as well, by insisting on a difference. He volunteered, "People talk about how I wear my hair, but I don't want to put grease on it."[15] The absence of grease suggested a small if crucial distinction between the Hollywood rebels' energy, perceived by adults as dangerous, and his own energy, which he claimed held the readiness to serve.

Recognizing the categories of star images epitomized by Stewart, Grant, and Dean in salient aspects of Kennedy's public persona does not require determining to what degree he calculatingly or even knowingly imitated them. A devoted fan of the movies, Kennedy was influenced by these actors' styles, and found in emulating them both a fantasy fulfillment of his private desires and the possibility of fulfilling those desires by appealing more to others. Enjoying romantic affairs and friendships with actresses such as Gene Tierney and Angie Dickinson, and associating with Frank Sinatra's Rat Pack (of whom brother-in-law Peter Lawford was a member), he acquired an insider/outsider's view of the trade. Kennedy moved in front of and behind the movie screen, sharing with the audience a view of Hollywood as a source of fantasy for an idealized self while sharing with the movie stars a knowledge of how to use those fantasies and live with them.

A politician who merely possessed good looks and a desire to emulate movie star glamor would likely have come off as vacuous and imitative. But Kennedy had early achieved a strong conception of what role he wanted to play in his private drama and of how that fit with his view of his audience. In *Profiles in Courage*, he had cast that role as hero-aspirant poised to revive the individualistic energies of democracy. Kennedy's approach to both the campaign and the presidency would be to enact his private desire in public, to project an image that each viewing citizen could emulate in his or her own way.

The distance between Eisenhower and Kennedy as star "types" was much greater than the small distance between them ideologically. In an era of constrained political debate, Kennedy positioned himself near the center, close to Eisenhower. But as a political candidate of the opposite party, Kennedy had to define himself as a radical version of Eisenhower's moderate centrist. The radicalism was not of an alternative ideology, but rather of intensity. Kennedy was a radical in the same way a Hollywood star playing a typical role in a genre film was a radical—in his projected scenario, he was playing a hero who faced a limited time in which to overcome obstacles. Kennedy identified himself with seemingly noncontroversial American desires for decency and aspiration, fairness and power, liberation and commitment, the individual and the family. But his urgency suggested that he was struggling to fulfill his own projected sense of self. Whereas a leader committed to a definite cause or agenda bonds with citizens as a group, aggrieved by some social injustice or frustration, Kennedy, committed to the fulfillment of his own image, bonded with individuals. He was constructing an image with the generalized virtue and conviction of movie heroes. Like the leading men of Hollywood, Kennedy projected these qualities through a winning combination of good looks, self-deprecating charm, earnest determination, and the appearance of common decency.

In the 1960 presidential campaign Kennedy brought together his efforts at self-presentation over the previous decade to project a vivid narrative before the American people. Kennedy sought to achieve through his image what he could not through his body. He created that image to satisfy frustrated aspirations in the culture at large, and he adapted his self by the methods of the film star. His own heroic fantasies; his identification with themes in the contemporary culture, from which he intuited discomfort with the Eisenhower ethos; and his recognition of the new importance of the visual media merged in his candidacy. Like a film star, Kennedy became a mirror image of the citizen's desire, an idealized reflection.

The 1960 campaign was remarkably devoid of disagreement within and even between the parties. Both Kennedy's contests with Humphrey in the primaries and his subsequent race against the Republican nominee, Vice President Richard Nixon, lacked substantial debate over either domestic or foreign policy. The cold war consensus imposed narrow ideological constraints. The liberal pluralists of the Democratic Party and the corporate liberals of the Republican Party held that their centrist positions were "reality." Their success in so defining their place in the political spectrum left small room for any candidate of the left or right to maneuver. Kennedy had little more than tactical quarrels with his opponents, and was motivated in his run for the presidency not by ideology but by the need to both please his father and fulfill his own heroic aspirations. Kennedy was not without ideology, but what he had was the same belief-system of anticommunism and domestic meliorism that guided the other major candidates, and thus was not a means of differentiating himself from his rivals.

Kennedy set himself apart by tapping into the resources of cultural energy found in the domains demarcated as literature, theater, and Hollywood. It had been not only the rivalry of television that prompted Hollywood to focus in the 1950s on genre films. The investigation by the House Committee on Un-American Activities (HUAC) into communist influence in the film industry had persuaded the studios to steer away from the social-problem films they had produced in the 1940s and to eliminate overt political content. Yet, as Peter Biskind has extensively documented in his study of the 1950s Hollywood film, the result was by no means a bland production of films presenting the same point of view.

The ideological consensus of the cold war was a lid pressed down on a wide spectrum of competing ideologies. Popular films—though on the surface lacking political content and reflecting the prevailing emphasis on domesticity and conformity—actually addressed the major issues of the day from the full variety of competing viewpoints. As Biskind puts it,

perhaps the most striking thing about films of the fifties is that they reflected not one but several warring ideologies, so that it is possible to speak of radical (left- and right-wing) films as well as mainstream films. Moreover, they waged this combat—slugged it out frame by frame—across a battlefield of sounds and images that stretched from one end of the country to the other, from Times Square to Hollywood and Vine—without explicit political allusions. Films of the fifties, in short, pitted different ways of being and acting against each other.[16]

Biskind analyzes the popular movies of the fifties according to how they organized the features of everyday life into "systems of ideas and values that are, finally, political." He demonstrates that films of the various genres—westerns, musicals, crime stories, and so forth—addressed the issues that were animating public debate in the realm of the news.

These films are far more powerful than overtly political ones because they answer questions that they have not even appeared to ask. Seeming to deal only with very specific and even remote problems, the films actually address such pressing issues of the fifties as "conformity, dissent, minori-

97

ties, delinquency, and sex roles."[17] Westerns such as *My Darling Clementine* (1946) and courtroom dramas such as *12 Angry Men* (1957), both starring Henry Fonda, might appear to be about ridding a town in the Old West of outlaws or saving a wrongly accused boy from the bigotry of jurors, but the interest of each was in the way it addressed the proper relation between consensus and dissent in a democratic society.

According to Biskind's analysis, *My Darling Clementine*, directed by John Ford, uses Fonda's star persona to portray a common-man Wyatt Earp whose authority derives from better-than-average professional skill, hard-earned experience, and a straightforward willingness to use necessary force. The main story of the film is not Earp's battle with outlaws but rather his forging a consensus with the elitist Doc Holliday. Once that unity is achieved, the outlaw Clantons can be swiftly dispatched in the gunfight at the OK Corral. Because it locates authority in the individualism and simple values of the common man, the film argues for the ideology of populist conservatism.

Director Sidney Lumet's *12 Angry Men*, by contrast, uses Fonda's trustworthy, sincere image to represent a pluralist manager whose authority rests in the dispassionate reason with which he cuts through prejudice and ideology to uncover complex reality and then forges a consensus through compromise, not force. *12 Angry Men* is less concerned with the fate of the accused boy than with demonstrating that corporate liberalism, with its ideology of the "end of ideology" in a complex modern world, can best solve the nation's problems through technocratic rationalism.[18]

If the seemingly apolitical world of fifties films was actually the setting of intense political debate on the pressing issues of the day, a debate waged through the portrayal of different styles of behavior as the "right" solutions to problems, then a director-actor whose film was played on the national news screen might present an even more vivid portrayal of the "right" solutions. The constraints on ideological discussion in the 1950s were every bit as strong in the realm of politics as in film. The ideological consensus of the cold war, enforced by the communist witch-hunt, reduced debate between candidates and within Congress and other forums to narrow consideration of means, not ends. Any politician—certainly one aspiring to the presidency—had to keep himself or herself within this circumscribed world of debate to be successful.

As Kennedy approached his campaign for the presidency with a strategy based on the construction of an image, he designed and performed that image within the same constraints as did creative figures in Hollywood.

But those boundaries likewise defined his opportunity for reaching into the same cultural pool in which they found their power. Kennedy's candidacy combined the major genres of storytelling that Hollywood held up to Americans. The result was a performance that reflected American politics through the prism of American fantasies.

Kennedy's famous "style," so powerful in its impact on citizens and yet so often contrasted by critics to a missing "substance," was of course a "way of being and acting." His style may be without substance in discussions of bills passed, programs administered, and policies executed. But if we discuss that style in the context of other styles of acting presented to Americans—the performance of star images in major roles upon the Hollywood screen—its substance becomes clear.

Kennedy's crisis politics has received considerable scrutiny from historians and biographers. Some have argued that Kennedy manufactured the crises of his presidency out of his own cold war ideology or to satisfy the needs of his own machismo. While such personal analyses can grossly distort history by failing to consider the various forces with which the individual actor has to contend, crisis was undeniably the paradigm of Kennedy's rhetoric and actions. He projected a vision of the 1960s as a time of crisis, and he typically responded to specific problems by shaping them into crisis situations.

Crisis was also a logical expression of his cinematic approach to the new politics made possible by television. A crisis, like a movie, took place within a compressed period of time, presenting clearly defined characters in a dramatic plot. By transforming a problem into a crisis, Kennedy could to some degree author it according to his preferred plot and position himself as hero figure. And by choosing narrative "scripts" and roles already proven at the box office, he could share with Hollywood directors and stars the improved odds of popular appeal.

His need since childhood to assert control amid the pressures and frailties that threatened him, his ambition to prove himself a leader, and above all his need to live up to his own projected image of the hero are the likely psychological sources of this characteristic strategy. Politics provided a stage on which to enact the fantasies he had found mirrored in romantic fiction, history, and the movies; he possessed a set of internalized scripts upon which to model his actions. This cinematic approach to politics does not mean that Kennedy manufactured his public actions. Such an approach was not easy. In the media world, political leaders interact in "live" encounters that merge social drama with public performance. The ability to project the script by which action will unfold and be perceived, and the ability to perform a role convincingly and with effect—when the other "characters" are also real people possessing wills and designs of their own—are strengths in the world of action too. In acting (simulating), Kennedy was also acting (doing). But it was nevertheless a doing that was inextricably bound up in representation.

Examining Kennedy's public performances, we can see that his assimilation of star images from the Hollywood screen was extended to his adoption of major genres. Above all, Kennedy, following 1950s Hollywood, relied on such images, story formulas, conventions of gesture, and other aspects of cinematic representation to convey deeper cultural messages than his specific political positions indicated. In the immediate contexts of the problems he was confronting, this strategy was probably motivated primarily by a desire to elicit admiration of and identification with his image in viewers who would recognize him as the hero of a story. But by drawing on the discourses of Hollywood, Kennedy also entered into those discourses. He became not only a more powerful candidate for the presidency but also a participant in the unspoken ideological combat waged on the film screen among different ways of "being and doing." Ironically, Kennedy's politics of style, which largely subdued issues of substance that would be divisive, sent him directly into the domain to which underlying social tensions—between the majority and minorities, male and female, authority and alternative ideas—had been driven.

This phenomenon is evident in a pivotal episode in the production of Kennedy's image during the 1960 campaign. On the eve of the Democratic convention, with the campaign against Nixon and the incumbent administration ahead of him, Kennedy had to respond to an attack from the titular head of his own party. Kennedy's response, a dramatic reply on live television, was so successful that he and his associates would in its aftermath be grateful the attack had given them such a well-publicized opportunity to confront doubts about Kennedy's qualifications. A reading of the "text" formed by this attack and Kennedy's response, in the context of the cultural environment of characters and stories familiar from the movies, can demonstrate both how Kennedy drew on the resources of Hollywood and how he began participating in its cultural war to determine the future behavior of Americans.

100

At a press conference on July 2, former president Harry S. Truman announced that he had resigned as a delegate to the convention because he did not want to "be a party to proceedings that had taken on the aspects of a prearranged affair." Decrying "the manner in which some of the backers of Joseph F. Kennedy [sic] have acted," he said that the "Democratic party must never be allowed to become a party of privilege." The 76-year-old former president then proceeded to pose a direct statement to the 43-year-old Kennedy: "Senator, are you certain that you're quite ready for the country or the country is quite ready for you in the role of President in January, 1961?" Claiming to foresee a great political future for Kennedy, Truman nevertheless urged him to be "patient," and warned that in the current difficult world situation the nation needed "someone with the greatest maturity and experience." Truman then listed a number of Democrats as examples, and called for an open convention where the party's "good men" could "be properly sized up."[19]

The last Democrat to occupy the White House had thus explicitly attacked Kennedy on the issues of class and experience, which next to religion were Kennedy's most vulnerable points. Moreover, Truman's coupling of the two issues articulated the suspicion that they were in this case really the same one. Truman called Kennedy a "victim" of some of those backing him. When a reporter pointed out the possible "Freudian slip" of his reference to Kennedy by his father's first name, he retorted that it was an accident and "the name of the young man is John." Nevertheless, Truman drew further attention to charges of Kennedy's weak relation to his powerful parent. When he went on to patronize Kennedy as a promising youth not yet ready to fill the role for which a number of his elders were clearly better suited, he was only doubling the humiliation of Kennedy as a mere rich boy.[20]

Before examining Kennedy's response to this attack, it is worthwhile to consider the more conventional courses that he might have chosen. Kennedy could have attempted to play down the significance of Truman's attack by ignoring it or making light of it. Kennedy's aides did not consider Truman's statement as serious a threat to Kennedy's nomination as it could be to his prospects against Republican candidate Nixon in the fall campaign; after all, Truman's attempt to stop the nomination of Adlai Stevenson in 1956 had failed.[21] Considering all this, the object of Truman's attacks might well have concluded that it was best to avoid prolonging the front-page headlines. A second obvious strategy would have been to rebut Truman's charges, providing a résumé of his experience as congressman and senator. Such a reply could have been adopted as a dignified and safe strategy for limiting the damage.

Kennedy's actual response was quite different, and it set the pattern that over the next three years would memorably impress itself upon the television audience. After requesting equal time on national television, Kennedy announced that he would reply to Truman at a press conference in New York on July 4th.[22] With this scenario, he chose not to downplay Truman's remarks, but rather to heighten them into a dramatic crisis. Sorensen recalled that he flew back to Hyannis Port from Los Angeles, where he was doing advance work for the convention: "I took with me a file on 'youth and age' containing rebuttal material for just such an occasion, and the Senator, looking relaxed and confident, interrupted his vacation to work on the text."[23]

With direct words, Kennedy rebutted Truman point by point, but the distinctive theme of his response was encapsulated by the *New York Times* the next day in the title and leading subtitle of its front-page report: "Kennedy's Reply to Truman Asks Young Leaders" followed by "Senator Contends 'Strength and Vigor' Are Required in the White House."

Kennedy began by refusing to "step aside at anyone's request." As the only candidate to "risk my chances in all the primaries," Kennedy declared that he had "encountered and survived every kind of hazard and opposition, and I do not intend to withdraw my name now on the eve of the convention." Further, he derided Truman's concept of "an open convention as one which studies all the candidates, reviews their records and then takes his advice."

Kennedy then turned to the "heart of Mr. Truman's objection," to which he devoted the following two thirds of his 1,600-word statement. He quickly summarized his accomplishments and experience before delivering the thrust of his reply. Referring to the youthful careers of such leaders as Alexander the Great, Napoleon, Jefferson, and Washington, Kennedy asserted that "the strength and health and vigor of these young men is equally needed in the White House." Older men could offer a president "their wise counsel of experience," but "the voters deserve to know that [the president's] strength and vigor will remain at the helm." Kennedy then asserted, "This is still a young country, founded by young men . . . and still young in heart," but "the world today is largely in the hands of men whose education was completed before the whole course of international events was altered by two world wars." He wondered aloud "who is to say how successful they have been in improving the fate of the world?" Looking both youthful and determined, Kennedy concluded: "The world is changing, the old ways will not do. . . . It is time for a new generation of leadership to cope with new problems and new opportunities."[24]

This vivid performance established before a national audience the image and theme that Kennedy would project as the Democrats' national candidate. Kennedy was thus performing as an actor in two senses: as a simulator of actions, for he offered a silhouette, spoke lines of dialogue, and enacted a plot familiar from western movies; and as a performer of actions, for his simulation successfully turned back Truman's attack and left Kennedy triumphant. As a dramatic narrative, this response—not only the words but also their delivery by one character to another in a specific situation—comprised a visual and aural text. That "text" was a social drama, in which real people enacted a conflict through the repertoire of scripts made available by their culture. It was at the same time a media performance, a use of images and words to convey a message to an audience. In his response to Truman, Kennedy drew on Hollywood's methods for both his internal compass and his desire to perform effectively for the viewer.

Psychoanalytic film theory has explored the means by which a viewer or subject is positioned as the desiring producer of a cinematic fiction. Various "lures" are employed to foster the identification of unconscious desires with desires generated in the film, so that the film seems to be the subject's dream, acting out his or her conflicts and wishes. The film star's attractive personification of a certain social type is a prime example of such a lure. Others include the use of a familiar genre or story type and the focus on a certain character's perspective or dilemma.[25] Combining his private fantasies with those made available by the movies, Kennedy shaped the problem of Truman's attack into a scenario pleasing to both himself and the public.

By his decision to treat Truman's charge as a powerful threat requiring a straightforward, immediate response, Kennedy transformed the political problem into a dramatic crisis evoking the showdowns toward which the western movies of the day invariably moved. Coming out to face Truman in the glare of the cameras, he was translating Truman's patronizing statement into the discourse of the western genre, walking into the open street of the town to face the villain's challenge. He further positioned himself as the western hero by emphasizing that he had proven his special worth through unique daring in entering a dangerous landscape ("I was the only candidate to risk my chances in all the primaries. . . . I have encountered and survived every kind of hazard and opposition"). Moreover, like a town marshal, he represented legitimate power conferred by the citizenry ("whatever support I've gotten has come by the free choice of the people"). Now he had been "called out" by the tyrannical old rancher who thought he owned the land and town because he was there earlier ("Mr. Truman regards an open convention as one which studies all the candidates . . . and then takes his advice"). As the genre dictates, the hero must go out into the open streets before the watching community and shoot it out with the villain ("I do not intend to step aside").

In his direct, clear presentation of his determination and righteous position, Kennedy even more clearly evoked the role that Henry Fonda had played in *My Darling Clementine* and that Alan Ladd had played in *Shane*. He "strode," as noted by the television announcer, into the conference room promptly at the appointed hour.[26] He looked calm and resolute, and directly confronted Truman's charges. Kennedy acted out the essence of Fonda's and Ladd's star images, particularly in their western roles as Wyatt Earp and Shane, and turned Truman into an Ike Clanton and Old Man Riker.

Yet Kennedy's performance also evoked another set of star images. As a youth complaining of being unfairly categorized and dismissed, Kennedy drew on his visual similarities to the sensitive young rebels of the fifties screen—Dean, Brando, and Newman. Like the heroes in such movies as *Rebel Without a Cause*, *The Wild One*, and *The Left-Handed Gun*, Kennedy could win the empathy of those viewers, especially the young, who felt unfairly treated or patronized by the dominant culture.

Kennedy's unusually youthful good looks, together with his knowing cool, lent themselves to obvious connection with these stars. As he had shown he was aware in his comment in the 1957 magazine article, his barely controlled hair, excessively long by the standards of the day, was saved from explicit identification with juvenile rebels only by not being slicked back. Kennedy's heavy-lidded, detached stare and slightly ironic smile also suggested the young rebel's attitude. These visual elements reinforced Kennedy's rebellious stance in chiding an elder former president as an authoritarian.

He therefore positioned himself beautifully—there is perhaps no better word for it, since the method and power were aesthetically designed—to appeal to two fundamental myths of American culture held up by Hollywood. Kennedy's "showdown" with Truman was a "preview" of the role that, eleven days later, he would in his New Frontier acceptance speech invite his viewers to join him in acting out.

Combining the western and the deliquency film in his narrative performance, Kennedy reached into the deeper similarities underlying the two seemingly disparate discourses. Both the western and the delinquency film assert that the problems their heroes encounter are extrinsic to the system. Troubles result from the natural fallibility and error of humans, not from the ideology and structure of the society. The western hero stands out in the street alone or at the head of a small group of supporters to face down the villain for the good of the community. Fonda in *My Darling Clementine* is a man willing and ready to use violence, and is originally motivated by a desire to avenge his murdered brother. But he does so as the duly constituted marshal of a town in desperate need of order, and thus represents a resolution of the conflict in the United States between individualism and authority. In his Truman performance, Kennedy also resolved this conflict. With references to his successes in the primaries, Kennedy positioned himself as the elected town marshal, the representative of the true community. And in pointed attacks on the former president's unfairness, he represented himself as the individual able to face down a powerful threat.

Kennedy and Sorensen thus used various lures and coded formulations to position the citizen as viewer of a western in which Kennedy was the legitimate authority using power against a lawless enemy of the community. But they also provided the viewer with a means of seeing Kennedy as the misunderstood boy rebelling against a bad adult. The discourse of the deliquency film seems on the surface quite different from that of the western. Yet they contain distinct parallels, and in certain films of the 1950s (most strikingly *The Left-Handed Gun*, a delinquent western), they had already been pulled together.

Both genres affirm the rightness of the individual and the rightness of the society at the same time. Any problems are displaced onto people failing to act according to the culture's ideology. The hero, whether popularly deputized wielder of force or restless youth, offers the viewer a fantasy fulfillment of individual power and right while affirming the power and right of the system. The delinquency film of the fifties, like the public concern that it reflected, was not really about the minority of "bad boys" that had always been around; it was a response to the discovery after World War II of a new youth culture, an unprecedented rejection by young people of the authority of their elders and institutions in favor of an alternative set of values and style of behavior offered by the particularly brash among their peers. In enacting the role of a Clift, Brando, Dean, or Newman as a sensitive youth daring to talk back to a figure embodying the authority of age and experience, Kennedy aligned himself with youth as a force for alternative values. By showing himself as an elected man of the people and yet also as a rebellious youth, Kennedy conflated the roles of Fonda and Dean

105

to portray Truman as a lawless, tyrannical enemy of an identification figure who like the nation (and thus the viewer) is constructed as "young."

Kennedy and Sorensen undoubtedly crafted the response to Truman with an eye to what would work most effectively with various audiences — silencing Truman himself, impressing the Democratic leaders, persuading the convention delegates, and appealing to various sections of the electorate. This is not the same thing as suggesting that Kennedy and his aide were consciously thinking of the western or the juvenile delinquent film, much less these genres' deeper meanings and affinities. But the unlikelihood of a completely conscious and calculated use of these elements does not leave their presence a mystery.

We have earlier examined the role of fantasy in Kennedy's consciousness and self-image, originally manifested in his love of romantic literature and history but also in his love of the movies and associations with Hollywood stars. We have also observed how Kennedy aligned his image with the forces identified with the dilemma of the individualistic hero. And we have explored how his developing image during the 1950s combined elements of the images of such star types as Cary Grant, Jimmy Stewart, and James Dean.

While I referred above to such westerns as *My Darling Clementine* and *The Left-Handed Gun*, Kennedy's response to Truman parallels even more exactly the plot of *Red River*. Billy Sutton, Kennedy's aide, roommate, and frequent companion on double dates during his years in the House of Representatives, has told us: "The way he loved movies was something else. Always going to the movies. His favorite movie in those days was *Red River*, with Montgomery Clift."[27] When a person is especially drawn to a movie, it is most probably because for that person, the film is analogous to a repeated or vividly recalled dream. The viewer, like a dreamer, presumably finds in the image-narrative a signification of emotions and ideas consciously or unconsciously held; it signifies deep anxieties or wishes. Of course, a dream is a personal fantasy that may or may not resonate strongly for others. To the degree it does, the waking dreamer who is a skilled artist can recast it as a poem, short story, painting, film, or other artwork. When the viewer contemplates not his or her own private dream but rather a public film, especially a broadly popular one, then the viewer can know that he or she is not alone in finding resonance there; the individual's fantasy interconnects with fantasies found throughout the community.

The young Kennedy should have had little difficulty finding in his favorite movie, *Red River*, a reflection of his personal conflicts and wishes.

In the film, a respected, powerful, but tyrannical rancher played by John Wayne attempts to bring a desperate cattle drive to successful completion through the individual force of will that has always worked for him in the past. Significantly, at the beginning of the film Tom Dunson, the John Wayne character, begins his transformation from lone scout to boss of a sprawling cattle empire with a loss. He leaves a covered wagon train to seek land for himself, despite the plea of the wagon boss that he made a contract and that his service is needed. He also resists the ardent requests of his young bride, who speaks of the domestic bliss they can share during the coming nights if he stays. Soon after, Wayne subdues attacking Indians, but he discovers that the Indians have in the meantime massacred the wagon train, killing his wife. His individualism triumphs at the price of the community he had agreed to serve, and along with that community he loses the possibility of forming a new one through a romantic and sexual relationship with a loving woman.

Next, a young boy appears. He is a survivor of the massacre, and the lone cow he brings with him signifies his appearance as the partial return of the "feminine" element Wayne has sacrificed in his single-minded pursuit of rugged individualism. The man's bull literally joins with the boy's cow to produce the cattle empire that is to replace the family the Wayne character would have had with his wife, had he stayed to protect her. A montage rapidly moves across time, informing us of the harshly triumphant progression of American history as the Wayne character ruthlessly but self-righteously builds his ranch into a cattle empire.

When the narrative settles back upon the characters, we are shown that the boy has grown into a young man, Matt Dunson, played by Montgomery Clift. Raised by the Wayne character, Clift has just completed an eastern education, but we also learn that he is distinguished by his youthful speed and accuracy with a six-gun. In the main plot that now begins, Wayne, with Clift as his lieutenant, leads the cattle in a desperate drive to Missouri. As the drive encounters terrible obstacles, Wayne becomes increasingly threatening to the community as he attempts to impose the autonomous solutions that worked for him in building the ranch (though at the sacrifice of his wife and potential children).

The climax comes when at last Clift reluctantly but decisively leads a mutiny against the man who has raised him as his own son. With an eastern education, a youthful optimism, and a more compassionate, "feminine," nature, the Clift character is more open to new possibilities for solving the problems of the cattle drive, and is far less willing to defer to injus-

107

tice because it is ordered by an older, "legitimate" authority figure. By the end of the film he has successfully completed the cattle drive and saved the Wayne character from the same impulses that earlier enabled the older hero to carve an American business from the frontier wilderness. A woman encountered along the way in a wagon train under attack by Indians—the full return of the feminine value carried by the slain wife—finally turns Wayne away from his determination to kill the rebellious Clift. The community represented by the reconciliation of the three signifies a progressive history for America from the rugged individualism of the early frontier represented by Wayne to the community service represented by Clift.[28]

One can easily infer why this film would have held a special fascination for the young Kennedy. The strong parallels between Clift's position in regard to Wayne and Congressman Kennedy's in regard to his father would have broken down only at the place in which Kennedy could have happily allowed his fantasies to follow the configuration of the rest of the film. In the Clift character Kennedy could see the same young, slight-of-build son that looked back at him from his mirror and from the mass media. (Kennedy, with his insider's knowledge of Hollywood gossip, may even have recognized a correspondence between the macho masquerade he himself performed to cover his "feminine" aspects and the homosexual actor's role as a gunslinging cowboy.) Both the Clift character and Kennedy were swept along by the drives of a powerful father who had created an empire through prodigious if ruthless feats. By the same token, Kennedy could see in the Wayne character the same rejection of domesticity and community that his father had enacted in living away from his family and humiliating his mother while creating a huge fortune. And during his experience in Britain as a college-age youth, Kennedy had been exposed to formative influences concerning aristocratic service beyond the purview of a father who had always rejected any endeavors that did not promise to serve his own interests.

While forming his admiration for the ideal of service he found among young British aristocrats (reflected in his love of Buchan's *Pilgrim's Way*, with its repeated elegies for youthful members of that class who died while serving the empire), Kennedy had watched his father wreck his political prospects by refusing—against the wishes of Roosevelt and the British—to bend from his rigidly isolationist stance at the outset of World War II. Kennedy's bonding during that war with the common men serving on the PT boats is also a factor here. Like the Clift character in his relation to the cattle drovers, Kennedy had formed a strong bond with a group that evoked in him an empathy and compassion missing from the father figure. Both admiring and severely critical biographers have emphasized the formative influence of Kennedy's wartime experience serving as part of a strongly bonded group of men. He thereafter worked to maintain that experience. Although he remained distant from women precisely by taking so many of them to bed, he gathered a close band of male friends around him.

The Kennedy of the late 1940s and early 1950s could see in *Red River* a reflection of his own experience as a callow, but perhaps more sophisticated and civilized, son dominated by a powerful father. That parallel ended at the point in the film when Clift mutinies, taking command of the drive and redirecting it. Yet that move and the subsequent plot of the film exactly parallel the course that Kennedy took with his public image. Whatever the reality behind the scenes—and certainly Kennedy continued to pay great attention to his father's ideas while pursuing exactly the goal that his father had in mind for him—when Kennedy, with Sorensen's help, began taking command of his image in the mid-1950s he moved it decisively away from his father's ideology toward the liberal pluralism of the reigning consensus. Like the Clift character, Kennedy separated himself from the authoritarian father and moved toward identification with the democratic ideals of a larger community. Matt Dunson accomplishes this by revolting against his father Tom and responding to news of a new, better route for the cattle drive; Kennedy did so by publicly disagreeing with his father's isolationism and by writing articles and taking public positions expressing a growing commitment to modern liberal ideas for domestic reform and international relations.

Debunkers characterize Kennedy's developing liberalism as no more than a "trick" played by Kennedy's father on the liberals.[29] Yet this is a matter of interpretation, and is belied by Kennedy's openness to new influences, particularly Sorensen. It seems more likely that Kennedy's persona was a projection of his actual struggle for independent statesmanship and his commitment to international policies that were anathema to his isolationist father. In the mid-fifties, Kennedy would enact the fantasy he had earlier enjoyed in the second half of *Red River*. He would pursue the father's goal by rebelling against his father's narrow and ultimately self-destructive rigidity, winning more broad-based support and achieving a more enlightened vision.

This plot is dramatically reenacted in Kennedy's response to Truman in 1960. Like Clift, Kennedy confronts an admired but aging leader, challenging the leader's authority by claiming his own identification with the

109

present community. Kennedy so identifies himself by emphasizing the votes that he won in the primaries and his membership in the younger generation that actually fought in the war. Kennedy's decision to confront Truman was risky, as it could have elicited charges of brashness. But it was rooted both in his personal fantasies and in his intuitive sense that those fantasies were shared by his fellow audience at the movies.

Kennedy's fascination with *Red River* reveals a connection between his psychology and his image. The ambassador's son's rewriting his father's defeatist stance into his own call to arms against the international threat of dictators, the young congressman's identification with the Oedipal themes of the Clift western, and the presidential candidate's response to Truman exchange places constantly, like scenes in a dream. This pattern suggests that we are witnessing not a progression but rather a repetition, a reenactment of a fundamental wish. Common to all three is a rebellious energy, a desire to enact an alternative to the way forced by the father while containing that forbidden rebellion by using it to save the father against his own will.

Kennedy could enact his personal fantasy in the image of the collective fantasy represented by popular films not only because he enjoyed it, but also because it made sense within his political strategy. A centrist politician speaks with several of the voices making up the political spectrum, acknowledging the influence of each yet avoiding choosing any one. But that centrist strategy is itself a product of unconscious needs, in this case the need to not admit the true rebellion, the true source of dissatisfaction. Truman had not anticipated that, by attacking Kennedy as a boy dominated by his father, he was putting himself in the dangerous role of that father.

Presenting himself as a wrongly treated youth ready to be an adult, Kennedy made himself into a signifier of what could not be openly admitted in national political discourse. Kennedy contained the dissent signified by the public construction of the juvenile delinquent by appropriating its energies to serve the system. But if the juvenile delinquent had been so used by the western hero, the western hero had been used as well by the juvenile delinquent. This was the electrifying tension locked within Kennedy's image.

Through such performances Kennedy was ultimately constructing his image as a popular text in which opposing elements of the culture could be held in dynamic tension. Into that image he projected his personal experience of the conflict Freud famously described between civilization and the discontents felt by its members. Kennedy made that projection through the discourses available in his culture, particularly the fantasies of Hollywood entertainment. The image was thus constructed textually in patterns that easily intersected with the viewing citizen's knowledge. The text inscribed upon the television screen and news pages by Kennedy's performance of the Truman crisis echoed and merged preexisting texts appropriated from the Hollywood screen, each of which represented a struggle between the ruling system and ideology and the deprivations felt by its members. Kennedy identified himself with the central beliefs and system of the United States, yet through the fantasy techniques of the movies he also identified himself with those most oppressed within that system.

Under the pressure of a social drama and media performance, Kennedy configured his psychological needs into a self-presentation mediated by the Hollywood discourses he shared with his audience. His political career had begun with his representation by John Hersey as a literary character with mythic resonance. Kennedy had seen himself portrayed as a figure of words and a function of narrative in which the reader could experience an extended state of liminal marginality on the way to being transformed. On the threshold of his nomination for president, Kennedy, with the aid of Sorensen, demonstrated that he could achieve the same power of representation through the visual and verbal form of "live" television. He invited the viewer to experience in his image a youth's triumph over humiliation by the father, and he was about to invite the public to make this exhilarating narrative the cohering narrative of the 1960s.

CHAPTER FIVE

The Erotics of a Presidency

Psychoanalysts use the term *imago* to denote a composite of impressions forming an internal image of an "ideal love." An encounter with someone who has, or seems to have, one or more of the traits making up the imago can trigger the projection of that silhouette upon that real-life person. "Falling in love" is a double act of the imagination: we make up an internal image and then shape our perception of another person to accord with that personal fiction.[1] As an act of the imagination, romantic love bears the weight of the whole of our past experiences and most fundamental yearnings and fantasies.

This analogy may help illuminate the relation of Kennedy to his audience that developed in the early 1960s. A prospective lover has a better chance of triggering others' romantic projections if he or she "performs" in accord with images already holding demonstrated appeal or, alternatively, presents an unexpected image that taps into yearnings not previously answered in the external world. Such self-presentation is a work of the aesthetic imagination seeking to match the imaginative work of a potential beloved's imago-making and projection.

Discussing the findings of sex researcher John Money, Virginia Wright Wexman has explored the role of Hollywood film in structuring the lover ideal held by members of a society. Wexman points out that "Hollywood has traditionally supplied a steady stream of such fictions."[2] As we have seen in the previous chapters, over the course of his political career Kennedy's image had been constructed according to ideal images in American literature, myth, and mass culture. He put those images together with his own personal traits to project a uniquely compelling persona. Kennedy's image was an electrifying complex of fused desires.

Writing from his observations at the nominating conventions in 1960, novelist Norman Mailer predicted that if the handsome young Democratic candidate were elevated to the White House, Kennedy's sex appeal would have a fundamental impact on American life. A Kennedy presidency would catalyze American myth to "emerge once more, because America's politics would now be also America's favorite movie, America's first soap opera, America's best-seller."[3] Whereas previous presidents had been father figures, Kennedy would be a romantic hero who would bring back to the surface of American life the yearnings and drives that had been forced underground during the domestic Eisenhower years.

Mailer's prediction that Kennedy's erotic appeal would turn politics into a form of romantic popular narrative, stimulating the American mythic imagination, was a prescient insight. The dynamic of Kennedy's image as it interacted with the public during his campaign and presidency had fundamental correlations with the magnetism of the images of film stars, which is to say with romantic love. John Ellis observes that Hollywood presents its stars as romantic ideals, producing "a relationship of desire between spectator and star performer that is intensified by the photo-effect of cinema itself."[4] Kennedy's impact created a similar powerfully complicated relationship. We can therefore by extension turn to psychoanalytic theorists and practitioners for help in identifying elements and dynamics making up the "chemistry" of the nationwide response to Kennedy. That response has heretofore been vaguely labeled, and often dismissed or even demonized, as "charisma." But to ignore as trivial or irrational the dynamic of this reaction is to rule out consideration of the uniquely powerful aspect of Kennedy's presidency.

It is also as narrow-minded as ignoring the significance of romantic love in the life of a person or couple. As psychiatrist Ethel Person points out, the "scientific attitude" has exhibited discomfort with love as a subject because of a predisposition of the human spirit to avoid engaging the deepest levels of inward experience:

Too easily, in the name of the good, or the rational, or the moral, or the Christ-ian, or the democratic, or even the merely socially acceptable, we blink away the actualities of our condition—the feelings, drives, dreams, and desires that express, with painful accuracy, the depths at which we really *live*. Not where we think or imagine we should live, or where society advises us to live, but where our lives are fueled and our deepest satisfactions experienced—this is what we disre-gard.[5]

A similar disregard has characterized most commentators' attitude toward the relation between Kennedy and the national citizenry, so analogous to that between a Hollywood star and the filmgoing audience. But an unwill-ingness to examine Kennedy's presidency in other than the conventional terms of policy formulation and decision-making echoes precisely the error that Person notes in the reluctance to take romantic love seriously. Kennedy's "style" was arguably the most important "substance" of his pres-idency, a dynamic that for better or worse changed America.

As romantic "lead," Kennedy, with his televised image as "hero-Presi-dent," elicited the audience identifications and projections accorded a Cary Grant or James Dean. But as this was the president, who was engag-ing them in the world of actual consequences, the audience could not for-get that choices of fantasy were bound up in choices of actual identity. Like a real-life romantic lover, Kennedy was offering the beloved (the audience) an opportunity to join him in enacting the fantasy he mirrored.

In 1960, in the new politics of television, the voters, now an audience, were essentially "feminine" in their relation to the masculine images of the candidates on the screen. They could choose from among the competing suitors, but they had little active relation to politics. As for a woman in the preferred cultural script of the time, the possibility of an active life for the citizen lay in the choice of a "mate," the candidate. The experience of fusion with the romantic Other could provide either a voyeuristic fulfill-ment or a sense of exciting partnership.

In this chapter we will examine the course of the fateful encounter of a dream lover and a nation through the 1960 campaign and the brief life of the Kennedy administration. Drawing upon the perspectives of both psy-choanalytic film theory and psychoanalytic theories of romantic love, we will explore the central dynamics of the shared fantasy through which Kennedy communed with his audience as candidate and president.

Kennedy's speech accepting the nomination at the Democratic convention in Los Angeles introduced his campaign slogan, "the New Frontier." As Richard Slotkin has shown in his monumental trilogy, "frontier" was in 1960 a widely current term loaded with ideological value brought down through four hundred years of Euro-American expansion accompanied by folklore, literature, and film transforming that historical migration into mythic story.[6] Kennedy introduced his New Frontier metaphor at a time when the Old Frontier had its strongest hold over American imagination. The gunfighter western in particular had been a hugely successful genre throughout the preceding decade. Defined by the films *The Gunfighter* (1950), *High Noon* (1952), and *Shane* (1953), this version of the western presented a hero possessing an exceptional expertise (the "fast draw"), operating in a vanishing area between a sense of individual masculine possibility and an encroaching society, and looking at that society with an ironic sense of its illusions and mystifications. The gunfighter western was central to a wide variety of films that appeared during the decade, and by the time Kennedy took office in 1961 provided the major formula for the thirty western television series that dominated the living-room screen.[7]

In challenging his audience to follow him into a frontier landscape, Kennedy seemed on the surface to be offering a tradition-sanctioned "map" as their shared guide. But Kennedy's New Frontier, like the westerns upon which it drew, was more complicated and deeply psychological in its implications than a simple affirmation of American power and virtue. As an invitation to join with him in entering a "new" and better version of the fascinating mythological/historical ground upon which the contemporary United States had been formed, Kennedy's vision of a New Frontier tempted his audience to experience with him the transcendence and transgression essential to the romantic experience. It offered the prospect of returning to the primal scene of the nation's mythic/historical experience, the frontier in which white Americans saw their forebears returning to nature in an act that revitalized civilization while also expanding it.

The westerns of Hollywood and television vividly conveyed the national mythology of the frontier. This mythology, as explained in 1893 by historian Frederick Jackson Turner in his famous "frontier thesis," told white Americans that the frontier was the site of America's formation. The frontier was, as Turner phrased it, the "meeting point between savagery and civilization," where the white European male regressed into savagery in a violent encounter with the Indian before emerging as a revitalized and triumphant new civilized man called the American. Turner, along with his fellow historian Theodore Roosevelt and the frontiersman-showman William F. "Buffalo Bill" Cody, had ushered Americans into the twentieth century with a firm sense of the frontier as their mythic place of origin. Kennedy's audience understood that the pioneers, their mythic/historical "parents," had thus created the American character.

Contemporary Americans were, however, well aware that among the legacies of their frontier origins was a good deal of "unfinished business." The frontier, the scene of the formation of American identity, was also the site of wounds to that identity that resonated down to the present day in severe social problems. The term "unfinished business" was central to Kennedy's 1960 campaign rhetoric, but it has an important meaning as well in psychological literature. This term was introduced by the founder of Gestalt Therapy, Fritz Perls, who was expanding Freud's identification of what he called the "repetition compulsion." The unconscious fantasy of a lover is that the new beloved will return the lover to the primal scene of the original relationship with the parents.

This compulsion may be a regressive scenario in which the lover seeks to use the beloved to remake the contemporary world in the image of a nostalgic memory. But in Freud's view it has a purpose that is ultimately progressive. The lover seeks to relive the past in order to be healed of its wounds. Thus the exciting possibility of transformation evoked by romance is accompanied by a pleasurable sense of necessary return. One goes after the new in the hope of reliving past conflicts in an idealized form in which unpleasant though repressed memories are healed and frustrated wishes fulfilled.[8]

The elements of this psychological explanation for the triggering of romantic love correlate with those visible in the 1960 encounter of John F. Kennedy with a national audience. He declared that it was "the responsibility of the next President of the United States to set before our country the unfinished business of our society."[9] Kennedy's use of the term "unfinished business" to denote a social and political agenda carried the unspoken weight of Perls's psychoanalytic meanings. Accepting the duty of righting historical and institutionalized wrongs would offer the pleasures accompanying a return to the founding episode of American life. On this exciting primal ground, white Americans could join with the hero to reenact the frontier ancestors' nation-making while at the same time wiping out the stain of the forefathers' sins, those historical acts that had blighted the promises of the Declaration of Independence. The New Frontier would be a thrilling opportunity to relive the Old Frontier and to revise it according to the deepest yearnings of American idealism.

Kennedy sketched the New Frontier as a site at which he and the audience he was wooing would experience precisely this combination of pleasurable return and exciting self-transformation. On the New Frontier they would together go back to complete the business their forebears had left unfinished, in particular to heal the wounds they now suffered as a result of the crimes committed by those original pioneers.

Kennedy's generation of white Americans had experienced the immediate postwar years as an anxious passage to adulthood. Even as they went about marrying, having children, and establishing a secure life for their families, they were told by their leaders that they must collectively assume the "responsibility" for preserving world peace and order. Unprecedented affluence and the confidence that they had been the decisive factor on the "right" side of a "good" war contributed to a feeling that the young nation had as a collective identity now entered adulthood, or at least late adolescence. Yet this generation of white Americans, like a young person finding that the legacy of childhood intrudes itself destructively upon attempts at mature happiness, soon found their postwar society showing symptoms of the wounds inflicted at the nation's founding.

The founders had declared that "all men are created equal" with the right to "life, liberty, and the pursuit of happiness." But the founders' sins—genocide and slavery, a rapacious exploitation of nature, a Puritan hostility toward sensual experience—had gradually risen to the collective consciousness, spoiling the self-satisfaction that might have accompanied the nation's triumphant accession to global power. The growing civil rights movement disturbed Kennedy's generation with reminders that the sweeping promises of the Declaration of Independence had not prevented racism from becoming fundamental to the formation of American identity. Symptoms of unease had not been expressed by black Americans alone. The Beats had taken to the road and to poetry to express a sense of something missing in American life even for privileged white males.

On the screens of both theaters and living rooms, westerns addressed major social issues of the 1950s through coded and displaced maneuvers. The widely expressed concern that the postwar American male, the man in the gray flannel suit, was losing his masculinity as he ran a corporate "rat race" at work and subjected himself to feminine social regulation at home in the suburbs was projected into the heroic self-sacrifice of the gunfighter. As the alienation of youth led to national concern over juvenile delinquency, the rebel male defined by Clift, Brando, and Dean entered the western as a particular version of the gunfighter. The growing civil rights movement led to westerns, such as John Ford's *The Searchers* (1956), dealing with issues of racism and bigotry.

The gunfighter western, the most visible context and the most immediate source of resonance for the metaphor of the New Frontier, was a mythological space within which Kennedy's audience had been prepared for the idea that they could somehow join a romantic hero in returning to the primal scene of American origins to heal the wrongs done by their forebears. White Americans approached the 1960s with a growing awareness that they were facing the results of abuses to the nation's ideals inflicted during the formative years of the nation's founding and expansion.

In his acceptance speech Kennedy first courted his listeners by reminding them of the frontier ancestors who had formed their society. In this way he evoked the nation's collective imago, the idealized image shaped by their mythic impressions of their forebears:

For I stand tonight facing west on what was once the last frontier. From the lands that stretch three thousand miles behind me, the pioneers of old gave up their safety, their comfort, and sometimes their lives to build a new world here in the West. They were not the captives of their own doubts, the prisoners of their own price tags. Their motto was not "every man for himself"—but "all for the common cause." They were determined to make that new world strong and free, to overcome its hazards and its hardships, to conquer the enemies that threatened from without and within.

With this summary of the impressions of their ancestors that Americans had gathered from textbooks and movies, Kennedy implicitly invited the audience to compare their frontier "fathers" and "mothers" to the compellingly youthful image before them. Kennedy was the lover who proposed that he and the audience he was wooing go together on a vital quest. He then directly turned to the great theme of love at mid-life, asserting that the excitement and challenges of youth are not over after all:

Today some would say that those struggles are all over—that all the horizons have been explored, that all the battles have been won, that there is no longer an American frontier.

But I trust that no one in this vast assemblage will agree with those sentiments.[10]

Kennedy was tapping the cultural concern often voiced during the affluent 1950s that Americans, in particular the mass of American men who had submitted to the "conformity" of social regulation by American women, were losing the frontier virtues that were their heritage. In so doing Kennedy was aiming at the dreams, feelings, and drives that he intuited made up the level at which Americans were really living. He was inviting them, in a supreme romantic leap, to leave behind the security and safety assured by the society their forebears had provided to take for themselves the excitement and self-transformation their forebears had enjoyed.

Kennedy came before the national viewing audience like a romantic lover whose appearance and words promised to return the beloved to the exciting scene of its origins to heal whatever wounds were incurred in those formative years. Like such a lover, he also excited the anticipation of expanding the self through breaking taboos. A central fantasy of romantic love is of violating the taboo surrounding the parents' marriage bed, daring to enact the pleasures of that sacred place. As psychoanalyst John Munder Ross states, mature romantic love "requires transgression, a symbolic sally at least across generational barriers into the forbidden domain of sensuality, the arena of the primal scene. There the lover rediscovers and revels in the once hidden sexuality of the parents and that of the imaginative oedipal child she or he once was."[11] If contemporary Americans joined Kennedy, they would together dare to return to the sacred space of American myth, where their fathers were imagined to have come together with the wilderness to create the American character. They would take for themselves the experience of creating American identity. Together, the new generation of Americans would perform an act analogous to Ross's "symbolic sally" into the arena of the primal scene.

Kennedy suggested that both domestic problems and foreign controversies were among the potential real-life settings for this metaphorical landscape. Yet he emphasized that the New Frontier would be neither a legislative agenda nor a foreign policy. Though Kennedy's administration would pursue reformist politics, expansionist economics, and cold war adventures, the New Frontier did not on its fundamental level denote any of those specific areas. Kennedy emphatically distinguished between the legislative agendas his Democratic predecessors had labeled with their slogans and the metaphorical setting he was naming:

Woodrow Wilson's New Freedom promised our nation a new political and economic framework. Franklin Roosevelt's New Deal promised security and succor to those in need. But the New Frontier of which I speak is not a set of promises—it is a set of challenges. It sums up not what I intend to offer the American people, but what I intend to ask of them.

Individuals tend to fall in love at certain times, particularly when they have experienced or anticipate separation from some previous bond or identity. Love signals that it is time for a change.[12] During the 1950s a father-figure president had reassured Americans of the maintenance of traditional domestic values amid the immense changes of the postwar world. But the cold war, with its institutionalization of vast bureaucracies and potential mass destruction, belied the assurance of paternal care. Technological and social change—television and automation, teenage culture and restive minorities—threatened the loss of traditional values.

Kennedy embraced change as his theme. He promised Americans that by going "boldly" with him into that change they would be both continuing and completing their history. Like a prospective lover, he represented an opportunity to make a break with the past and promised the excitement of a new narrative in which the future opens up as a dramatic culmination:

But I tell you the New Frontier is here, whether we seek it or not. Beyond that frontier are the uncharted areas of science and space, unsolved problems of peace and war, unconquered pockets of ignorance and prejudice, unanswered questions of poverty and surplus. It would be easier to shrink back from that frontier, to look to the safe mediocrity of the past, to be lulled by good intentions and high rhetoric—and those who prefer that course should not cast their votes for me, regardless of party.

But I believe that the times demand invention, innovation, imagination, decision. I am asking each of you to be new pioneers on that New Frontier. My call is to the young in heart, regardless of age.[13]

Cloaked within the images of continuity was an acknowledgment of past wounds, the "unfinished business" of American ideals resulting from the wrongs done by the pioneers. "Science" and "space" reminded Kennedy's listeners that a dramatic new setting awaited those willing to risk new experience. "Prejudice" and "poverty" alluded to the racist and classist barriers in the United States. Kennedy's New Frontier offered the opportunity to loosen the hold of the past and reorganize the American superego to better acknowledge errors and adjust American ideology accordingly.

Kennedy offered Americans a shared romantic journey in which together they would meet the challenge of completing the unfinished business of American life. The New Frontier was a perfect image for this opportunity. The poetic metaphor re-created the original scenario of the national experience, returning Americans to the excitement of their revolutionary and frontier origins, but with the anticipation of joining with the hero to revise their forebears' mistakes. The national wounds would be healed. As the Democratic Party's nominee for president, Kennedy was presenting himself as the means of returning to the foundations of the American nation.

Psychoanalytic theorists of love account for the feeling of completeness that accompanies romance by focusing on the phenomenon of opposites attracting. One of the primary wounds suffered in childhood is caretakers' disapproval, either explicit or implicit, of certain aspects of the personality. A common reaction is to "lose" a part of ourselves, repressing traits and yearnings that are not in accord with society. In compensation for this "lost" self, we develop a persona that can successfully meet the expectations of those around us. We tend to fall in love with someone in whom we see some of the traits of the Lost Self.[14]

Kennedy's public image was more than a meeting point of American myths. Kennedy's private myth, driven since childhood by fantasies of British adventurers, was an important influence on the public image he projected; it contributed elements—aristocratic style and sophistication, rebellious impatience with authority—that had been disowned by the official culture of the Eisenhower fifties but that survived in the star images of Cary Grant and James Dean, respectively. But these images were also conflated in the contemporary western with which his New Frontier metaphor was aligned. The gunfighter was characterized by a self-assured, if self-tormented, bearing, a personal style that ennobled an edgy alienation with the superior character and ability of a "natural aristocrat."

Romantic love is never only a repetition of childhood relationships, nor is it only a matter of projected ideals. However much a lover seems to fit the silhouette carried around in the beloved's head, the lover is likely to contain a good deal that is new. Ross states this succinctly:

122

Not all loves are revivals and not all lovers are "revenants." They are also irreducible—new people, unique. They bring distinct personal histories, teach new knowledge, expand experience in unexpected ways. The lover must be prepared, sure enough of his or her own psychosocial identity, to take them in.[15]

Kennedy's personal history, both public and private, brought an intense new element to the image upon which the public gazed. If Americans took him as their president, they would make a choice that would expand their experience in ways difficult to predict.

Kennedy's daring campaign strategy—to offer himself as a candidate bringing adventure and challenge rather than paternal gifts—was as exciting and frightening for a potential voter as the prospect of falling in love. Persuading a majority of the public to overcome their caution and choose him over his Republican opponent would be the work of the fall campaign.

Kennedy's heroic aspirations addressed the uneasiness that had been increasingly voiced by opinion makers. By mid-1960 the concern that the United States was drifting had led to a nationwide debate in newspapers and periodicals concerning the "national purpose." The debate was not so much about what this purpose should be as about how to articulate and revive the sense of purposefulness among the populace. And for this debate Kennedy was a candidate who had arrived at the perfect time.[16]

Shortly after his New Frontier speech accepting the nomination, Kennedy responded to an invitation from *Life* to define the "national purpose." In his opening he drew an analogy between a nation and an individual. Safely wrapping his observations in the familiar wisdom of Socrates, Kennedy may well have been thinking of his own private self-contemplation during his hospitalization, and his decision to labor on *Profiles in Courage*:

In all recorded history, probably the sagest bit of advice ever offered man was the ancient admonition to "know thyself." As with individuals, so with nations. Just as a man who realizes that his life has gone off course can regain his bearings only through the strictest self-scrutiny, so a whole people, become aware that things have somehow gone wrong, can right matters only by a rigidly honest look at its core of collective being, its national purpose.

If Kennedy perceived that his life had for a time gone off course, perhaps he was thinking of how he had allowed himself to drift during the illness-plagued years of his early political career, surrendering his public image to his father's control. Or perhaps he was thinking of how at Harvard he had failed to apply himself fully to his literary and political interests until he found that his prospective fiancée was marrying a successful young jour-

123

nalist. As Kennedy proceeded to scrutinize the political and literary texts articulating American principles and goals, he concluded that "our national purpose consists of the combined purposefulness of each of us *when we are at our moral best*: striving, risking, choosing, making decisions, engaging in a pursuit of happiness that is strenuous, heroic, exciting and exalted. When we do so as individuals, we make a nation that, in Jefferson's words, will always be 'in the full tide of successful experiment.' "[17]

Kennedy was using the language of liberation, of desire, in the narrative of a hero's journey of service. He urged Americans to make their lives the meeting point between the culture they had been given and the aspirations they felt within. He was thus offering a vision of democracy that would have at its center what it has been most criticized for lacking: a spiritual quest. In so doing he spoke as the dream lover, the man who reawakened the idealistic dreams of the nation's infancy while promising an exciting shared journey to heal what had been neglected, violated, or otherwise abused.

In the article, Kennedy described the 1950s as a time in which "the very abundance which our dynamism has created has weaned and wooed us from the tough condition in which, heretofore, we have approached whatever it is we have had to do." The post-World War II United States had become overcivilized, like a threatening woman who used her pleasures and comforts to create dependency as she "weaned and wooed." Masculine leadership was needed "to remind us of our national purpose, to direct its shaping for current ends, to spur us to new efforts, to encourage and, if need be, to exhort."[18] Kennedy offered himself as a supportive teacher and guide, an ideal figure in whom the public could find their own aspirations to cross into their own frontiers. Following this heroic dream lover, they could leave behind the temptation of staying with a society figured as wife/mother, a choice that would mean the life-in-death of wasted potential.

When after Labor Day the fall campaign began, Kennedy experimented with his theme while listening to the response he was getting from crowds. By all accounts, Kennedy was centrally involved in the writing of his campaign speeches. According to Joseph Kraft, an important member of the team of speechwriters who furnished Kennedy and Sorensen material, Kennedy's "prime concern was to evoke a response," and he was "terribly good" at altering his speeches according to what he inferred from his audience: "If he found that a particular line was exciting people, he was getting them interested, he would move on to that in a hurry. If it happened by accident, he'd note it immediately. I think that that was his primary concern. It was to reach people all the time."[19] Sorensen, Richard Goodwin, and other members of Kennedy's speechwriting "factory," and the responses of the audience, contributed to Kennedy's choices as he refined his theme and thus the image he was projecting.

In his early appearances Kennedy rather awkwardly tried to relate the New Frontier to his various settings. On September 2, he spoke in New Hampshire of being in "a section of the United States that Bernard De Voto said 30 years ago was a finished place. I talk in this State also of the new frontier." In Maine on the same day he similarly referred to "living in an old section of the United States but still in a new frontier." The next day, in Alaska, he again took advantage of the local relevance of his slogan, but this time he used it as a point of departure for explaining the meaning of the term: "This is, in a great way, a new frontier, and in another way it is the last frontier. But what I was talking about earlier was a state of mind. Those people in this country who do not want things done for them, but want to do them themselves."

Three days later, on September 6, he moved a step further from the New Frontier defined in the acceptance speech and closer to the "Ask not what" line that would appear in his Inaugural Address: "When I talk about the new frontier, I don't mean just a physical reality, I mean all of those who believe that they want to serve our Government and serve our system, who want to join with us not because of what we are going to do for them, but for the opportunity that they will have to serve our country."[20] When Kennedy found audiences responding to his challenges to service, he quickly gave up his clumsy attempts at relating his New Frontier to the parochial identities and concerns of his listeners.[21] By the first debate with his opponent, Vice President Richard Nixon, on the evening of September 26, Kennedy had become convinced of the power of his theme and of the image with which he could project it.

Dramatic and important events in Kennedy's campaign occurred both before and after the initial one-on-one confrontation with his Republican opponent. On September 12 he had directly confronted the religion issue by facing a sullen gathering of 300 Protestant ministers in Houston, strongly asserting both his commitment to individual freedom of conscience and his own right as an American Catholic to run for president. In late October he would solidify his support among black Americans with telephone calls from himself and his brother Robert expressing concern for the safety of Martin Luther King Jr., incarcerated in Georgia, that helped achieve King's release. But all historians agree that the turning point of the campaign was the first of the four Kennedy-Nixon debates. Public opinion polls, the responses of leaders in both parties, and the dramatic changes in the crowds the candidates drew confirmed that Kennedy was the winner. The subsequent three debates added up to a draw, and thus failed to change the crucial "first impression" made by the opening debate. The importance of this debate to the 1960 election can hardly be exaggerated. Kennedy went into it the underdog, an unproven leader facing the heir apparent of a highly popular administration; he emerged the favorite.

How did Kennedy win the debate with Nixon? Again, commentators have agreed on the essential points. First, Kennedy addressed the audience, taking his central campaign theme to the viewer, while Nixon addressed Kennedy, responding "me too" to Kennedy's central theme before rebutting Kennedy's specific claims in standard debate fashion. Second, Kennedy simply looked better. He appeared crisp, confident, handsome, earnest, and sincere, where Nixon appeared bland, worried, sallow, distracted, and untrustworthy.

In the days immediately following the debate, reporters witnessed a huge increase in both the size and the intensity of the crowds Kennedy drew. They were particularly impressed by the phenomenon of "jumpers." In *The Making of the President 1960* Theodore White offered the following account:

The jumpers made their appearance shortly after the first TV debate when from a politician Kennedy had become, in the mind of the bobby-sox platoons, a "thing" combining, as one Southern Senator said, "The best qualities of Elvis Presley and Franklin D. Roosevelt." The jumpers were, in the beginning, teenage girls who would bounce, jounce and jump as the cavalcade passed, squealing, "I seen him, I seen him." Gradually over the days their jumping seemed to grow more rhythmic, giving a jack-in-the-box effect of ups and downs in a thoroughly sexy oscillation. Then, as the press began to comment on the phenomenon, thus stimulating more artistic jumping, the middle-aged ladies began to jump up and down too, until, in the press bus following the candidate, one would note only the oddities: the lady, say, in her bathrobe, jumping back and forth; the heavily pregnant mother, jumping; the mother with a child in her arms, jumping; the row of nuns, all jiggling under their black robes, almost (but not quite) daring to jump; and the double-jumpers—teenagers who, as the cavalcade passed, would turn to face each other and, in ecstasy, place hands on each others' shoulders and jump up and down together as a partnership.[22]

Kennedy's triumph in the debate had clearly had an erotic effect. He had successfully wooed the television audience with the methods of a prospective lover.

By addressing the audience, Kennedy gave the viewer his energy and attention; whereas Nixon worried about Kennedy, Kennedy pursued the viewer. Such pursuit is flattering, particularly when the pursuer mirrors the pursued's fantasy, appears to see in the pursued the mirror of his own, and offers a compelling vision of the fantasy they could achieve together in relationship. In the statement opening the debate, Kennedy offered the viewer his vision of their joining to meet a challenge of exalted proportions. He began by sketching the present election as an opportunity to reenact the achievement of the supreme American patriarch, though on a larger scale:

In the election of 1860, Abraham Lincoln said the question was whether this Nation could exist half slave or half free.

In the election of 1960, and with the world around us, the question is whether the world will exist half slave or half free, whether it will move in the direction of freedom, in the direction of the road that we are taking or whether it will move in the direction of slavery.

I think it will depend in great measure upon what we do here in the United States, on the kind of society that we build, on the kind of strength that we maintain.

Kennedy returned to this theme at the close of the statement, making clear that he had an idealized image of his audience, and that he believed he and they should join together to embark on an exciting journey that would transcend normal domestic concerns:

In 1933 Franklin Roosevelt said in his inaugural that this generation of Americans has a "rendezvous with destiny." I think our generation of Americans has this same "rendezvous." The question now is: Can freedom be maintained under the most severe attack it has ever known? I think it can be, and I think in the final analysis it depends upon what we do here. I think it's time America started moving again.

In between these exhortations Kennedy insistently repeated "I'm not satisfied" as he listed concerns ranging from economics to national strength to racial injustice. Kennedy's words aimed at eliciting emotions of incompleteness and at offering himself as the partner with whom the audience could journey to fulfillment. By creating this scenario, Kennedy made himself the lover with whom the television audience could return to a thrilling moment in the American past in order to go forward.

This suit was more stirring than the sensible replies of his rival, who said that while he agreed with Kennedy's themes, he disagreed with the "implications" that America had "been standing still" and that Democratic solutions would be better than Republican efforts. Yet it has been noted that the majority of those who listened to the debate on the radio rather than watching it on television were inclined to call it a draw or declare Nixon the winner. However astute Kennedy's handling of the rhetorical terms of the debate, to a listener Nixon appeared to mount an adequate rebuttal.

For the far larger audience of television viewers, the decisive additional element was the contrast in the appearance of the two men. Kennedy looked confident, urgent, self-possessed. When Nixon made his rebuttals, Kennedy regarded him coolly with a slightly sardonic expression. While Kennedy spoke Nixon was seen shifting his eyes about nervously. By all the signals of appearance and mannerism available to viewers watching two rival suitors in a Hollywood romantic comedy, Nixon was obviously the wrong one.

To fully understand the viewers' choice in the debate, we must view it in terms of the man whom either Kennedy or Nixon would be chosen to replace. Despite the emphasis on Kennedy's youth, the two men were of the same generation, with Nixon only a few years older. When one of the questioners challenged Kennedy with the Vice President's accusations that Kennedy was "naïve and at times immature," Kennedy correctly observed that he and Nixon had entered Congress at the same time. Nixon was subsequently asked about a notorious statement of Eisenhower's at a press conference a month earlier. Asked to give an example of a major idea of Nixon's that he had adopted, the President had replied: "If you give me a week, I might think of one. I don't remember." Nixon was forced to attempt a deferential explanation. He suggested that the President had made what was probably a "facetious remark," and that it "would be improper for the President of the United States to disclose the instances in which members of his official family had made recommendations, as I have made them through the years, to him, which he has accepted or rejected." In any event, Nixon said, "The President only makes the decisions."

In this context, Nixon and Kennedy appeared with Eisenhower as characters in a familiar situation of such 1950s Hollywood family dramas as *East of Eden* (1955) and *Cat on a Hot Tin Roof* (1958). Kennedy looked like the sexy rebel son who is the right one to replace the father. Because he dared to rebel, the father views him as dangerous. But Nixon, the good son chosen by the father for his loyalty and obedience, lacks precisely the traits that could make him a worthy successor, capable of an independence and power commensurate with the father's. Not even the father designating him his successor can summon any enthusiasm. For the young woman in these dramas, and for the audience, the sexy, dissatisfied son driven by urgent inner demands is obviously the right one. Kennedy's and Nixon's rhetorical positionings in regard to this scenario with Eisenhower were all to Kennedy's advantage. But the words of either could only assert their positions. When combined with the contrasting appearances of the two men, their roles in this biblical drama seemed simply fact.

Standing beside the worried and shifty Nixon, Kennedy seemed the *one* for whom the audience had been looking. Together he and the audience would heal the wounds inflicted by history while realizing a national, shared fantasy. Kennedy closed the debate by reiterating his desire "to set before the people the unfinished business of our society" and his promise of shared fulfillment: "I think we're ready to move. And it is to that great task, if we are successful, that we will address ourselves."[23] His idealized mirroring of the audience he so ardently wooed validated the beloved: the nation was worthy of such a suitor.

In the end, Americans chose Kennedy over Nixon by one of the smallest popular-vote margins in history. Considering that the youthful challenger was running during a time of peace and unprecedented prosperity against the shrewd vice president of a popular administration, the victory was a remarkable achievement. Even more remarkable was the manner in which Kennedy immediately began broadening and intensifying the nation's identification with him as their romantic hero. His victory speech, with his beautiful, young, pregnant wife at his side, in which he spoke of now turning to prepare for a "new administration and a new baby," and the subsequent public search for a cabinet and advisers consisting of the "best and the brightest" in the land, began the projection of an idealized White House court that would one day be named Camelot. But most crucial was the Inaugural Address.

While the Address was written in collaboration with Sorensen, and drew upon suggestions solicited from many sources, Kennedy took an intense interest in it and must be seen as the primary writer and true author. Most important, he is its speaker, performer, and primary subject. The Address elegantly distills the campaign themes of challenge and sacrifice, elevating them to the cadences of ritual and ceremony. It also condenses the parallel life journey taken by the historical Kennedy and his double—the public image—that had led to this dramatic moment in which he now presented himself as the personification of the nation.

The often-quoted and -replayed third paragraph of the Address announces the speaker Kennedy as the mythic hero in whom the public can see its collective destiny. Here the successive stages of the production of the Kennedy image—achieved up to now through historical, journalistic, and literary narrative; photographs and television; and campaign rhetoric—are evoked in a single sentence of poetic declamation:

Let the word go forth from this time and place, to friend and foe alike, that the torch has been passed to a new generation of Americans—born in this century, tempered by war, disciplined by a hard and bitter peace, proud of our ancient heritage—and unwilling to witness or permit the slow undoing of those human rights to which this nation has always been committed, and to which we are committed today at home and around the world.

The announcement that "the torch has been passed to a new generation of Americans," made by a coatless Kennedy on a cold winter's day as his outgoing predecessor Eisenhower sat huddled in coat and scarf, begins the conceit that the speaker personifies all those of his age. Kennedy's personal history and the collective history of his generation are then yoked together in poetic images that work as synecdoches for the major texts of the Kennedy myth: "born in this century" (Henry Luce's foreword to *Why England Slept* had emphasized that the young author represented the readiness of his generation to defend freedom); "tempered by war" (John Hersey's "Survival" had shown the brash youth chastened in the wartime fire and water of the PT boat catastrophe); "disciplined by a cold and bitter peace" (*Profiles in Courage* had demonstrated the new seriousness and self-control with which the recently married senator had emerged from his extended confinement to the hospital bed); "proud of our ancient heritage" (Kennedy's campaign rhetoric had evoked the model of defenders of freedom reaching from classical times to the frontier forebears); and "unwilling to witness or permit the slow undoing of those human rights to which this nation has always been committed, and to which we are committed today at home and around the world" (Kennedy's facing up to Truman, the Protestant ministers in Houston, and the imprisoners of Martin Luther King Jr. in Georgia had dramatized his commitment to the individual's aspirations against artificial barriers, whether they were ones of age, religion, or race).

The culminating lines of the Address bring this mythic personification of a generation's collective biography to an assertion of a climactic role now being accepted through the voice of the speaker:

In the long history of the world, only a few generations have been granted the role of defending freedom in its hour of maximum danger. I do not shrink from this responsibility—I welcome it. I do not believe that any of us would exchange places with any other people or any other generation. The energy, the faith, the devotion which we bring to this endeavor will light our country and all who serve it—and the glow from that fire can truly light the world.

And so, my fellow Americans: ask not what your country can do for you—ask what you can do for your country.

In the decades following his death, historians have ranked Kennedy as a president only somewhat above average. Yet Kennedy was enormously popular during his time in office, and that popularity has grown with each succeeding president who has tried to supplant him in the national consciousness. The "rational" judgments of political observers during his presidency as well as those of historians in its aftermath have been irrelevant to a nation swept away by Kennedy's mirroring of the national imago. Kennedy reached the White House a master of the various elements available for the production of his presidency. He used those elements to project glamorous images and a dramatic narrative in which the public enjoyed a thrilling relationship with this idealized reflection of their deepest yearnings. He made superb use of words, actions, and setting to construct the presidency as a cinematic narrative of elevated power and significance. Winning the adoration of large numbers of people, he took them through vicarious experiences of the crises into which he characteristically shaped events.

Early in his administration, Kennedy took the controversial step of deciding that his press conferences would be broadcast "live" on television. Many critics worried that this practice would result in dangerous gaffes

131

with repercussions in foreign affairs. But Kennedy's thorough preparation, witty ability to think on his feet, and cool management of his emotions displayed a mastery of self, of facts, and of reporters that dazzled the nation. The press conferences enhanced Kennedy's increasing intimacy with the American public. It was not the intimacy of Franklin Roosevelt's fireside chats, in which American families during the depression and war had gathered around the radio to hear the warm reassurance and direction of a father figure. It was rather the intimacy, or illusion of intimacy, afforded by the movie screen, onto which each member of the audience could see his or her dreamed self projected as an idealized image. Because the movie and television screens project only a phantom image, not a bodily presence, the viewer can more easily identify with the spectral presence as a reflection of the self. Kennedy's curious mixture of abstracted intensity and detached emotion heightened this power of his movie-star image to be the object of the projection of his audience's inner desires. Because Kennedy's image was only electric, two-dimensional, it could more easily mirror the viewer's dreams.

The picture magazines were eager to cooperate in Kennedy's presidential production. Kennedy's extraordinary appeal made him a more highly attractive commodity with each passing day of his administration. The novelty of a beautiful young wife and two vivacious young children in the White House increased this aura. *Life* already used the white middle-class family as a heightened, universalized image of the American way of life. Throughout the 1940s and 1950s the Luce publication mirrored American ideology, and mixed the public with the personal, by portraying an idealized family in which the father worked, the mother managed the domestic household and embodied a refined elegance, and the children blissfully played in the backyard and in front of the television set. This projected norm offered a resolution of events and conflicts of the cold war era. *Life* juxtaposed such presentations with alluring features on the wilder lives of movie stars and other celebrities. In effect, the scandalous affairs of personas like Elizabeth Taylor were presented as the tempting alternative that could be appreciated yet kept outside the normal happiness of domestic life in the United States.[24]

With the same movie-star quality, Kennedy and his family presented a version of this scenario. Kennedy carefully controlled the production of photographs to ensure that he was always presented as the character he had chosen to play. No photographs were allowed showing him eating, smoking cigars, playing golf, or kissing his wife. On the other hand, whenever their protective mother was away he allowed his children to be photographed playing with their pony Macaroni or cavorting under his desk at the Oval Office while he did business. He also made the press aware of his crises as they were happening, so that they could present him as someone valiantly struggling with the pressures of work. His wife's chosen project, the restoration of the White House based on a reverence for its history, offered a heightened version of the domestic role of the average housewife. Kennedy's sexual appeal was acknowledged only in the glowing enthusiasm of young women in crowds, or in a kind of joke, like when friends surprised him at Madison Square Garden by having Marilyn Monroe sing "Happy Birthday." His sarcastic acknowledgment of her singing in such a "sweet, wholesome way" duplicated the attitude of the disconcerted but finally responsible reader of *Life*, or the Tom Ewell father/husband in the Marilyn Monroe film *The Seven-Year Itch* (1955). In the eyes of the public, Kennedy was acknowledging the illicit temptation but holding it at bay.

Kennedy and his wife collaborated closely in displaying images of excellence. Besides their lonely, wounded childhoods and their children, they most deeply shared a love of literature. Jacqueline added to this her love of the arts. Though Kennedy's tastes in music and the visual arts ran toward Broadway tunes and inspiring seascapes, he was committed to elevating the nation's sense of its creative potential. The President and First Lady's patronage of the arts climaxed in the dinner for recipients of the Nobel Prize. Pablo Casals emerged from his self-imposed exile from the United States to give a White House performance. Kennedy wittily pronounced that there had never before been such an assemblage of brilliance under the White House roof, with the exception of those evenings when Thomas Jefferson dined alone. The values of America's great artists and writers were publicly embraced as part of the proud heritage of its government.

Kennedy enthusiastically promoted excellence of the body as well. His physical fitness campaign included exhortations to American schools to include calisthenics as part of the daily schedule. Despite his own periodic debilitation (a few months into office he seriously strained his back during a ceremonial planting with a shovel, and was for a period returned to dependence on crutches), he managed to provide photographers with many images of his zest for physical activity. He was photographed swimming off the coast of Florida and sailing off Cape Cod. His regular use of the swimming pool in the White House was much noted. Photographs of him in the rocking chair he used in the Oval Office to relieve the pressure on his back conveyed his restless determination to work despite his injury.

The advocacy of fifty-mile hikes, with his brother Robert and other members of the administration providing examples, became the most famous symbol of the strenuous life in the Kennedy years. But the many images of Kennedy's restless and enthusiastic pursuit of both work and fun, rendered poignant by the public's knowledge of his bad back and earlier scrapes with death, made the president himself the prime model of the pursuit of toughness. The images of excellence were an important part of the erotics of the Kennedy presidency.

Even more than the dramatic rhetoric and the appealing images, crisis marked Kennedy's New Frontier. Indeed, it was in the successive crises during his administration that Kennedy brought his appreciation of rhetoric and spectacle together with his need to perform in the other sense of the word—to achieve. Kennedy had not sought the presidency to create a show devoid of actual accomplishment. He saw the office as the arena in which he could fulfill his deepest aspirations. He wanted to demonstrate his masculinity and his self-worth; he wanted to show that his idealism was matched by his "toughness"; he wanted, as a successor to other generations who had fought for liberty, to shape the destiny of the contemporary United States. The fundamental significance of John F. Kennedy's constructing a public image and bringing that image to the presidency was that this merged the world of art into the world of action.

The citizenry that was now connected to national politics mainly as a spectating audience gathered before the television screen. Kennedy, the identification figure, was repeatedly compelled to prove that his role had substance through his dramatic "real-life" performance. Viewers could recognize each succeeding episode of Kennedy's presidency as a testing of his character. As Kennedy sought to make problems unfold according to the ideological scripts he had projected, his role as hero was powerfully determined, in part, by what he perceived as the end desired by the audience. It was also determined, in part, by what Kennedy desired—from the deepest sources of his personality—to make of himself. Thus the Kennedy administration developed according to the logic of an intense love affair, a kind of shared dream. The wishes of Kennedy and his audience drove the narrative. Like a romantic lover, Kennedy self-consciously performed according to his perception of the yearnings of the beloved (his public) and according to his own desires.

Kennedy did not create the problems that unfolded during his presidency. They had been developing for some time: the civil rights movement had been gathering momentum since the 1954 desegregation order by the

Supreme Court; Cuba, Berlin, and the Congo were all problems presented to Kennedy, not created by him. Yet though Kennedy did not create these problems, it was not inevitable that they should have all been configured into crises.

Crisis was the Kennedy method. He had begun practicing it during his campaign, and it worked well for him. The attraction to crisis probably had its psychological source in Kennedy's need since childhood to feel in control of situations otherwise defined by his mother or his doctors. Like his many romantic intrigues, crisis may also have given him the "high" of a felt intensity, of maximizing every moment of a life expected to be short. But as a political method, it had the further risky but compelling advantage of placing problems before the public as dramatic narratives in which Kennedy played the role of heroic protagonist.

A crisis is a conflict situation in which life is intensified by the requirements of drama. The limited time span within which to resolve a clear conflict requires the protagonist to make decisions and to act, however ambiguous the opposing forces or frightening the alternatives. The deadline similarly forces the viewer to go along with these choices or give up the object of identification—the sense of seeing one's ideal self in the protagonist. Romantic love resembles fiction precisely in the experience it affords of feeling with, or imagining that one feels with, another person.[25] Romantic love also typically resembles narrative in being a charged experience in which the lover/reader must either remain steadfast through shared adventures or give up identification with the beloved.

It was essential to Kennedy's politics of identity that his responses in these crises, at least those visible to the public, also adhere to scripts that would enable him as the hero to retain the identification of the public. *Profiles in Courage* had focused on the disaster that befalls politicians who lose such identification. In his opening and closing chapters Kennedy had emphasized that such martyrdom was not what a politician should seek, but rather what he should be prepared to risk as the ultimate price for integrity if he and the public turned out to be hopelessly divided in their perception of a great issue. Thus the crises of the Kennedy administration were tests of Kennedy's character, but they were also tests of the cultural scripts that he shared with his public. As long as the viewer could maintain identification with Kennedy while he performed what he perceived to be the right actions, the scripts were held intact or favorably altered.

The conflicts with historical forces in the crises of Kennedy's presidency were experienced by the public as the hero's application of expertise, ide-

135

alism, and emotion to problems at the point at which choices had to be made. The knowledge, belief, and direct experience of the hero appeared to reflect back on the citizen, who identified in Kennedy the capabilities that the citizen would like to believe she or he would have brought to the situation. Lured into identification with this hero as a projection of his or her best self, the viewer experienced the resolution of contradictory historical forces as a personal choice. The citizen, as viewer, experienced a vicarious confrontation with the forces of the time.

What Jacqueline Kennedy would subsequently call Camelot was, then, a narrative spectacle made up of a series of vivid episodes. Camelot names the sense that an episode that occurred briefly in time seems somehow to be timeless. Psychoanalysts explain the perception in a romance that normal time has been transcended as a result of the psychological dynamic of déjà vu—the encounter with the romantic lover triggers regression to one's childhood origins. The Kennedy administration triggered a sense of returning to America's legendary origins, the terrain of the movies, particularly the westerns in which the American frontier is nostalgically filtered through present American dreams.

"Toughness" was a central preoccupation of both the private Kennedy psyche and the public Kennedy mystique. The term was among the criteria listed on forms evaluating candidates for positions in the administration. New Frontiersmen were reminded by Robert Kennedy that "we're liberal but we're tough." The President styled himself a "liberal without illusions" and a "pragmatist." Kennedy's stance powerfully appealed to the broad mainstream of his audience, for it resolved the contradictory strains within the national ideology in a style familiar from popular culture: that of the tough-guy detective, a twentieth-century descendant of the nineteenth-century western gunfighter. The private eye brings distinctively American values forward into the urban and institutional milieu of modern American society.

The toughness of this hero is shaped by those values. As Rupert Wilkinson has observed, toughness is not usually defined because "personal concerns with toughness often come through to us as a matter of style and aura—a wisecrack, a grimace, or a tone of voice—rather than in systematic statements that invite analysis. Yet styles and mannerisms reflect cultural values no less than do explicit declarations." The appeal of the tough guy in American culture is based in part on the assumption that the environment is dangerous but provides an opportunity for the lone individual to prove he "can handle" himself. The tough guy is masterful (can "manage situations"), dynamic (celebrates action), can "take it" (copes well with stressful challenges), is a "stand-up guy" (a living reproach to approval-seeking society), and has "class" (achieved through "aura and performance") yet in the sociological sense is "classless" (his styles are drawn from ethnic and lower-class idioms).[26]

By the time of his assassination, Kennedy had exhibited his toughness in dramatic crises in each of the major areas of the national life—economic, social, and foreign affairs. The U.S. Steel Crisis, the Civil Rights Crisis, and the Cuban Missile Crisis were the three most dramatic events of the Kennedy presidency. In each case, Kennedy responded to a problem that he had hoped to avoid, even deny, by defining a clear plot, including a deadline, in which he played the role of hero in the decisive confrontation. In each case his dramatic actions enabled him to play the role of a tough guy in a suspenseful story familiar to filmgoers and television viewers. In the fundamental plot of the hardboiled detective story, the tough-guy hero discovers during the course of his investigation that the extent of the villains' corruption and perfidy is far greater than he originally imagined. The hero defines his idealism when he responds by confronting that evil, identifying it, clearly judging it, and taking action against it. In the presentation to the American people of the U.S. Steel Crisis, the Civil Rights Crisis, and the Cuban Missile Crisis, Kennedy in each "case" began with a relatively naïve view of his antagonist. In the Steel Crisis he thought that he could trust the word of the steel-company executives, but he learned the hard way that their "pursuit of private power and profit exceeds their public responsibility."[27] In the Civil Rights Crisis he began by believing that Southern whites had been victims during Reconstruction and therefore deserved his sympathetic treatment as they both dealt with the rowdy demands of the protesters, but he learned through his dealings with contemporary Southern governors and the televised face of Bull Conner what black Americans had endured at their hands. In the case of Cuba, Kennedy began by believing the promises of the Soviets, but with the discovery of missiles in Cuba he encountered the deceit of Soviet leaders. In each of these major crises, Kennedy took his discovery to the American people in a dramatic televised speech, revealing the beating he, and they, had taken at the hands of the criminals he now identified and judged, and immediately announcing the tough actions he was taking against those criminals.

The Cuban Missile Crisis made the most vivid impression, as it was played for unprecedented stakes. Kennedy's performance was necessarily enacted with a constant awareness of audience. For both domestic and foreign political reasons, Kennedy could not consider allowing the Soviet Union's covert introduction of offensive nuclear missiles into Cuba to succeed, or even appear to succeed. While advisers differed on the degree of actual change in the strategic balance of power the missiles represented, Kennedy knew that if they remained in Cuba, the effects on the global perception of American resolve and on the domestic perception of his presidency would be devastating.

Once the missiles were discovered, the major pressure exerted on Kennedy was to remove the missiles with a surprise air strike as strongly advocated by elder statesman Dean Acheson, probably accompanied by a full-scale invasion of Castro's island. While Kennedy's ambassador to the United Nations, Adlai Stevenson, urged a diplomatic solution that offered removal of obsolete American missiles in Turkey for the removal of the Soviet missiles in Cuba, Kennedy was determined that he and the United States not be seen as having buckled under pressure from Premier Khrushchev's reckless international gamble.

His chosen response was subsequently portrayed as relatively moderate, positioned between a surprise attack and an offer of a deal. But the decision to blockade Cuba and give the Soviets a limited time to remove the missiles was not inherently a moderate course; in contrast to the *fait accompli* that a missile strike would have presented, Kennedy's choice of action heightened the situation in Cuba to a major confrontation between the two superpowers in which each was under pressure to call the other's bluff. Kennedy's strategy did in the end result in the removal of the missiles without war, but not all have agreed that it was the wisest way of dealing with the Soviet gambit.

As a political decision on how best to define the problem for the American viewing audience, however, Kennedy's course of action was both characteristic and shrewd. In the televised address with which Kennedy informed Americans of the crisis, he positioned himself in the classic role of the tough-guy detective. He had discovered that he and the public were victims of a clandestine and dangerous plot. Now holding incontrovertible evidence of Soviet and Cuban perfidy, he was exposing the crime, judging it before the court of world opinion, and directly confronting the criminal. As the opening scene in the public's knowledge of the crisis, the announcement of a quarantine with a clearly drawn line and a limited time frame for the removal of the missiles created a scenario that conformed to the requirements of Hollywood narrative: a hero seeks to achieve a goal before the expiration of a deadline. The "quarantine" of the island, announced in

Kennedy's speech first informing Americans of the missiles in Cuba, immediately created this suspenseful situation.

It also implicitly created the secondary romantic plot of classic American cinema. In Hollywood films, the hero typically wins the "girl" through his character-proving performance as he pursues the goal set up by the plot. In this case the "girl" was the feminized citizenry, the viewing audience. They understood that Kennedy must focus on achieving the goal of the removal of the missiles without starting World War III. Only if he succeeded, in terms they could accept with self-respect and self-validation, would they continue to embrace their hero.

Kennedy's quarantine immediately defined the problem of the Soviet missiles as a suspenseful story. The Russian ships steaming toward an American blockade and the limited time afforded the Soviets before American action would be taken to remove the missiles riveted the eyes and emotions of the audience. When the Russian ships stopped in the water short of the waiting American ships, they had "blinked"—in the famous "eyeball-to-eyeball" phrase used by a member of Kennedy's cabinet. When Khrushchev at last agreed to remove the missiles, the crisis was brought to the resolution expected at the end of the classic American film: the hero had achieved the goal and won the admiring embrace of the girl.

Since then, as more information has gradually become available concerning the crisis and its context, Kennedy's "standing up to the Russians" in Cuba has been both softened and muddied somewhat. We now know that his administration had been sponsoring covert activities against the Cuban regime that may have at least partly inspired Khrushchev's gamble, and we know that Kennedy's successful forcing of the missiles' removal was finessed with his secret indication that the U.S. missiles would at a later date be removed from Turkey. But these revelations have not changed the basic story. Under great stress, Kennedy withstood both domestic and foreign pressures while achieving the removal of the Soviet missiles short of war.

The mystique of the Cuban Missile Crisis has been based on the understanding that Kennedy stood up to both the intimidation of the Soviets and that attempted by the militaristic forces in his own government. In "now-it-can-be-told" accounts of the crisis subsequently published, Kennedy made sure that he was portrayed as wisely steering a rational but firm course between the "militarists" and the "appeasers" in his own government. The story of his brother Robert's objecting to Acheson's demand for an air strike by saying that he did not want Jack responsible for a "Pearl Har-

139

bor in reverse," and the characterization of Stevenson's willingness to consider a diplomatic trade of missiles for missiles as "Adlai wanted a Munich," served this purpose. Kennedy's publicizing of these two anecdotes established the roles he did not want to play. Whether or not either of these courses would have been preferable as a cold-war decision, either would have been in serious conflict with the mythic and mass-culture scenarios through which Americans understood their role in history. Kennedy instead shaped the problem into a crisis with a familiar storyline in which he could play the preferred role of the American hero.

In his Inaugural Address, Kennedy had defined his stance in the cold war with the balanced admonishment, "Let us never negotiate out of fear. But let us never fear to negotiate." He asked "that both sides begin anew the quest for peace, before the dark powers of destruction unleashed by science engulf all humanity in planned or accidental self-destruction." Kennedy achieved the removal of the Soviet missiles from Cuba without letting fear, of either the threat of force from outside or the possibility of weakness inside, govern his actions. When his tacit promise to remove the obsolete American missiles from Turkey became apparent to Americans at a later date, it simply confirmed for most that he had shown a reasonable flexibility in solving the crisis.

Kennedy entered the Cuban Missile Crisis with the image that each hero of American cinema has brought to the various scenarios of Hollywood movies. He possessed the expertise, the emotion, and the direct experience in which the audience could see reflections of their ideal movie-screen selves. When he brought precisely those traits to the solution of a crisis that had the highest possible stakes, the viewer vicariously experienced a confrontation with the deepest elements of the self. Kennedy's choices on behalf of the people he represented were successful, and thus validated Americans' highest sense of self.[28]

As Person observes, "love creates a situation in which the self is exposed to new risks and enlarged possibilities; it is one of the most significant crucibles for growth."[29] Kennedy saw the need to show his public an image of their shared narrative of return and transformation on the New Frontier. He sought with the help of a cooperative national press to provide Americans with contemporary heroes—the astronauts, the Peace Corps, and the Special Forces, or "Green Berets"—who could be seen acting out the values of the New Frontier. Each of these sets of heroes was depicted as enacting the values of self-sacrifice, the doing of good works, and the resurgence of vigor that were at the core of the New Frontier ideology. Space, the undeveloped nations of the Third World, and particularly Indochina offered specific sites upon which the landscape of the New Frontier could be projected. In each of these areas, Kennedy's rhetoric and the journalists following his cues could depict the drama of heroic Americans going boldly into the 1960s, giving up their security and comfort but winning a revitalized and pleasingly revised American identity.

Kennedy particularly emphasized the Special Forces, irregular military adventurers who could reincarnate the warrior-aristocrats that he had so admired on the frontiers of the British Empire. Kennedy gave the Special Forces the mission of counterinsurgency: they would enter the frontiers of the cold war represented by former colonial nations to do battle with communist insurgents. He took a personal interest in the adventurers' training and equipment. The press responded during 1961 and 1962 with a series of articles celebrating the Green Berets and their mission. Such popular periodicals as *Newsweek, Saturday Evening Post, Saturday Review,* and *Look* portrayed the work of the Green Berets in the resonant images of American frontier mythology: the adaptation of a few brave individuals to a wilderness to redeem it from savagery. The setting of Southeast Asia possessed further resonance as the setting of the 1958 best-seller *The Ugly American.*

As presidential aspirant, Kennedy had urged every American to read this potboiling novel by William Lederer and Eugene Burdick. *The Ugly American* portrayed a few contemporary American individualists, strikingly similar in characterization to such vigorous and egalitarian heroes of mythic American history as Benjamin Franklin and Davy Crockett, contending in the complacent Eisenhower era with a far larger number of racist, materialist, and bureaucratic Americans. These ugly Americans were, through their contemporary faithlessness to the traditional American character and mission, aiding the ruthless Soviet organization men portrayed as misleading the pastoral natives of Southeast Asia.

The new Kennedy administration presented the Green Berets in Vietnam as symbols of a resurgence of the traditional American spirit of the frontier and the Declaration of Independence against this "ugly" prejudice, complacency, and careerism. Thus, Vietnam was drawn in the national media of 1961 and 1962 as a thrilling re-creation of the frontier that also promised a redemptive cleansing of the ugly stain of racism from American heritage. Defying the organizational tables and career ladders of the Pentagon, these "new" frontiersmen were implicitly depicted as following the original pioneers in escaping the restraints and corruptions of

141

civilization to struggle with savagery; unlike their ancestors, however, they would save and help the darker-skinned native peoples, not dispossess them. Vietnam promised ultimate validation of the American frontier journey as a progress toward the enlightened liberal values of egalitarianism and diversity.[30]

Psychoanalysts assure us that the notoriously transitory mood we call romantic love is followed by disillusionment as the lover gradually discovers that the beloved is a real person with virtues and faults as well as a personal agenda not devoted to the healing of the lover's wounds. With this loss of romantic dreams, the lover either moves on to another object of projections or develops a mature regard for the flesh-and-blood human being.

Kennedy's brief administration lasted long enough that political observers discerned a mixture of positive and negative traits. Kennedy's centrist politics inevitably dissatisfied both ends of the political spectrum. Faced with a coalition of Southern Democrats and Republicans, Kennedy was unable to get his legislative agenda through Congress. But his politics of exalted images and suspenseful handling of crises sustained a sense of promise and expectation. The aura of his image transcended any specific failures or frustrations.

For most Americans, the romantic phase of their love affair with John F. Kennedy had not faded into anything like a disillusionment or even a mature regard when he was shockingly taken away. They were left standing alone on the symbolic landscape of the New Frontier, the re-created mythic space of American origins, bereft of the beloved with whom they had been re-experiencing the deepest expectations and desires. Reeling from a terrible new loss, they were left to struggle uncertainly, alone, with the mechanics of healing the national wounds that Kennedy had presented as fresh challenges.

As American history deteriorated into increasingly painful experiences of domestic riot and foreign war, those wounds only became greater. Vietnam, in particular, became the site of a massive reopening of the primal wounds of American culture. Kennedy had encouraged the press to depict Vietnam as a specific landscape in which American involvement visibly enacted the terms of the New Frontier. In the years after his death, Vietnam mirrored original American sins in horrific images. The fate of Native Americans, blacks, and nature in the frontier expansion of the nineteenth century was revealed in the Vietnam images on the nightly news.

Kennedy became an obsession. If he had lived, would we have indeed been able, with him, to "heal" our wounds, pulling away from Vietnam and instead journeying out endlessly into the true New Frontier of noble ideals and meaningful existence? The obsession redoubled in intensity as revelations about the "real" man behind the projections came to public awareness. His sexual preoccupations, involving deceit and promiscuous conquest of women, seemed impossible to reconcile with the idealized image of the nation's lover. Yet the memory of that lover—the powerful experience of relationship with the Kennedy image—could not be put out of mind.

CHAPTER SIX

An Assassination and Its Fictions

John F. Kennedy was assassinated in Dallas, Texas, on Friday, November 22, 1963 at 12:32 P.M. His head was torn apart, his body wrenched, his actual person killed. Three days later his horribly mutilated body was buried. But his public image was transfigured. The representation of John F. Kennedy, aesthetic and erotic in his lifetime, now became also religious.

Confronting, along with the nation, the horror and the subsequent disorder in Dallas, his widow designed a funeral that would assert the transcendent meaning of John Kennedy's life and death. The riderless horse, the eternal flame, and her dignified bearing as the beautiful widow with her young children were in the same classical mode as the elegant phrases of her husband's Inaugural Address. She directed and performed a silent drama that asserted the tragic universality of her husband's personification of his generation as "proud of its ancient heritage" and welcoming the knowledge that "the torch has been passed."[1]

Like her husband, she knew the power of a few carefully selected words. In the aftermath of the funeral, she gave her sole interview to Theodore White, the journalist who had written the penetrating but romantic story of her husband's triumph in the 1960 election. Asserting her authority to pronounce John Kennedy's epitaph, she invoked the grand intimacy of the

145

White House bed. Before they would go to sleep, she revealed, her husband would sometimes put on the soundtrack album of a Broadway musical. He loved the lines about never forgetting that for "one brief shining moment" there had been the magical kingdom of King Arthur and the Knights of the Round Table. While there would be "great Presidents again," she said, there would never be "another Camelot."

She offered the public what she believed was the right way to understand the Kennedy administration, and thus the seeming absurdity of its abrupt end. She informed her listener that once, when she had read history, she had become "bitter." But Jack, she said, "had this hero idea of history, the idealistic view." For him, history was "full of heroes."[2] Thus she explained her determination to have the eternal flame burn over his grave in Arlington. Not history, which recorded particular stumbles and failures, but myth, which preserved the recurring will to struggle toward the ideal, was the meaning of John F. Kennedy.

Jacqueline Kennedy's evocation of Camelot was the first attempt to transcend the apparent meaninglessness of John Kennedy's death. It would begin a process that has haunted the public consciousness of Americans through the final third of the twentieth century and shows no sign of abating as we move toward the twenty-first.

Three major phenomena have evolved over the decades since the assassination, all of them aspects of our mythic and religious sensibility. One is the dream of resurrection, the return of the hero from the grave. Another is demonology, the search for the principle of evil that slew the hero. The third is blasphemy, denial that this incarnation of the ideal was what it is purported to have been.

The dream of resurrection has been apparent in the ceaseless attempts to place Kennedy once again in the White House. These have ranged from the campaign of his brother Robert in 1968 to that of Gary Hart in 1984 to that of Bill Clinton in 1992. The dream has not been confined by political allegiances or traditions, for it has included Ronald Reagan's 1980 invocations of John F. Kennedy and Dan Quayle's misfiring self-comparison to Kennedy in 1988.

The second phenomenon, demonology, has been the fury of speculation concerning conspiracy swirling around the assassination. Every conceivable agent of the horror has been identified in a theory spun out to fill a book. None are proven, and the vehemence with which a person holds a particular theory to be true reveals more about their fundamental ideology, even their deepest philosophy of life, than about the demonstrated facts of the case.

The phenomenon of blasphemy has been evident in the literature of tabloid revelation and revisionist debunking of Kennedy's character and decision-making. Inevitably, the magnification of Kennedy's character and achievements after his death led to reaction among the skeptical, and the post-Watergate era of investigation resulted in discoveries of hidden aspects of Kennedy's presidency that have provided considerable material for desecration of the hallowed image. But this new material has succeeded only in constituting a blasphemy that confirms the broader belief.

The Kennedy obsession started early in the twentieth century, in one boy's bedridden dreams as he read romantic history. The obsession has endured as the fevered dreams of a nation reading the history of his life and death. From the beginning to the present, narrative has been the distinguishing aspect of the Kennedy mystique. Storytelling is both the compelling vehicle for the fundamental ideas and beliefs of a culture and the site where a writer or reader reworks that ideology in relation to personal experience. The attempts to somehow bring Kennedy back to life, the search for the true story of who killed him and why and what it means, and the investigation of the "real" Jack behind the image have all essentially been efforts to complete the Kennedy story that, from its origins in the young Kennedy's private imaginings and John Hersey's experiment in novelistic reportage, had been driven by narrative. The impulse toward shaping plot to confer meaning upon life has been common to them all.

To bring the part of that story in this book to an end, then, it seems appropriate to turn to self-conscious fiction. By exploring the consciously fictive Kennedy produced in novels and film, we can more clearly see both the Kennedy produced in the purportedly factual areas of political campaigns, conspiracy theories, and biographies and the ideas and emotions artists have brought to the contemplation of this subject. While I will discuss other works along the way, this chapter focuses on the three texts that most thoroughly exemplify and comment upon the theologies of the Kennedy image in the afterlife of the man himself: Don DeLillo's novel *Libra* (1988), Oliver Stone's film *JFK* (1991), and D. M. Thomas' novel *Flying in to Love* (1992).

With several highly cerebral novels exploring the mass culture of the contemporary United States, Don DeLillo has attained eminent standing among literary and cultural critics. His novel about the Kennedy assassination brings both the insights and the limitations of postmodern theories of language and image to what is arguably the defining moment that showed how the televisual and the real were inextricably mixed up in our "live" experience. Postmodern theorists have made the fictiveness of all experience, even of nature, their only bedrock. For DeLillo, the essential fact of our experience of Kennedy's assassination is that the murdered "subject" was a culturally constructed image.

In his "Author's Note" following *Libra*, DeLillo separates his novel from the goal of assassination theorists: "This is a work of imagination. While drawing from the historical record, I've made no attempt to furnish factual answers to any questions raised by the assassination." In a final two paragraphs, inexplicably dropped from the paperback edition, DeLillo explains what his goal is:

In a case in which rumors, facts, suspicions, official subterfuge, conflicting sets of evidence and a dozen labyrinthine theories all mingle, sometimes indistinguishably, it may seem to some that a work of fiction is one more gloom in a chronicle of unknowing.

But because this book makes no claim to literal truth, because it is only itself, apart and complete, readers may find refuge here—a way of thinking about the assassination without being constrained by half-facts or overwhelmed by possibilities, by the tide of speculation that widens with the years.[3]

DeLillo presents his fiction as "a way of thinking about the assassination" that has a purpose other than the obsessive need to know what "really happened." Reflection upon that need and its relation to Kennedy's image is DeLillo's goal.

The plot of *Libra* consists of three major separate narrative strands: Lee Harvey Oswald's mock-heroic progress as he seeks to become a world historical figure; the conspiracy launched by a disaffected CIA operative, Win Everett, to bring about a changed Cuba policy by orchestrating a spectacular failed attempt on the president's life that will be traced back to Castro; and the desperate attempts twenty-five years later of Nicholas Branch, a retired analyst contracted by the CIA to write the "secret history" of the Kennedy assassination, to construct the narrative that will fully explain the "holy" event that "broke the back of the American century."

Kennedy appears as an actual consciousness only for the few brief pages in which he arrives at Love Field outside Dallas and rides in the fateful motorcade. Even then DeLillo's narration lets us see that consciousness only in terms of its relation to the crowd. The emphasis is on the Kennedy image with which both its flesh-and-blood performer and its viewers are obsessed:

He reached a hand into the ranks and they surged forward, looking at each other to match reactions. He moved along the fence, handsome and tanned, smiling famously into the wall of open mouths. He looked like himself, like photographs, a helmsman squinting in the sea-glare, white teeth shining. There was only a trace of the cortisone bloat that sometimes affected his face—cortisone for his Addison's disease, a back brace for his degenerating discs. They came over the fence, surrounding him, so many people and hands. The white smile brightened. He wanted everyone to know he was not afraid. (392)

The crucial observation is "he looked like himself, like photographs." Kennedy's "self," certainly for the crowd but perhaps also for the self-regarding object of their gaze, cannot be located in any place, including Kennedy's person. It is an abstraction, an idea, that produces and is produced by the mass of representations of Kennedy. These reproductions of Kennedy's image, like the idea of "a helmsman squinting in the sea-glare," are themselves images of images.

In the glimpse DeLillo gives of Kennedy's interior, we are shown that the man himself is made up of stories:

Here he was among them in a time of deep division, the country pulled two ways, each army raging and Jack having hold of both. Were there forebodings? For weeks he'd carried a scrap of paper with scribbled lines of some bloody Shakespearian ruin. *They whirl asunder and dismember me.* Still, it was important for the car to move very slowly, give the crowds a chance to see him. Maximum exposure as the admen say, and who wants a president with a pigeon's heart? (393)

The "scrap of paper" is a textual token of the ideology of the romantic hero in history, which is the innermost filter for Kennedy's psyche. Kennedy's obsession with heroic sacrifice, first inspired by adventurers found in English history, provides his self-concept the costume of Shakespearean drama. Mixed with this aristocratic British ethos is the voice of Hemingway. Kennedy's fear of showing a "pigeon's heart" echoes Papa's macho

149

posings. "Maximum exposure" is a phrase Hemingway used in *The Sun Also Rises* to describe a bullfighter's honorable confrontation with danger;[4] Kennedy's recognition that it is also what the "admen" want asserts his knowledge that in the political arena the crowd is both the audience and the source of danger.

Otherwise, not Kennedy but Kennedy's image is a character in the novel, the object of desire that elicits murderous longings. DeLillo sees Kennedy's image becoming an object of assassination through the same process by which it became an object of adulation. Through the force of its idealness, Kennedy's image invites desires of all kinds. As a product of resonant stories preexisting in the culture, it lures the audience's projections of individual fantasies. As the crowd greets the motorcade winding slowly through Dallas, DeLillo describes a production of energy threatening to rupture the social fabric:

A contagion had brought them here, some mystery of common impulse, hundreds of thousands come from so many histories and systems of being, come from some experience of the night before, a convergence of dreams, to stand together shouting as the Lincoln passed. They were to be an event, a consciousness, to astonish the old creedbound fears, the stark and wary faith of the city of get-rich-quick. Big D rising out of caution and suspicion to produce the roar of a sand column twisting. They were here to surround the brittle body of one man and claim his smile, receive some token of the bounty of his soul. (393–94)

Among these "systems of being" are the angers and fantasies of the waiting assassins. One of the conspirators, Guy Bannister, is portrayed early in the book as raging at the power Kennedy exerts through his image:

It's not just Kennedy himself. . . . It's what people see in him. It's the glowing picture we keep getting. He actually glows in most of his photographs. We're supposed to believe he's the hero of the age. Did you ever see a man in such a hurry to be great?

Bannister, a racist former FBI agent, recognizes that Kennedy projects his image as a reflection not only of his desired self but of the nation he is attempting to author. Bannister is horrified by Kennedy's attempt to rewrite American identity in Kennedy's own idealized image:

He thinks he can make us a different kind of society. He's trying to engineer a shift. We're not smart enough for him. We're not mature, energetic, Harvard, world traveler, rich, handsome, lucky, witty. Perfect white teeth. It fucking grates on me just to look at him.

The initial plot of which Bannister is a part intends a failed assassination attempt that will result in the revelation of Kennedy's secret plotting on Castro's life. Bannister sees Kennedy's glowing image as depending on the suppression of such "secrets":

Do you know what charisma means to me? It means he holds the secrets. The dangerous secrets used to be held outside the government. Plots, conspiracies, secrets of revolution, secrets of the end of the social order. . . . Strip the man of his powerful secrets. Take his secrets and he's nothing.   (67–68)

Bannister and his cohorts in DeLillo's fictional conspiracy theory do not at first seek to murder Kennedy but rather to put on an illusory "show," a "spectacular miss" that will initiate a chain of events eventually exposing the backstage manipulations of Kennedy's production. Washington is described as "the theater of the Kennedys, the capital city that measured itself to a certain kind of manliness, a confidence and promise, the grace to take the maximum dare."

Everett, the originator of the conspiracy, seeks to expose Kennedy's act by authoring his own fiction. He will purposely construct a character whose trail will lead investigators to Kennedy's secrets:

The pocket litter, the gunman's effects, the sidetrackings and back alleys must allow investigators to learn that Kennedy wanted Castro dead, that plots were devised, approved at high levels, put into motion, and that Fidel or his senior aides decided to retaliate. This was the major subtext and moral lesson of Win Everett's plan. (53)

Everett depends on the devices of realistic fiction to construct his fictional gunman: "He would put someone together, build an identity, a skein of persuasion and habit, ever so subtle. He wanted a man with believable quirks" (78). But when he sends a fellow conspirator to find a model for this character, the conspirator discovers that the fiction is already present in the world: "It was no longer possible to hide from the fact that Lee Oswald

151

existed independent of the plot." Everett's attempt at secretly controlling events is thus answered by a hint of an uncontrollable complexity of fictions outside the conspirators' private rooms:

Lee H. Oswald was real all right. What Mackey learned about him in a brief tour of his apartment made Everett feel displaced. It produced a sensation of the eeriest panic, gave him a glimpse of the fiction he'd been devising, a fiction living prematurely in the world. (178–79)

Oswald himself has been constructing a fictional version of his life. Perceiving that "a family twists you out of shape" through the expectations of their gaze, he has used the texts of Marxist theory to give himself a plot by which to script an autonomous identity for himself: "The books were private, like something you find and hide, some lucky piece that contains the secret of who you are" (41). He adopts a secret name for himself and enjoys a fantasy life, "the powerful world of Oswald-hero, guns flashing in the dark" (46).

As a Marxist, Oswald has considered exerting power through authorship: "I want to write short stories on contemporary American life" (160). Married to pretty, Russian Marina, Oswald finds himself working as writer when she asks him to translate magazine stories about the Kennedys: "He didn't mind doing it and sometimes added details not in the stories." But his creative embellishments to Kennedy's image pale before the power of his listener's additions. The experiences Marina brings to these articles connect with the eroticism of Kennedy's image: "In the pictures taken near the sea, with the wind ruffling his hair, the President looked like her old boyfriend Anatoly, who had unruly hair and kissed her in a way that made her dizzy." In Marina's consciousness Kennedy becomes a phantom lover whom she awaits in her marital bed:

She wondered how many women had visions and dreams of the President. What must it be like to know you are the object of a thousand longings? It's as though he floats over the landscape at night, entering dreams and fantasies, entering the act of love between husbands and wives. He floats through television screens into bedrooms at night. He floats from the radio into Marina's bed. There were times when she waited for him, actually listened late at night for a few words of a speech or a news conference recorded earlier in the day, waited for the voice of the President, the radio on a table near the bed.

Even as Marina "thought of the President sometimes, in pictures taken near the sea, while Lee was making love to her," her husband begins to see in Kennedy's image his own reflection. Reading about Kennedy, he selectively focuses on correspondences with himself: "Lee was always reading two or three books, like Kennedy. Did military service in the Pacific, like Kennedy. Poor handwriting, like Kennedy. Wives pregnant at the same time. Brothers named Robert" (336). Ironically, Oswald and Marina both find in Kennedy's image fantasized compensation for Oswald's inadequacies. Oswald's gaze, like the conspirators', will produce murder.

As the conspiracy unfolds, some of the plotters add their own motivations to Everett's plan and decide to kill the president. As one of them meditates on Kennedy's appeal, he equates admirers' attempts to possess some aspect of Kennedy's image for their own psychological use with the conspirators' need to attack him: "Goes to Dallas next month. The man's a serious traveler. And wherever he goes, somebody wants a piece of him. Deep sweats of desire and rage. I don't know what it is. Maybe he's just too pretty to live" (365).

DeLillo's Oswald is brought into the conspiracy as the "patsy" the actual Oswald claimed to be, but after he is arrested he begins to see his cell as a private room in which he can at last forge his world historical role: "After the crime comes the reconstruction. He will have motives to analyze, the whole rich question of truth and guilt. . . . This was the true beginning. They will give him paper and books. He will fill his cell with books about the case" (434–35). Oswald now sees himself and Kennedy as "partners" in the production of the true Oswald. As opposed to his social identity, Lee Oswald, he sees himself reborn in the media as they announce his existence through the use of his full legal name: "His life had a single clear subject now, called Lee Harvey Oswald" (435). Lee Harvey Oswald is on the threshold of becoming a production even as John Fitzgerald Kennedy had been one.[5]

These two plots—Oswald's life and the conspiracy—are enacted by men obsessed with the idea that there is a "world within the world," an assertion that is repeated often within the text and represented by the characters' placement in small rooms. The conspirators want to take power and have an impact on events, use their private rooms to design plots that will reshape the public world. Kennedy's image is viewed as an illusion authoring their world; they want to wrest from Kennedy the power he exercises through this carefully controlled image. Win Everett, who conceives of the original conspiracy, wants to create a fiction that will change politics.

153

Oswald wants to write his life as history, live as in a book. Win loses as JFK loses: he cannot control life through imposition of a fiction—too many competing and diverging fictions overdetermine the conspiracy.

Oswald follows JFK to the grave, when the image he has won invites Jack Ruby's fantasy aspirations. Marina wonders what it is like to enter others' dreams, as JFK does hers, but she soon enters the dreams of others through television. The Win and Oswald plots mirror the JFK story: like their target, the two men each attempt to extend fiction and the fictive idea of the self into the world, and for all three this world-authoring ends in unexpected consequences, the inviting of the ferocious gaze. DeLillo critiques the JFK illusion of control while showing that Kennedy's "secret" becomes available to all. Each of these plots goes out of control in the course of the novel, each slips away from its presumed author's desire.

Libra includes a third plot, Nicholas Branch's frustrated attempt to fulfill his contract with the CIA to write the secret history of the assassination. The retired analyst is a surrogate for our obsessive need to know, and know definitively, what happened and why. Branch is in the ideal position only dreamed (or claimed) by the assassination theorists, for he is the privileged recipient of all available documents. Indeed, he knows the answers to the questions of who shot the President and why. Yet, far from providing him the rest we seek, the knowledge has overwhelmed Branch:

> He sits under a lap robe and worries. The truth is he hasn't written all that much. He has extensive and overlapping notes—notes in three-foot drifts, all these years of notes. But of actual finished prose, there is precious little. It is impossible to stop assembling data. (59–60)

As the privileged holder of the facts, authorized to write a "secret history," Branch is the perfect foil to DeLillo himself. Obsessed with the desire to know for certain what the assassination meant, he is tied to whatever patterns the world offers: "Branch is stuck all right. He has abandoned his life to understanding that moment in Dallas, the seven seconds that broke the back of the American century." The facts keep offering mysterious new patterns of connection:

> Branch has become wary of these cases of cheap coincidence. He's beginning to think someone is trying to sway him toward superstition. He wants a thing to be what it is. Can't a man die without the ensuing ritual of a search for patterns and links?

> The Curator sends him a four-hundred page study of the similarities between Kennedy's death and Lincoln's. (379)

His quest for absolute certainty and understanding leaves him in the trap of a small room like those the plotting Everett and Oswald tried to use as sources of power:

> But he persists, he works on, he jots his notes. He knows he can't get out. The case will haunt him to the end. Of course they've known it all along. That's why they built this room for him. The room of growing old, the room of history and dreams. (445)

DeLillo sees that the Kennedy image was a product of drawn-together fantasies, of obsessive dreams. As we have seen, that process was intensely underway in the production of Kennedy's private myth and in its subsequent reproduction through the public myths of American mass culture. DeLillo's focus is on the infinite power that came together when the separate members of a mass audience were so successfully lured into projecting their own fantasies upon that image. In contrast to Branch, and to the conspiracy theorists he parodies, DeLillo offers us a self-acknowledging fiction of the assassination. Only in the relative simplicity of even the most complex of fictions, he argues, can we gain "rest"—however illusory— through the production of a world in which we can know everything about what happened, and why it happened.

We recognize that such a world is made of illusions. Through his imagery, DeLillo insists upon the religious status of the assassination. He depicts the religious experience as a product of an infinitely complex meeting of fantasies, dreams, and other obsessions. In DeLillo's view, Kennedy's image must be understood as a historically produced cultural construct, and our response to his assassination must therefore be understood in those terms as well. We can only stop obsessing over the Kennedy assassination, futilely spinning conspiracy theories and other arcane theologies, when we recognize that what we are really mourning is our own illusions.

DeLillo's novel is penetrating, even brilliant, in its insights. As an attempt to affect the consciousness of its time, however, it lacks the emotional resonance of its subject. The producers of the Kennedy image, most especially Kennedy himself, constructed a mass-culture myth that included both ideas and emotions. DeLillo's novel offers his analysis of this product, but while

155

the determinedly cerebral approach can help us better understand the collective depression produced by the assassination, it is powerless to dispel it. Even understood as an idealized representation, the Kennedy image—and thus the awful image of the assassination—continues to haunt us.

If DeLillo speaks to us in the dispassionate tone of a psychoanalyst, in making his film *JFK* director Oliver Stone brought to his subject the emotional intensity and calculations of a therapist convinced that a patient's troubles are consequences of childhood abuses repressed by memory and the lies of the abusers. His aim was not to give us rest from our trauma but rather to awaken us to our victimization in history. Stone's target is the "official myth" of the assassination, which he asserts the Warren Commission placed between us and the reality of what happened on November 22nd. Making skillful if histrionic use of every possible film technique for manipulating mass emotions and ideas, Stone succeeded in reviving the repressed torments of the nation. The film was a huge box-office success and the subject of columns and letters that filled the *New York Times* editorial and op-ed pages for months; and it forced Congress to respond with legislation to reveal remaining classified documents relating to the investigation of the assassination.

The opening segment of the film, showing Kennedy at play with his wife and children, unabashedly returns to us the Kennedy of the original image system. He is the perfect man, the embodiment of the traditional ideals of masculinity. This physical reflection of the American imago is violated, and ultimately disembodied (his brain disappears), by corrupt forces. Perversion, as depicted in Stone's homophobic terms, is the opposite of Kennedy in *JFK*. Kennedy's impulses toward peace are secretly opposed by the CIA and the military-industrial complex. The perverters of democracy use a cabal of homosexuals to perform the violation of Kennedy's body with the assassin's bullets.

The power of this film lies not in the spurious factuality of its claims, but in its skillful cinematic assertion of the emotional logic set forth in the climactic summation speech by heroic district attorney William Garrison (played by Kevin Costner). Like that speech, the film weaves spurious "facts" about who is responsible for the crime based on the pain it has caused us. Because Kennedy was so wonderful, because he promised to heal our wounds and fulfill the American mission at home and in the world, he must have been killed by a vast conspiracy of the forces that have frustrated that healing and fulfillment.

The certainty of Stone's emotional logic cuts through the endlessly pro-liferating facts and patterns that frustrate DeLillo's Nicholas Branch. Dur-ing the darkest moment of his investigation, the film's hero is summoned by a possessor of inside knowledge and told to follow the question "Who benefited?" In constructing the plot for his movie, Stone has actually fol-lowed the inverse corollary: "Who suffered?" His answer is himself, the young man who was sent by Lyndon Johnson to Vietnam to endure a war that failed to earn the expected validation of his manhood by his country.

Stone had already told the essential story structuring *JFK* in *Platoon* (1986). In that Vietnam film, Stone used realistic texture to lure the audi-ence into a romantic parable in which an earnest, naïve young soldier finds himself torn between two father figures, "good" and "evil" sergeants. The good sergeant is an excellent warrior but is also nurturing and self-sacrific-ing; he has a warm bond with his fellow soldiers, and restrains them from brutality toward civilians. The evil sergeant is a powerful soldier but is rigid and brutal, taking pleasure only in violence. The young soldier is led away from the influence of the good "father" by the evil sergeant, who assassi-nates his rival during a battle. Eventually, the youth realizes that the evil father killed the good one. The soldier finds redemption by confronting the evil sergeant and avenging the slain good father.

Upon its release in 1987, *Platoon* was greeted by the media as the realis-tic Vietnam film that put to shame the outsized mythmaking of such previ-ous films as *The Deer Hunter* (1978) and *Apocalypse Now* (1979), not to mention the revisionist fantasies of the MIA films exemplified by *Rambo: First Blood Part II* (1985). But Stone actually used the compelling devices of realism and his claims to authority of experience as a Vietnam veteran to convey a vision of the Vietnam War every bit as romantic and mythic as those of previous directors. Like the aforementioned films, *Platoon* employs an allegorical story to explain the significance of Vietnam within the con-text of the American national mythology of a unique frontier nation.

Stone's explanation of the problem presented by Vietnam—the loss of Americans' assurance of special grace—is that in Vietnam Americans' noble impulses, epitomized by the good Sergeant Elias (William Dafoe), were deviously and brutally wiped out by the darker longing for power epit-omized by the evil Sergeant Barnes (Tom Berenger). The climax of *Pla-toon*, the avenging by Chris (Charlie Sheen) of his good father, provides the viewer the satisfying, if tragic, closure denied in actual history by the fall of Saigon. In Stone's mythic parable of Vietnam, America's lost war becomes a crucible for moral self-discovery, choice, and growth.

In *JFK*, Stone applies this mythic understanding to the Kennedy assassination, though once again the true subject is the meaning of Vietnam in American history and thus to the American identity. Sergeant Elias, who possessed the frontier-hero traits Kennedy and the press had idealized in the Green Beret, becomes Kennedy. Sergeant Barnes, who celebrated the military as a "machine," becomes the military-industrial complex that expresses itself through Lyndon Johnson. Chris becomes the earnest district attorney Jim Garrison (Kevin Costner), who comes to see all good living Americans as "Hamlets, children of a fallen king."

The persuasive strategy of Stone's mythmaking in *Platoon* depends on the devices of realism, strengthened by the authority derived from the director's well-publicized personal experience in Vietnam, combined with the subtle use of resonant images drawn from traditional American representations of the frontier and war. In *JFK* Stone turns to the authority of familiar documentary and Hollywood images, specifically by his repeated use of the Zapruder home movie of the assassination and his casting of eminent stars in cameo roles. Our shared experience of the assassination, along with the images of Kennedy and Hollywood stars, becomes the source of felt authority. Stone understands, at least on an intuitive level, that the public has not put together an acceptable story of the Kennedy assassination less because of problems with the facts than with the narrative. Whenever he has been confronted with his manipulative distortions of and selections from the facts, Stone's response has been that he was not producing a documentary but rather a "countermyth" opposing the "official myth" constructed by the Warren Commission. Stone's argument is that it required someone using the power available in film to impress upon Americans that the interpretation of the facts carrying the authority of the establishment—the government and national media—is not necessarily definitive.

He is correct that the Warren Commission, and certainly the government agencies it depended on, were driven by a desire to construct a whole and complete story. Nevertheless, in *Case Closed* (1994), Gerald Posner has more recently turned the same scrutiny the conspiracy theorists have applied to the Warren Commission Report upon the theorists' accounts, carefully studied all the evidence now available, and declared Oswald guilty. The footnotes in Posner's book are an essential part of his account, for they form an investigator's relentless explanation of why alternative "facts" or "patterns" have not held up under scrutiny. Oliver Stone, by contrast, selects his evidence and draws his conclusions according to an emotional, mythic logic. The story, or myth, that he produces is based upon a need for simplicity, for blacks and whites, for heroes and villains—not a need for accuracy.

The authority of the Zapruder film is that of an undeniable fact transfigured into collective rite. We suffered the loss of Kennedy in history, but it has become a religious experience through the collective pain we continue to experience in it. Stone's repetitive use of the home movie makes it a ritual. As we return to the moment of assassination many times in the course of *JFK*, our re-viewings join us with Garrison/Costner as our surrogate in this suffering.

The use of venerable actors such as Jack Lemmon, Walter Matthau, and Donald Sutherland lends the prestige of their enduring star personae to Stone's controversial project. More subtly, their presence refers to the experience of Camelot as an incarnation of Hollywood in actual American life. Significantly, each of these stars plays a crucial role in guiding Garrison's suspicions. Stone had originally planned to have Kennedy's ghost appear to Garrison. Instead, he chose to have Kennedy be the only figure in the film played by himself (Steve Reed merely sits in for Kennedy during reenactments of the Dallas motorcade). Having an actor play Kennedy as ghost would have only reduced the force of his ghostly presence in documentary film. In addition, any actor playing Kennedy would have failed to reproduce the Kennedy charisma; only indirectly could Hollywood stars make us feel the allure of the star presence in the White House that the assassination removed. It is this "fact," the remembered experience of Kennedy's administration as an incarnation of American myth, that Stone uses as the grounding verisimilitude for *JFK*. Everything else in the film develops out of the logic of that psychology, the memory of gazing upon the American-ideal-made-televisual-reality horribly betrayed and murdered.

Stone had already made heavy use of Christian symbolism in *Platoon* in his portrait of Sergeant Elias, who is first shown walking with his arms thrust over the M-16 that he carries across his shoulders and who expires with his arms raised out to his sides. More essential, Stone characterizes Elias as a contemporary reincarnation of the ideal American frontier hero first represented in the stories of Daniel Boone and James Fenimore Cooper's Leatherstocking Tales. *Platoon* is Stone's vision of the frontier hero, the ideal American, forsaken and crucified in Vietnam by a military machine that betrays the best American self. In *JFK*, Stone begins the film with a prologue establishing Kennedy's New Frontier as the incarnation of the ideal America in the body of the beautiful man. Kennedy promised to

159

usher in an era of change in which racial justice and world peace would confirm the best possibilities implied by the American Constitution. The repeated replaying of the motorcade's fateful journey, climaxing in Kennedy's head being blown apart in the Zapruder film, invite analogies to Christ's passion and crucifixion. Stone insists on this comparison by re-creating the Parkland hospital scenes in which Kennedy's body is carried away in bloody sheets.

The autopsy scenes in Washington, in which Kennedy's body is shown being penetrated and opened up, defiled in the interests of deceitful manipulation, make Kennedy's corpse a metaphor for the body politic of the United States and its Constitution, as the examination is manipulated into a lie protecting the murderers. Thereafter Kennedy's image is all that is left to us. But it refuses to stay buried, as the mounting catastrophes of the 1960s—particularly Johnson's Vietnam policies—catalyze Jim Garrison's suspicions about why Kennedy is dead and why the wrong man is sleeping in the White House bed.

Viewed in terms of historical fact, the revelation of Vietnam as the motivation for Kennedy's assassination is the most ludicrous aspect of Stone's film. Those desiring a full-scale war in Vietnam, for crass motivations of money and power, are named as the ultimate conspirators not because this interpretation is plausible but because it touches the deepest and broadest wound of postassassination America. Once the war became unpopular, the question of what Kennedy would have done if he had lived became crucial to historical meaning. Claims have been made by a couple of Kennedy intimates that he confided plans to get America out of Vietnam after the 1964 election. But such confidences are worth little in revealing what Kennedy truly intended, or even if he knew what he would do. Kennedy's public pronouncements and actual decisions were far more ambiguous. Whatever he might have eventually done, certainly those on the political right had little reason in November 1963 to feel he needed to be assassinated in order to ensure a war in Vietnam. But it is Vietnam that Americans most often think about when they lament Kennedy's assassination as the turning point of the American century. Kennedy might very well have followed a far less disastrous course in Vietnam than did Lyndon Johnson. The evidence of his presidential record suggests that Kennedy would never have tolerated a protracted escalation with no foreseeable conclusion. In the many previous problems that reached such serious proportions during his presidency, he chose either to force a dramatic crisis demanding resolution within a defined period of time, or to negotiate a face-saving defusion of the issue. It is also difficult to imagine Kennedy, so sensitive to the Third World, following policies—continuously bombing a small country—that would have so conflicted with the idealized image he had constructed for himself and the nation he represented. But accepting this evidence is not the same thing as leaping past historical knowledge to the fictional conclusion that Kennedy was planning to withdraw from Vietnam in 1963 and was therefore killed by the military-industrial complex. Stone chooses this explanation because it mythically constructs a powerfully simple version of the more complicated, ambiguous conclusion that things would have been better if Kennedy had lived.

In the climactic prosecution summary concluding the film, Stone has Garrison himself name *Hamlet* as the true story of the Kennedy assassination. In terms of proving both the guilt of the single man Clay Shaw who is on trial and of the huge conspiracy of the military-industrial complex that Garrison "reveals," the Garrison/Costner speech does not do enough to provoke such emotion. What is effective in this oration, accompanied by the Zapruder film and documentary-looking dramatizations of claims about it, is the emotion itself. With *JFK*, Stone brilliantly employs film to articulate the obsessed replayings, and the accompanying imaginings, of the Kennedy assassination and of the dream of Kennedy's restoration and reincarnation that have dominated American life during the last decades of the twentieth century. *JFK* attempts to position us as Hamlet in a play not yet finished, a drama in which the audience—like the film's hero—can play the tough-guy detective who will find those responsible for arresting the development of a generation, and in doing so at last take the Kennedy image into the self.

Stone's film completely ignores the revelations about Kennedy's own involvement in conspiracy and his extraordinary promiscuity that surfaced in the aftermath of the Watergate inquiries in the mid-1970s. Congressional investigations into CIA involvement in foreign assassinations led to revelations of attempts on foreign leaders' lives during Kennedy's administration, as well as of his "friendship" with a woman who was also connected to a Mafia leader.

Since those revelations, a second JFK has come to haunt American consciousness. This Kennedy is a hypocrite, a cynic, and a sexual libertine. Discussing Hollywood stars, Richard deCordova has pointed out that sexual revelation holds a privileged place in our perception of character:

161

The star system, and arguably twentieth-century culture in general, depends on an interpretative schema that equates identity with the private and furthermore accords the sexual the status of the most private, and thus the most truthful, locus of identity.[6]

The discord between the image produced for and by Kennedy during his lifetime and the image produced in the revelatory literature after his death correlates with deCordova's observation. Kennedy's image during his career, certainly during his presidency, centered on visual representation; it came to the audience like a movie. The hagiography written by Kennedy aides and others after Kennedy's death attempted to add depth to the public images, showing a private Kennedy in accord with the public one. But revelations concerning his sex life follow the logic of going yet deeper into the private to find the "real" man. The biographies that have produced this private Kennedy vary somewhat in their interpretations, but they consistently portray a man whose private amorality is impossible to reconcile with the image projected during his lifetime and amplified after his death.[7] Popular novels and films have brought this Kennedy into the realm of fiction, where the reader or viewer is invited to either identify with or voyeuristically observe this Tabloid JFK as he either connives or bullies his way through back rooms and bedrooms.

The most cynical of these is Michael Korda's *The Immortals* (1992), which strips the portraits produced by the revelatory biographical literature of any trace of sincere emotion or idealistic motivation to present a John Kennedy who is a character out of Harold Robbins' *The Carpetbaggers*, a product of a world moved solely by crass calculation and desire. Robert Mayer's comic reworking of the Kennedy mythology offers a considerably more sympathetic but hardly admirable interpretation. His novel *I, JFK* (1989) is narrated by Kennedy from heaven. Kennedy's confession follows the view that Kennedy was simply the weak son of a powerful father who pursued sexual liaisons and cold war confrontations to allay masculine insecurities. Only the wryly self-aware perspective of the Kennedy who reflects from the tranquility of heaven earns some trace of redemption for his having been a "fake."

162

George Bernau's potboiling novel *Promises to Keep* (1988) attempts to reconcile the two JFKs by moderating them into two sides of a flawed romantic hero. Bernau's novel begins with the assassination in Dallas, but in this fictional world Kennedy (called John Trewlaney Cassidy in the novel) is not killed. Instead, the bullet lands four inches away from the fatal spot in actual history, incapacitating but not slaying the young president. Forced to give up the presidency, Cassidy/Kennedy's struggle to overcome his physical wound parallels the Vietnam War's tearing the nation apart under his successor Johnson's policies. As he recovers, Cassidy is portrayed in an extramarital dalliance with all the trappings of a romantic novel (he and the woman are out riding horses in Ireland). As he nears full recovery, Cassidy overcomes his romantic weakness and reconciles with his wife, achieving the maturity of full commitment. He then also accepts the need to challenge his successor's Vietnam policies and attempt to heal the nation's wounds by running for president in 1968.

In the meantime, a subplot of the novel has developed the possibility of a conspiracy in the Dallas assassination attempt. During the 1968 campaign, Cassidy is confronted with the discovery that the assassin (an Oswald figure) was one of a small number of men whom Cassidy had authorized the CIA early in his administration to train for assassination of foreign leaders. Cassidy is forced to face that his near-fatal wounding, and the subsequent disaster of Johnson's policies, originated in his own endorsement of subterfuge and violence. This plot parallels our understanding of the journey Robert Kennedy made after his brother's assassination.

By having the John Kennedy character survive and make the journey of self-discovery himself, Bernau rewrites the disastrous 1960s into a distinctly American wish fulfillment, the second chance, but with the nation's and the president's mature self-knowledge and changed character achieved through suffering. The reward offered the reader of *Promises to Keep* is that at the June victory celebration of the Cassidy win in the California primary in Los Angeles, Cassidy is saved from the assassination attempt that in history felled John Kennedy's brother Robert. The John Kennedy character survives both Dallas and Los Angeles to redeem himself, and Bernau's novel provides its reader with a pleasurable and thoughtful meditation upon how the romantic president might indeed have healed our wounds and made us whole. Bernau's novel has a more complicated view of Kennedy than a black-and-white Camelot-genre story, such as Stanley Shapiro's inventive science-fiction novel *A Time to Remember* (1986), in which a time-traveling hero's prevention of the assassination in Dallas ensures an idyllic American future. In *Promises to Keep* Kennedy must first suffer and mature, healing his own wounds, before he can become the true fulfillment of our dreams, the lover who will complete our unfinished business.

Bernau's novel is a thoughtful and sophisticated vehicle for popular fantasy, but its reconciliation of the two JFKs decisively mutes the revelations of Kennedy's compulsive and impersonal sexuality. The portrait thus offers an unconvincing resolution. In real life, outside the realm of such wish-fulfilling softening of revelations about the private Kennedy, we remain caught in the divide between our original image of Kennedy as ideal American and the Tabloid JFK in a Dr. Jekyll and Mr. Hyde scenario impossible to resolve.

British author D. M. Thomas, best known for his novel of the Holocaust, *The White Hotel*, has made the gulf between the two JFK images central to his novel *Flying in to Love* (1992). Thomas combines postmodern manipulations of time and space with sensational sex and violence. The novel is centered on the assassination, but the subject is more precisely the two irreconcilable Kennedy images and their relations with the American public.

Thomas explores the Kennedy image as a figure of the public's dreams. As the double meaning of the title suggests, the premise of the novel is that when Kennedy flew into Love Airport outside Dallas on November 22, he flew as well into the complex dynamic of a love obsession. The assassination transformed those erotic energies into a religious event. Thomas's novel successfully condenses the energies that have driven the afterlife of John F. Kennedy in American culture.

In exploring what *Flying in to Love* has to say about the obsessions of John F. Kennedy and our obsessions with him, I will be making special use of the work of Polly Young-Eisendrath, an analyst and psychologist who has revised the central concepts of Carl Jung in light of contemporary feminist theory. *Flying in to Love* works with both individuals' dreams and the collective dreams we call "myth," and Jungian approaches have always focused on how these personal and culturewide stories are linked. At the same time, the novel opposes the appeal of John F. Kennedy to the subsequent transformations in our ideals of masculinity and femininity wrought by the feminist movement. Young-Eisendrath's feminist revision of Jung's ideas in her exploration of love affords a historically and socially specific framework in which to view Thomas's treatment of the Kennedy image.

Young-Eisendrath avoids the universalist and mystical tendencies of Jung's thought, finding the origins of his fundamental concepts in specific situations:

Archetypes, in Jung's last theory, are not mysterious forms that lie outside experience. They are not Platonic ideals or aspects of a fuzzy collective unconscious.
They are ordinary human experiences of emotionally powerful images that predis-
pose us to action. Such an image is a cue, a stimulus, that re-presents a highly
charged relational theme.[8]

Cultural definitions of gender are categories that shape consciousness, creating archetypes. The "archetypal feminine" has been traditionally defined
as the "province of relating and caregiving"; "it concerns joining, attach-
ment and involvement with people, things, and ideas." The "archetypal
masculine" is the "domain of distancing and separating," where the
emphasis is on "binding off, separating from, and aggression toward nature
and human beings for survival purposes."[9] Young-Eisendrath emphasizes
that these archetypal categories are neither essential nor universal, but
rather categories of human capacities arbitrarily defined by a culture as the
realm of one sex or the other. She similarly emphasizes that a person's situation and history must be viewed within the context of a specific culture.
In her view, a "psychological complex is a collection of associations from
past experiences held together by an emotional core."[10]

Young-Eisendrath uses the term *strange gender* to denote "the way we
imagine the opposite sex." Based on early impressions, this concept sharp-
ens when we discover that the opposite sex is a club from which we are
excluded: "With this realization, the strange gender begins to transform
into 'dream-lovers': the specific images of those Others we fear and desire
because we imagine they are *different* from us." These "subjective impressions" of the opposite sex become powerful parts of our unconscious, seemingly manifest in, but actually projected by us upon, real-life members of
the opposite sex. Young-Eisendrath concludes that "dream lovers are
uniquely important complexes" that "link our strange gender to the dramas
of our early lives . . . and to our dreams and wishes for the future."[11]

Thomas begins *Flying in to Love* by making it clear that dream will be
his central subject: " 'Ten thousand dreams a night,' a Dallas psychologist
told me, when I dined with her and her black lover, 'are dreamt about
Kennedy's assassination.' " The narrator also indicates that the novel will
itself be a dreamlike experience: "fiction is a kind of dream, and history is
a kind of dream, and this is both."[12]

Thomas's self-conscious opening establishes the parallel between his
novel and his subject. The Kennedy assassination catalyzes dreams
throughout the culture. Dreams are representations in which operations of

165

the unconscious transform the events of waking life, adding to them and changing them according to the deepest yearnings and fears of the dreamer. History and fiction, although composed by authors who are apparently awake, are nevertheless "kinds of dream" in that consciousness is never fully in control. Unconscious forces, of both psychology and ideology, shape the composition of history and fiction as much as they shape dreams. Thomas thus argues for the validity of his postmodern fictional mode.

Flying in to Love merges the realms of historical research and fictional invention. Indeed, in a brief prefatory acknowledgment, Thomas cites several sources, concluding with the remark that "Only the last of these, a fine novel, is openly a work of fiction; but every book about the assassination of John F. Kennedy has mingled reality and fiction, and mine is no different." Thomas exploits the full resources of the dreamlike process of composition to take his novel beyond plausible representation of what supposedly happened in Dallas on November 22, 1963. He moves the novel back and forth between a "realistic," history-based realm and a "possible" realm. In the portions of the novel making up the latter, the assassination attempt is foiled, and we follow Kennedy through the remainder of his Texas trip. The juxtaposition of nightmarish history with dreamlike wish fulfillment is further complicated by movement back and forth between November 1963 and several anniversaries of the assassination and Kennedy's birthday, as we follow the vicissitudes of the Kennedy image through the consciousness of two nuns, Sister Agnes and Sister Beatrice, who are among its major characters. Thomas also includes characters' explicit dreams in his text. Thus the plot of *Flying in to Love* is suffused with the logic of dream, transforming our notions of reality at various levels.

If dream is the crucial mode of Thomas's text, love is the subject, the central thematic concern. Beginning with the title, the word *love* appears on nearly every page of the novel. Thomas sees that the American public has since 1960 had a relationship with the JFK image analogous to romantic love. Dreams and romantic love both derive from the unconscious, transforming external reality into representations important to the dreamer. Thomas uses the mode of dream to explore the "love" dynamic between Kennedy and our perception of him.

166

After his opening discussion of history and fiction as "kinds of dream," Thomas asserts that since his novel is both it can begin at any number of points. After introducing several possibilities, he self-consciously suggests "let's begin with the soul, Kennedy's soul, and the priest" (3). Depicting the scene in Parkland hospital after the doctors have given up trying to save the president's life and turned over Kennedy's body to a caretaker of the soul, Thomas shows the hapless priest's attempt to reassure the widow: " 'I am convinced,' he whispers, 'that the soul . . . you know . . .' " By beginning with the unsolvable mystery of where Kennedy's soul has gone, Thomas removes the subject of the "essential" or "real" John F. Kennedy—his self or "soul"—from the book. We are left instead with a creature of memory and fantasy, necessarily a product in part of our consciousness and thus of our projections. Hearing the priest's words, Jacqueline finds her thoughts returning to the night before as she remembers how her husband joked with her lovingly as he kissed her goodnight. Thomas's fiction immediately moves from the question of Kennedy's soul to Kennedy as an image refracted through—and inevitably transformed by—another's consciousness. Kennedy is gone; we are left with his image in characters' memories and fantasies, including those of the author and ourselves.

Thus, the Kennedy in the novel is like the Kennedy we know outside the novel, a subjective impression, an image. Thomas's character is not the actual or "essential" Kennedy postulated by the idea of his "soul," but rather "our" Kennedy, more precisely our Kennedys, the wildly contradictory images of him that we have formed from the projections of the mass media.

Thomas reinforces this status of his Kennedy character by emphasizing the impressions of him in the consciousnesses of three characters: Jacqueline, and the fictional Sister Agnes and Sister Beatrice. Since they are all female, the novel emphasizes the gender dynamic in the relation between the public and Kennedy. The portrait of Kennedy in the novel is really a portrait of the "dream lovers" that we have projected upon him. As we have seen in previous chapters, Kennedy and his aides worked hard at presenting an image that would trigger our projections. Bobby Kennedy is depicted in the novel as saying: "We created a myth; or we let the media create one. And my brother died because of it. We're just rich boys with an ambitious father and time on our hands" (191).

The "dream lovers" projected upon Kennedy by Jacqueline, Sister Agnes, and Sister Beatrice represent the dream lovers we as a nation have projected upon him. We first meet Sister Agnes before she learns of the assassination, as she muses about having met the president along the Dallas motorcade.[13] Her Kennedy is the perfect man of the Kennedy presidential image. For Sister Agnes, Kennedy is what Young-Eisendrath designates the Hero dream lover, "the man a woman would be: He is courageous, long suffering, virtuous, idealistic, and sensitive to feelings."[14]

In Jung's theory, the animus is the realm of the masculine within a woman's psyche, manifesting itself in projections upon men. Young-Eisendrath identifies five stages of animus development: 1) Animus as Alien Other; 2) Animus as Father, God, Patriarch; 3) Animus as Youth, Hero, Lover; 4) Animus as Partner Within; 5) Animus as Androgyne. In the first stage the woman feels herself threatened by male power, and in the second she feels sacrificed to it. In the third, Animus as Youth, Hero, Lover, "The woman experiences herself as surrendering to the animus. This is more active than being sacrificed, and she feels more like she is entering into a relationship in a lively way. . . . Still, her identity as a woman is incomplete and largely reflected by the animus."[15]

Writing to her parents about her brief encounter with the president while she watches her pupils work at their desks, Sister Agnes gushes that when she shook President Kennedy's hand she "felt dithery and there was a roaring in my ears" (15). Twenty years later (but only some thirty pages farther into the narrative), we find her acknowledging her passion: "Yes, she had felt his sexual magnetism. And had responded to it. If he had not died, she would have been forced to confess it" (46).

Sister Agnes, as a Catholic nun in 1963, is an apt representative of a woman's standing in the traditional patriarchy. She is clearly placed in the second of Young-Eisendrath's stages of the animus. With her vows of celibacy and nun's habit, she has sacrificed her sexuality to the service of the Church Fathers and God. As teacher of children, she confines her energies to the role of caregiver prescribed for women. But her undeniably romantic and sexual attraction to the young Catholic president makes him a projection of her Hero dream lover. Kennedy, triggering a new "story" for her relation to her animus, presents the possibility of a vital relation to her own excluded aspects of gender identity.

Sister Agnes' Kennedy is the ideal Kennedy projected during his political career and in subsequent hagiographic literature. According to Young-Eisendrath, "The main emotions involved with the Hero dream lover are joy, expansiveness, love, excitement, courage, curiosity, disappointment, fear, and anger."[16] Sister Agnes writes to her father that Kennedy "seemed immeasurably kind and gentle and *interested*. We're very lucky to have him as our President. I look at my hand, and think that an hour ago it held the hand of President Kennedy" (15). Acknowledging that "I know I've been writing like a gushing schoolgirl," she compares her feelings about this "memorable day" to how her parents must have felt on the day of their wedding (15).

Years after the assassination, Sister Agnes—like other members of the public that idealized Kennedy—finds her joy and expansiveness turning to sadness and disappointment over both the "lies" told about the assassination and the revelations of Kennedy's sexual affairs. She has with a struggle forgiven him the latter, accepting the excuse of his living with pain and the prospect of early death. Instead, she obsesses over the possibility of a conspiracy, founding and editing a journal devoted to the assassination and guiding her pupils toward the topic. She continues to carry high the "torch" of Camelot, convinced that "Kennedy wasn't a myth; people grieved for him because there had been a single lantern in a dark, stormy field, and someone had come along and kicked out its frail light" (199).

Sister Beatrice serves as a foil to Sister Agnes' idealization of Kennedy. Well before the assassination, she had been embittered toward men by a tyrannical stepfather and the rejections resulting from a disfiguring facial birthmark. The one man who had promised her love confessed his perverted desire when he broke off the relationship for a woman more seriously disfigured by burns. Sister Beatrice had actually planned to kill herself in front of this man on November 22, 1963. When Kennedy's assassination results in her former lover's not showing up at the appointed hour, Sister Beatrice decides not to commit suicide; her life is ironically saved by Kennedy's death. Years later, she has become a radical feminist who idolizes Sylvia Plath and hates Kennedy. She ritualizes her rage by masturbating with the remote control while watching the Zapruder film on the VCR, replaying the assassination until she achieves orgasm at the moment Kennedy's head blows apart.

Sister Agnes' obsession with the assassination represses her own sexual longings for the president; this repression in turn covers over the reality of her childhood. As a Catholic convert who has doubled that rejection of her Southern Protestant heritage by becoming a nun, Sister Agnes nevertheless feels no conscious antagonism toward her parents. She idealizes her father, a teacher himself, who taught her to read and whom she understands to be a martyr for liberal idealism. She believes that he lost his job when she was a child because he taught a poem that had a "dirty" word in it. But disconcerting elements present themselves to her consciousness. She remembers when she was a teenager finding pornographic magazines hidden among his belongings. And as she innocently writes her parents about meeting Kennedy even as he, unknown to her, is being assassinated, she is troubled by having caused her father to be hurt in an accident, though she seems blissfully ignorant of the Freudian hint of the accident's being an expression of repressed hostility.

The climax of the Sister Agnes sections of *Flying in to Love* comes, appropriately enough, in a dream. Her unconscious presents a repulsive, beer-bellied man who confesses to her that he was the member of the conspiracy who fired the fatal shot that blew Kennedy's head apart. After begging her to forgive him, he molests her, a sexual violation that brings her to orgasm. The logic of this perverse response lies in her conflation of Kennedy's assassin with her own father and with Kennedy himself, the hidden Kennedy who used women. She correspondingly identifies herself with his wife:

He used her, as he had used all women. She's just an ornament for him, with her personable looks and shy smile and whispery complaisant voice. Sister Beatrice has been right about him all along. Weeping, as she dries her hands, she desperately wants her father's arms around her. Sitting down on her bed, she picks up *November 22*, finds the arrival of the Kennedys at Love Field, and rips it out.

Sister Agnes releases herself from her obsession with Kennedy's assassination and the "lost" dream he represents. But she retreats from her relation to Kennedy as lover to Young-Eisendrath's second stage of the animus, "desperately" wanting "her father's arms around her." Ironically, we subsequently see Kennedy, moments before the assassination, remembering that Sister Agnes's father lost his job because he taught black children to read with pornographic magazines. In bitterly deciding that the idealized Kennedy was really a corrupt villain, Sister Agnes has only continued to hide from herself a far darker truth, that good and evil are fathers to us all. Just as the public has been unable to reconcile its idealized image of Kennedy with the revelations about his private sexuality, the teenage Sister Agnes "couldn't align the magazines with her cultured father" (28). Only many years later does she perceive that her father might have been seeking solace for a lack of sexual giving from her mother.

170 The characterization of Kennedy himself that has emerged from the biographical literature repeats the portrayal of Sister Agnes's father: a splitting of the anima into idealized and degraded projections resulting from the withholding of love. In terms of Young-Eisendrath's dream lovers, Kennedy is driven by his Terrible Mother to overlook the actual woman who is his

wife and pursue either of two extreme projections, a Mistress Lover or a Maiden Lover. Both of the latter images of woman result from his ambivalence toward religion and sex, and they represent the contradictory images of Kennedy as idealistic President and rapacious womanizer.

In Young-Eisendrath's scheme, the Terrible Mother complex is the most common obstacle to a man's achieving intimacy with women and comes in various negative experiences of the mother. She may be experienced as disempowering, suffocating, or manipulative and seductive. This analysis is explicitly stated in *Flying in to Love* in a paper on "The Kennedy Myth" written by a female psychologist. The paper ends in a discussion of Kennedy's relation to his mother:

He was emotionally split already as a result of his background: the sexually rapacious, energetic and capitalistic father; the undemonstrative, puritanical, intensely religious mother. He had no proper home; woman was his only home, or rather it was her womb and her vagina where, for the last time, his mother had truly hugged him. So he kept wanting to find it again, and the women were all too eager. Home is where, as Frost said, if you have to go there, they have to take you in.

The mother, Rose, is the central person in his life; the woman he always sought in vain: most determinedly through his marriage to the similarly cool Jacqueline. He was reputedly a bad lover because there was an element of punishing his mother in every act of "love."

Yet he kept trying.   (196)

The split between the desire to "punish" the withholding mother and the desire to fulfill her religious demands is reflected in Kennedy's pursuit of women upon whom he projects either the Mistress Lover or the Maiden Lover.

Early in the novel Thomas presents us with a scene in which Kennedy has a nocturnal encounter with his Mistress Lover. She comes in the form of a wealthy Texas woman named Catherine who offers him sexual gratification while manipulating him toward his destruction the next day in Dallas. The encounter begins with Kennedy acting the macho bully, the rapacious lover seeking to "punish" his victims:

"I want you to know I don't make a practice of this."

"I don't give a damn whether you do or not." He stretched forward, slid his hand up her thigh under her cream skirt.   (6)

As she undresses, Catherine uses her seductive power to manipulate the insecurities beneath Kennedy's macho façade:

As she removed her jacket and laid it carefully on a chair back she turned away from him, towards the window. "I'm glad it's raining; I hope it goes on. I didn't come here just to offer you sex, Mr. President, though I can't say this isn't a dream come true. I'm worried about Dallas. People like my husband hate your guts. Anything could happen there." Her skirt, unhooked, slid slowly to the floor. "I guess if it's rainy you'll have to have a top on your car?" (7)

Catherine proceeds to inform Kennedy that she was afraid that if the weather was sunny he would refuse the bubble top to avoid Texans' finding him "chicken."

Catherine simply repeats the role that Mistress Lovers from Circe and Eve of ancient myths to the heroines of modern films such as *Double Indemnity* and *Body Heat* have played: she uses her surface beauty to destroy a man. Young-Eisendrath states that a man's "attraction to Mistress Lover fantasies and projections is less about the fear of death than it is about the fear of losing power among men."[17] In this dreamlike episode, Thomas distills the psychological analysis of Kennedy's machismo into a projected archetype. Kennedy's bullying of Catherine is pathetically weak before her seductive manipulation of his insecurities. The Circe figure embodies the needs driving his will to power.

The portrait of Catherine as Mistress Lover is inspired by the revelations of Kennedy's apparently innumerable one-night stands. The portrait of Kennedy's opposite dream lover in *Flying in to Love* has no such obvious source among his mistresses. In one regard, Thomas's imagining of Kennedy's seeking an affair with Sister Agnes is simply a parody of the president's reputed disregard of moral boundaries (his aide exclaims, "Not a nun, Mr. President!" [32]). But Kennedy imagines that their relationship will be a meeting of her spirituality with his sensuality, a joining of their quests for love. Just as he is Sister Agnes' Hero dream lover, she triggers his projection of his Maiden Lover. This term for what is commonly called the soul mate labels a complex driven by "narcissistic motives to reproduce what is loved in oneself and to avoid what is detested and depreciated."[18] Young-Eisendrath explains that the search for a soul mate outside of an existing relationship may be an avoidance of true commitment, and indeed a way of staying tied to the mother. Kennedy's desire for a relationship with Sister Agnes ("a long one—perhaps as long as a year") is a fictional exploration of his intense attraction to an abstract idealism. As a beautiful nun, she is actually a stand-in for the highly attractive yet puritanically withdrawn mother Kennedy knew as a boy. His pursuit of this nun in *Flying in to Love* links Kennedy's political idealism to his mother's intense religiosity.

Amid the complex projections making up the stories of Sister Agnes, Sister Beatrice, and Jack Kennedy, the portrayal of Jacqueline Kennedy is poignantly simple. The dominant note is sadness, as she grieves over the losses of her baby Patrick and husband Jack. In the scenes with her husband she is shown trying to be a supportive wife and wistfully wondering why he is seemingly unable to say "I love you." When he asks her if she slept with Onassis while vacationing on his yacht, she says no and points out that they have sworn to be faithful to one another. Jackie works sincerely and hard at the woman's traditional role, but she is only victimized—by nature (the death of her baby), her husband (his infidelities and, more generally, his withholding of committed love), and the world (the conspiracy that takes her husband's life).

In her waking moments, Jackie projects no obvious dream lovers; she displays uncomplicated and authentic emotions. But the assassination turns her life into nightmare, and Thomas gives Jackie a four-page dream that concentrates both the method and the theme of the book as a whole. A merger of history and fiction, it is a representation of Jackie's unconscious sending her—and us—a message. Thomas constructs the dream from facts and fictions of Kennedy lore and of Jackie's life. The association of Jack and Bobby with Marilyn Monroe, Grace Kelly's visit to Jack's hospital bed after his back operation, Joseph Kennedy's lobotomizing of his daughter Rosemary, Jackie's future life with Onassis in Greece, her love of horses—all these elements figure in the dream. Thomas uses Freud's familiar dream mechanisms of fusion, condensation, and displacement to order these elements. He further uses one element of Jackie's consciousness—her interest in Greek mythology—to present the dream in allusive imagery that enables readers to experience it—as we did Jackie's design of the funeral—as having culturewide meaning.

The dream moves from Jackie's problem toward her solution. Along the way, it progresses through symbols, controlled by the deeper logic of her unconscious, that reveal the source of her troubles as the gender hierarchy into which she was born. The dream is structured as a classic dream/myth quest, as Jackie seeks to bring her husband back to life. In the course of her journey she travels through expanses of her past and future, but the continuing motif is her relation to the male hierarchy and, finally, her own animus—her own "masculine" qualities repressed in accord with the traditional script. The dream moves toward her achieving partnership with that animus.

Jackie's dream occurs in the White House on the night of the assassination, after an honor guard has been put in place around her husband's casket in the East Room. Injected with Amytal, she falls asleep alone on the double bed, and the dream begins:

"Why are you all facing away from him?" Jackie asked the Marine Corps officer, stiffly at attention. "Surely you should be facing your President?"

The young officer's face turned red; his lips moved but at first could say nothing. Then he whispered, "Because we're embarrassed. It doesn't seem right."

"There's no need to feel embarrassed," she said, turning her head towards the catafalque. What she saw made her cry out softly, "Oh no! . . . Yes, I see what you mean!"   (211–12)

Jackie discovers that the casket has been replaced by a bed, upon which her husband is making love with Marilyn Monroe. Relieved that he is alive, she suffers from "horrible embarrassment and resentment." After failing to dissuade Charles de Gaulle from going to see her husband, she goes out to find thousands of people lined up to see Jack. She pleads with Bobby Kennedy to do something. Bobby, unhappy over his brother's sleeping with the woman Bobby loves, suggests that they get the retarded sister Rosemary to replace Marilyn, since "A sister, a family member, would be OK." Bobby worries about Marilyn, however, and suggests a family conference to see if she could be given a "lot of money." At the conference, Joseph Kennedy insists that Jack must be saved at all costs: "But Rosemary doesn't know how to, one of the girls said. And harshly he replied, Then she'll have to learn quick!"

This opening section of the dream conflates Jackie's grief over the loss of her husband with her fear of future revelations of his infidelities. Unable to

stop him, she is reduced to asking others to either not see him or help her get him to stop so that the multitude will not know. This episode recapitulates her role as political wife and First Lady, in which her primary concern had to be presentation. In the dream she confronts three male figures: De Gaulle, Bobby, and the Kennedy patriarch. None are concerned with her.

De Gaulle, famously charmed by Jackie in Paris, nevertheless in her dream overrides her request, bluntly insisting on his own wish to see. Bobby is concerned with his own "love" for Marilyn and the family reputation. His suggestion that the solution lies in giving Monroe a "lot of money" to let the daughter Rosemary replace her is a displacement of the father's having Rosemary lobotomized in the 1940s and his reputedly giving Jackie a million dollars not to divorce Jack in the 1950s—both actions supposed to have been motivated by a desire to protect the family's image. These "facts" of the Kennedy legend are fused to present to Jackie the single disguised truth that she—and all women—are being sacrificed to the demands of patriarchal power: "Jackie felt resentful, and she was consumed with thirst" (213). She realizes that she is being denied the source of an authentic life.

The second section of the dream takes Jackie to Jack's hospital room, where he is making love with Marilyn as a blood-covered priest gives him the last rites. Jackie has returned in her dream to the scene of Jack's near-death in 1954 from his back operation. She recognizes that the woman is not Monroe, but rather Princess Grace. She thought it was Monroe because of the poster of Monroe she had placed on the wall to boost Jack's morale. Grace Kelly's sex act with Jack is a distorted image of the actual hospital visit she paid him at Jackie's request: "It was hopeless, the princess said, tearful, looking down at the clothed President in his casket, the priest babbling over him.—I thought maybe I could revive him. I must be losing my touch." Jackie thanks her for trying to help, then, "Dressed in black, numbed with grief, she was in a Greek museum with her sister Lee and Aristotle Onassis" (214).

This abrupt shift begins the third section of the dream, with the "Greek museum" representing a simultaneous move into her future relation with Onassis and into the antiquity of classical Greek myth. After she notices a bust of Socrates turn and speak to one of Plato, Jackie tells Onassis, who replies, "It's possible; the dead can come alive in Greece. Our myths prove it. Euridice. Alcestis" (214).

What transpires, however, is a revised myth of Ariadne, Theseus, and the Minotaur. Jackie asks Onassis if he can help her "bring the dead to life." When the multibillionaire shrugs and asks who she has in mind, Jackie looks at her sister Lee and decides: "It had to be their father. That would be wonderful, it would console her for Jack's loss. My father, she said" (214).

Onassis informs Jackie that they must go to Crete, where they enter the labyrinth: "Far underground, they were threading their way through a maze, moving ever closer to the secret at the heart of it." When she asks if

175

they will find the Minotaur, Onassis tells her, "Not the minotaur—your father. His voice echoed many times." Finally, in a central room they come upon a magnificent black horse:

I told you, Onassis said. Shall I leave you with him?
  But this isn't my father.
  He looked taken aback. "But his name is Black Jack. This is Black Jack." (215)

When she tearfully explains that Black Jack was only a nickname for her father, Onassis apologizes for being an "ignorant Greek" and relinquishes his role as guide:

"The riderless black horse can lead you to its master in the underworld. Mount it, and it will guide you to your husband."
  Full of hope again, she sprang on to Black Jack's back, tugged its mane, and it was bounding off. They flew through the Cretan landscape of stony mountains.

The movement in the Greek section is a regression leading to progress. Thomas uses recognizable elements of Jackie's biography after the assassination: She did in fact place the riderless horse named for her father in the funeral to represent her fallen husband, marry Onassis and move to the Greek islands, and depart from Onassis' world to become an independent woman. Thomas dramatizes Jackie's unconscious reworking of these facts into a dream that reveals her changing relation to her animus. Onassis, her dead father and husband, and the horse are all images of her relation to the masculine. In marrying the much older and incredibly powerful Onassis, Jackie was apparently seeking the security of a return to the father. However, she left that marriage possessing the wealth that enabled her to live an independent life. Her riding the horse to which Onassis has led her suggests her partnering with her own animus, the part of her psyche gendered by her culture as masculine, which she has previously projected out upon her chosen males. The horse leads her where she wishes to go, but she (her conscious mind) rides it. Significantly, in leaving the labyrinth on the flying horse she leaves behind the Theseus-Ariadne story of the slaying of the Minotaur, in which Ariadne was a mere helpmate to the masculine hero Theseus. Our Ariadne figure takes the hero role herself.

As she flies away, she sights another symbolic animal:

She saw a brown deer leap away anxiously, and she suddenly thought: There are no deer in Greece! This landscape is familiar; I was here with Jack before the Inauguration. It's Johnson hill country! It's Johnson Hill Country! The wind taking her hair, she threw her head back and laughed in sheer relief. It was nothing but a dream, a trance. She and Jack were in the Hotel Texas. She had dreamed of his death because Dallas was worrying, they weren't looking forward to it. (215)

The deer that Jackie sees "anxiously" fleeing suggests an image of her husband as potential victim, and its significance is amplified by two subsequent recurrences as the novel draws to a close.

Several pages after Jackie's dream, in the "possible" realm in which the assassination is foiled, Kennedy proceeds on his Texas trip to a stay at the Johnson ranch. As Kennedy finds himself compelled by his host to hunt a deer, he meditates upon a Robert Frost poem:

He liked the whole poem, about those two lovers who are climbing a mountain at dusk—seeing at the last moment an image of themselves in the form of a buck and a doe. A kind of spell in which the lovers feel the love of the earth for them. Jackie had first acquainted him with the poem, and then the old man had read it to them at a White House dinner. (225–26)

Soon he and Johnson sight a deer. Johnson tells him to "shoot the sonofabitch." Kennedy is caught between the "feminine" voice of poetry and the "masculine" voice of the old frontier:

He raised his rifle and looked through the telescopic sight. The eyes of the buck seemed to be directly on him. He aimed steadily between those brooding, innocent eyes, and imagined they were filled with love for him. And that he himself felt love for it.

This was foolishness. It was the effect of the poem, and you couldn't let poetry rule your life. He eased his finger against the trigger. He saw the tender, intimate eyes glaze instantly in death. God, he hated death. He fought it with all he knew; every time he got inside a warm pussy he was fighting it. He loathed it, much more than Communism. Still, this had to be done, for Lyndon's sake.

At the moment of firing he jerked the rifle up. The buck bounded away and vanished behind a hill. (227)

177

Jung identified the deer as a common object of projections of the anima, the feminine component of a man's mind. In other passages of the novel Johnson talks about possessing women sexually in the same rough language with which he here urges Kennedy to "take" the deer. Through the hunt, a central ritual of the American frontier myth and ideology, Kennedy joins Johnson so that they confirm each other's masculinity. According to Manchester's *Death of a President,* in an actual hunt on Johnson's ranch shortly after the 1960 election, Kennedy regretfully killed a deer to prove "his mettle" to his host, but "the memory of the creature's death had been haunting, and afterward he had relived it with his wife, *vider l'abcès*, to heal the inner scar."[19] Here, in this imagined second chance, as Kennedy projects his own repressed longings for intimacy and tenderness upon the deer, he chooses to let the animal live. Thomas links this act to the possibility that Kennedy might have survived to turn back from the fateful errors in Vietnam and guide the nation through the changes of the civil rights movement.

In Thomas's imaginings, Jackie dreams herself toward partnership with her animus, while Jack survives Dallas to turn away from repressing his anima. Thus Jack and Jackie represent the possibility of a transition in the gender hierarchy, both within a private psyche and without in the collective structure of a society.

But of course in the historical world, the world in which things actually happen, Kennedy was shot. Thomas concludes the novel with a one-page chapter that brings us back to the question of where the "essential" Kennedy has gone. It is Sunday night, sixty hours after the assassination, and Jackie lies in the double bed, reaching over to "the empty space":

Later, still unable to contemplate sleep, she wanders out into the grounds. She gazes up through a tree's bare branches at the stars, cold and brilliant. She wonders where, in the vast cosmos, he is. Is it possible he is nowhere? She whispers his name. She is only aware of the silence. Then she hears a rifle shot, and as it echoes she sees a small deer, racing away through long grass, vanishing.   (261)

When Jackie, in her mind, sees the "small deer" running out of view, we know she sees not the actual John Kennedy but her projected image of him. The novel began with acknowledgment that any "essential" JFK is lost to us, and it ends with the image of our poignant pursuit of an elusive projection.

Thomas's novel deals with the Kennedy obsession as a complex phenomenon of projections, both Kennedy's and ours. The strong implication is that we need to take back our projections and analyze what they tell us about ourselves. By focusing on gender, *Flying in to Love* compels us to recognize how much the narrative that Kennedy projected for us was a reflection of a masculinist ideology that has held sway as the American identity. The implication of the novel seems to be that we should rethink those obsessions and myths, balancing them with the values and traits that have been gendered as feminine and labeled inferior, even terrifying.

Flying in to Love leaves us, after all the pain and anxiety circulating around the image of John F. Kennedy's assassination, to face the fact of his absence, to contemplate the meaning of the story that Kennedy and his collaborators projected as his image, the story of each of us—including Kennedy—who invested our yearnings in that image. Through these retellings, we are perhaps engaged in the project of rethinking the national identity.

Preface

1. Quoted by Theodore White in C. David Heymann, *A Woman Named Jackie* (New York: New American Library, 1990), 430.
2. Theodore H. White, "For President Kennedy: An Epilogue," *Life*, 6 Dec. 1963, 159.
3. For brief meditations on the projection of Kennedy's image, see "The Leading Man: A Review of *JFK: The Man and the Myth*" in Norman Mailer, *Cannibals and Christians* (New York: Dial, 1966), 165–71; Jerome Klinkowitz, *The American 1960s: Imaginative Acts in a Decade of Change* (Ames: Iowa State University Press, 1980), 3–19; Thomas McEvilley, "Ask Not What," *Artforum* Feb. 1986: 68–75; and Bruce Mazlish, "Kennedy: Myth and History" in *John F. Kennedy: Person, Policy, Presidency*, ed. J. Richard Snyder (Wilmington, Del.: Scholarly Resources, 1988), 25–34.
4. On myth, see Mircea Eliade, *Myth and Reality*, trans. Willard R. Trask (1963; reprint, New York: Harper & Row, 1975); Marshall Sahlins, *Historical Metaphors and Mythical Realities: Structure in the Early History of the Sandwich Islands Kingdom* (Ann Arbor: University of Michigan Press, 1981); James Oliver Robertson, *American Myth/American Reality* (New York: Hill & Wang,

1980). See also the introductions to Richard Slotkin's three volumes: *Regeneration Through Violence: The Mythology of the American Frontier, 1600–1860* (Middletown, Conn.: Wesleyan University Press, 1973); *The Fatal Environment: The Myth of the Frontier in the Age of Industrialization, 1800–1890* (New York: Atheneum, 1985); *Gunfighter Nation: The Myth of the Frontier in Twentieth-Century America* (New York: Atheneum, 1992). On ideology and its relation to art, literature, and popular culture, see Roland Barthes, *Mythologies*, trans. Annette Lavers (1957; reprint, New York: Hill & Wang, 1972); Janet Wolff, *The Social Production of Art* (New York: New York University Press, 1984); Frederic Jameson, *The Political Unconscious: Narrative as a Socially Symbolic Act* (Ithaca: Cornell University Press, 1981); Raymond Williams, *Marxism and Literature* (Oxford: Oxford University Press, 1977). For works more specifically concerned with the mass media and popular culture, see Adrian Forty, *Objects of Desire* (New York: Pantheon, 1986); Tony Bennett and Janet Woollacott, *Bond and Beyond: The Political Career of a Popular Hero* (New York: Methuen, 1987); Walter Benjamin, "The Work of Art in the Age of Mechanical Reproduction" in his *Illuminations: Essays and Reflections*, ed. Hannah Arendt, trans. Harry Zohn (1955; reprint, New York: Schocken, 1969), 217–52; *The Culture of Consumption: Critical Essays in American History, 1880–1980*, eds. Richard Wightman Fox and T. J. Jackson Lears (New York: Pantheon, 1983); *American Media and Mass Culture: Left Perspectives*, ed. Donald Lazere (Berkeley: University of California Press, 1987); *Studies in Entertainment: Critical Approaches to Mass Culture*, ed. Tania Modleski (Bloomington: Indiana University Press, 1986); John Fiske, *Understanding Popular Culture* (Boston: Unwin Hyman, 1989), and John Fiske, *Reading the Popular* (Boston: Unwin Hyman, 1989). For an overview of theoretical approaches to the image, see *Semiotics: An Introductory Anthology*, ed. Robert E. Innis (Bloomington: Indiana University Press, 1985). The moving image is explored in Christian Metz, *The Imaginary Signifier: Psychoanalysis and the Cinema*, trans. Celia Britton et al. (1977; reprint, Bloomington: Indiana University Press, 1982).

Prologue: A Bedside Visit

1. "Chapter 1. The Meaning of Courage," Manuscripts—*Profiles in Courage* folder, Box 27, Item 1, John Fitzgerald Kennedy Personal Papers, John F. Kennedy Library.

2. Letter, Theodore C. Sorensen to author, 17 August 1990.

3. Heymann, *A Woman Named Jackie*, 170.

4. This anecdote has been told in Ralph G. Martin, *A Hero for Our Time: An Intimate Story of the Kennedy Years* (1983; reprint, New York: Ballantine, 1984), 89; Peter Collier and David Horowitz, *The Kennedys: An American Drama* (1984; reprint, New York: Warner, 1985), 253; Heymann, *A Woman Named Jackie*, 170.

5. Joseph Campbell, *The Hero with a Thousand Faces* (1949; reprint, Princeton: Princeton University Press, 1973), 69, 71–72.

1. How Kennedy Awoke: Jack's Reading and *Why England Slept*

1. The fullest and most vivid account of this episode may be found in Doris Kearns Goodwin, *The Fitzgeralds and the Kennedys* (New York: Simon and Schuster, 1987), 309–12.
2. Richard J. Whalen, *The Founding Father: The Story of Joseph P. Kennedy* (New York: New American Libary, 1964), 169.
3. James MacGregor Burns, *John Kennedy: A Political Profile* (New York: Harcourt, 1959), 20.
4. Goodwin, *The Fitzgeralds and the Kennedys*, 142–47; 174–89.
5. Rose Fitzgerald Kennedy, *Times to Remember* (Garden City, N.Y.: Doubleday, 1974), 94, 122.
6. Burns, *John Kennedy*, 20; Goodwin, *The Fitzgeralds and the Kennedys*, 352; Burns, *John Kennedy*, 28. For a fully developed, and relentlessly negative, psychological explanation of Kennedy's health problems, see Nancy Gager Clinch, *The Kennedy Neurosis* (New York: Grosset & Dunlap, 1973), 108–12.
7. Nigel Hamilton, *JFK: Reckless Youth* (London: Random, 1992), 50.
8. Goodwin, *The Fitzgeralds and the Kennedys*, 461.
9. Burns, *John Kennedy*, 21; Kennedy, *Times to Remember*, 153; Collier and Horowitz, *The Kennedys*, 212.
10. See Ralph G. Martin and Ed Plaut, *Front Runner, Dark Horse* (Garden City, N.Y.: Doubleday, 1960), 122; Herbert S. Parmet, *Jack: The Struggles of John F. Kennedy* (New York: Dial, 1980), 17; Frances Trego Montgomery, *Billy Whiskers: The Autobiography of a Goat* (New York: Dover, 1969); Kennedy, *Times to Remember*, 110–13.
11. Ibid.
12. Goodwin, *The Fitzgeralds and the Kennedys*, 752; Kennedy, *Times to Remember*, 111–12.
13. Burns, *John Kennedy*, 24.
14. Oral history interview of Ralph Horton, Jr. by Joseph Dolan, 1 June 1964, page 2, John F. Kennedy Library.
15. On *Kim* see Edward W. Said, *Culture and Imperialism* (New York: Knopf, 1993), 132–62; on *Ivanhoe*, see Clare A. Simmons, *Reversing the Conquest: History and Myth in Nineteenth-Century British Literature* (New Brunswick, N.J.: Rutgers University Press, 1990), 76–87.
16. Arthur M. Schlesinger, Jr., *A Thousand Days: John F. Kennedy in the White House* (Boston: Houghton Mifflin, 1965), 80.
17. See Collier and Horowitz, *The Kennedys*, 117, and Hamilton, *JFK*, 147–52.
18. See Joan Meyers, ed., *John Fitzgerald Kennedy . . . As We Remember Him* (New

York: MacMillan, 1965), 17; Kennedy, *Times to Remember*, 180–83; Parmet, *Jack*, 35–38; Goodwin, *The Fitzgeralds and the Kennedys*, 486–89.

19. Hamilton, *JFK*, 129–30.
20. Goodwin, *The Fitzgeralds and the Kennedys*, 505; Parmet, *Jack*, 45–47.
21. See Hamilton, *JFK*, 297–98.
22. Schlesinger, *A Thousand Days*, 87.
23. David Nunnerly, *President Kennedy and Great Britain* (London: Bodley Head, 1972), 17.
24. Bradford Perkins, *The Great Rapprochement: England and the United States, 1895–1914* (New York: Atheneum, 1968), 84–86.
25. Ibid., 82.
26. See Slotkin, *Gunfighter Nation*, 265–71.
27. Hamilton, *JFK*, 286–87.
28. Meyers, *John Fitzgerald Kennedy . . . As We Remember Him*, 35.
29. Hamilton, *JFK*, 320–21.
30. Ibid., 306–19.
31. John F. Kennedy, *Why England Slept* (1940; reprint, Westport, Conn: Greenwood, 1981), 5.
32. This psychological theme is incisively discussed in James David Barber's *The Presidential Character: Predicting Performance in the White House* (Englewood Cliffs, N.J.: Prentice-Hall, 1972), 305–7.
33. Kennedy, *Why England Slept*, xxi. Subsequent references are made in parentheses in the text.
34. Burns, *John Kennedy*, 44.
35. See, for example, Joan and Clay Blair, Jr., *The Search for J.F.K.* (New York: Berkley, 1976), 60–61; and Martin, *A Hero for Our Time*, 35.
36. Blair, *The Search for J.F.K.*, 86.
37. Hamilton, *JFK*, 342.
38. Ibid., 358–59.
39. Blair, *The Search for J.F.K.*, 94.
40. Ibid., 107.
41. Collier and Horowitz, *The Kennedys*, 213–14.
42. Hamilton, *JFK*, 520.
43. David Cecil, *The Young Melbourne: And the Story of His Marriage with Caroline Lamb* (New York: Bobbs-Merrill, 1939), 149–50.
44. Ibid., 162.
45. Ibid., 163.
46. Ibid., 155.
47. Hamilton, *JFK*, 449.
48. Ibid., 473, 630.
49. Ibid., 544–45.
50. Schlesinger, *A Thousand Days*, 87.

51. Martin, *A Hero for Our Time*, 35–36.
52. John Buchan, *Pilgrim's Way: An Autobiography* (1940; reprint, New York: Carroll and Graf, 1984), 212.
53. Blair, *The Search for J.F.K.*, 124.
54. Adrian Caesar, *Taking It Like a Man: Suffering, Sexuality and the War Poets Brooke, Sassoon, Owen, Graves* (Manchester, England: Manchester University Press, 1993), 8.
55. Ibid., 6.

2. John Hersey's "Survival": A Literary Experiment and Its Political Adaptation

1. See Blair, *The Search for J.F.K.*, 241–78; without analyzing it, Hamilton, *JFK*, describes Hersey's article as containing "writing of a very high order."
2. For a full theoretical exposition of my approach to works combining journalistic material with fictional technique, see John Hellmann, *Fables of Fact: The New Journalism as New Fiction* (Urbana: University of Illinois Press, 1981). In addition to drawing on my own theoretical work, I have been influenced in this chapter by John J. Pauly's suggestion that we might "interpret a work of reporting as a *social behavior*, without precluding close textual analysis." Elaborating, Pauly advocates studying the venues of publication, the process of research and writing, and how that process "implicates writer, subjects, and readers in relationships beyond the text." See John J. Pauly, "The Politics of the New Journalism," in *Literary Journalists in the Twentieth Century*, ed. Norman Sims (New York: Oxford University Press, 1990), 112. For two theories of literary reportage differing from my own, see Mas'ud Zavarzadeh, *The Mythopoeic Reality: The Postwar American Nonfiction Novel* (Urbana: University of Illinois Press, 1976) and Eric Heyne, "Towards a Theory of Literary Nonfiction," *Modern Fiction Studies* 33 (1987), 479–90.
3. Blair, *The Search for J.F.K.*, 268–276.
4. See Whalen, *The Founding Father*, 368; Goodwin, *The Fitzgeralds and the Kennedys*, 657–58.
5. Blair, *The Search for J.F.K.*, 293.
6. Hamilton, *JFK*, 254, 286–87, 320, 546, 550.
7. Ibid., 643–44.
8. John Hersey, A Reporter at Large, "Survival," *The New Yorker*, 17 June 1944, 31–43. All specific references to "Survival" in this chapter will be to this text. In my analysis of Hersey's article I am using the original *New Yorker* text, rather than the *Reader's Digest* condensation, both because it offers me the fullest opportunity to show Hersey's intentions and because it represents not only what the earliest readers encountered but also what many subsequent writers used in their research for articles and books on Kennedy. When my focus switches to the electorate in Kennedy's 1946 congressional district, it is the *Reader's Digest*

185

version that is most relevant, since that is the text that was used as a campaign · material. At that point, all relevant aspects of my analysis of the original *New Yorker* text remain valid, since the condensation retained all of the major elements and structure of the original. Besides deleting isolated sentences and paragraphs, the condensation eliminated the frame tale in which Hersey originally recounted how he obtained the story; it substituted the letter in which an officer lamented the loss of Ross and Kennedy as the frame opening, lifting it from its original position after the crash, and thus even more greatly emphasized the experience of Kennedy and his crew as one in a suspended zone between life and death.

9. Blair, *The Search for J.F.K.*, 333. As biographers who were looking for the truth *behind* the tale, the Blairs pay no discernible attention to Hersey's comment.

10. Hersey interview, Blair inventory, page 3, American Heritage Center, University of Wyoming.

11. See "The Art of Fiction XCII: John Hersey," *Paris Review* 98 (1986): 245, 228–29.

12. Quoted in Blair, *The Search for J.F.K.*, 333.

13. "The Art of Fiction," 232.

14. Hersey interview, Blair inventory, American Heritage Center, University of Wyoming, page 3.

15. See "The Art of Fiction," 228.

16. Quoted in Hamilton, *JFK*, 644–45.

17. See Blair, *The Search for J.F.K.*, 342.

18. John Hersey, *Here to Stay* (New York: Knopf, 1963), 85.

19. Victor Turner, *The Ritual Process: Structure and Anti-Structure* (1969; Ithaca: Cornell University Press, 1977), 129.

20. See Blair, *The Search for J.F.K.*, 331–37; Hamilton, *JFK*, 641, 644.

21. Goodwin, *The Fitzgeralds and the Kennedys*, 698.

22. John F. Kennedy, ed. *As We Remember Joe* (privately printed, 1945), 5.

23. Paul B. Fay, Jr. *The Pleasure of His Company* (New York: Harper and Row, 1966), 141.

24. Collier and Horowitz, *The Kennedys*, 176.

25. Spalding interview, page 22, Clay Blair inventory, American Heritage Center, University of Wyoming.

26. Collier and Horowitz, *The Kennedys*, 43–54, 177–87; Blair, *The Search for J.F.K.*, 443–557; Goodwin, *The Fitzgeralds and the Kennedys*, 706–21; Parmet, *Jack*, 125–62.

27. John Hersey, "Joe Is Home Now," *Life*, 3 July 1944, 66–80.

28. Martin and Plaut, *Front Runner, Dark Horse*, 134–35.

29. Kenneth P. O'Donnell and David F. Powers with Joe McCarthy, "*Johnny, We Hardly Knew Ye*" (Boston: Little, Brown, 1970), 66–67.

3. The Old Man and the Boy: Papa Hemingway and *Profiles in Courage*

1. "Dear Senator Oldtimer," manuscripts—*Profiles in Courage* folder, Item 4 [C], John Fitzgerald Kennedy Personal Papers, John F. Kennedy Library.
2. John F. Kennedy, *Profiles in Courage*, (1956; reprint, New York: Pocket, 1963), 1.
3. See Wendy Kozol, *"Life's" America: Family and Nation in Postwar Journalism*, (Philadephia: Temple University Press, 1994).
4. Eric F. Goldman, *The Crucial Decade—and After: America, 1945–1960* (New York: Vintage, 1960), 303–5.
5. Malcolm Cowley, "A Portrait of Mister Papa," *Life*, 10 Jan. 1949, 93– 94.
6. Ernest Hemingway, *Across the River and into the Trees* (New York: Scribner's, 1950), 234.
7. "A Great American Storyteller," *Life*, 1 Sept. 1952, 20.
8. Gerry Brenner, *The Old Man and the Sea: Story of a Common Man* (New York: Twayne, 1991), 15–16.
9. Kenneth S. Lynn, *Hemingway* (1987; reprint, New York: Ballantine, 1988), 566–70.
10. "The Old Man Lands Biggest Catch," *Life*, 8 Nov. 1954, 25–28.
11. John Raeburn, *Fame Became of Him: Hemingway as Public Writer* (Bloomington: Indiana University Press, 1984), 151.
12. Parmet, *Jack*, 307–15.
13. Schlesinger, *A Thousand Days*, 105; Philip Young, *Ernest Hemingway: A Reconsideration* (University Park: Pennsylvania State University Press, 1966), 273n.
14. See Goodwin, *The Fitzgeralds and the Kennedys*, 708–19.
15. Parmet, *Jack*, 163–95.
16. David E. Koskoff, *Joseph P. Kennedy: A Life and Times* (Englewood Cliffs, N.J.: Prentice-Hall, 1974), 393.
17. Victor Lasky, *J.F.K.: The Man and the Myth* (1963; reprint, New York: Dell, 1977), 131–69; Parmet, *Jack*, 163–95; Blair, *The Search for J.F.K.*, 562–81; Collier, *The Kennedys*, 188–210.
18. Joseph Alsop, "The Legacy of John F. Kennedy: Memories of an Uncommon Man," in *J. F. Kennedy and Presidential Power*, ed. Earl Latham (Lexington, Mass.: D. C. Heath, 1972), 266.
19. Blair, *The Search for J.F.K.*, 539–40.
20. Burns, *John Kennedy*, 128; William Manchester, *Portrait of a President: John F. Kennedy in Profile* (1962; reprint, New York: McFadden, 1964), 69; Arthur M. Schlesinger Jr., *A Thousand Days*, 87; Theodore C. Sorensen, *Kennedy* (New York: Harper and Row, 1965; 1988), 14.
21. Goodwin, *The Fitzgeralds and the Kennedys*, 744–49.
22. Sorensen, *Kennedy*, 11.
23. Blair, *The Search for J.F.K.*, 547.

24. Mary Barelli Gallagher, *My Life with Jacqueline Kennedy* (New York: David McKay, 1969), 16–17.

25. Paul F. Healy, "The Senate's Gay Young Bachelor," *Saturday Evening Post*, 13 June 1953, 26.

26. Edward Klein, *All Too Human: The Love Story of Jack and Jackie Kennedy* (New York: Pocket, 1996), 84; Christopher Andersen, *Jack and Jackie: Portrait of an American Marriage* (New York: Morrow, 1996), 138.

27. Ibid., 116, 117; Klein, *All Too Human*, 158.

28. "*Life* Goes Courting with a U.S. Senator," *Life*, 20 July 1953, 96.

29. *Person to Person.* CBS television program, 10 Oct. 1953.

30. J. L. McConaughy, "The World's Most Exclusive Clubmen," *Life*, 19 April 1954, 114.

31. Manchester, *Portrait of a President*, 68.

32. See transcription and actual notes, "Doodles 1955" folder, Item KS-11, John Fitzgerald Kennedy Personal Papers, John F. Kennedy Library.

33. Parmet, *Jack*, 298–325; Heymann, *A Woman Named Jackie*, 174.

34. Burns, *John Kennedy*, 156–57; Parmet, *Jack*, 309–13; Collier and Horowitz, *The Kennedys*, 251; Goodwin, *The Fitzgeralds and the Kennedys*, 775–76.

35. Collier and Horowitz, *The Kennedys*, 253.

36. Parmet, *Jack*, 324–29.

37. Oral history interview of Hugh Fraser by Joe O'Connor, 17 Jan. 1966, page 12, John F. Kennedy Library. Kennedy aides Kenneth P. O'Donnell and David F. Powers make similar observations in their memoir, written with Joe McCarthy, "*Johnny, We Hardly Knew Ye*" (Boston: Little, Brown, 1970), 103–4.

38. Burns, *John Kennedy*, 157.

39. Parmet, *Jack*, 323.

40. Garry Wills, *The Kennedy Imprisonment: A Meditation on Power* (Boston: Little, Brown, 1982), 135.

41. Martin and Plaut, *Front Runner, Dark Horse*, 201.

42. Ernest Hemingway, *The Old Man and the Sea* (New York: Scribner's, 1952), 126–27.

43. Kennedy, *Profiles in Courage*, 1–2.

44. Ibid., 5, 4.

45. Ibid., 208.

46. Ibid., 250–51.

47. Hemingway, *The Old Man and the Sea*, 75.

48. Parmet, *Jack*, 356.

49. Oral history interview of James A. Reed by Robert J. Donovan, 25 June 1964, page 38, John F. Kennedy Library.

50. Parmet devotes a full chapter to this production. See *Jack*, 479–88.

51. "Texts of Kennedy and Johnson Speeches Accepting the Democratic Nominations," *New York Times*, 16 July 1960, late city ed., 7.

52. A. E. Hotchner, *Papa Hemingway: The Ecstasy and Sorrow* (New York: Morrow, 1963), 281.

53. *Ernest Hemingway: Selected Letters, 1917–1961*, ed. Carlos Baker (New York: Scribner's, 1981), 915.

54. Jeffrey Meyers, *Hemingway: A Biography* (New York: Harper and Row, 1985), 554.

55. Bernice Kert, *The Hemingway Women* (1983; reprint, New York: Norton, 1986), 500; Lynn, *Hemingway*, 589; Meyers, *Hemingway*, 550.

56. *Hemingway: Selected Letters*, 916.

57. John F. Kennedy, *Public Papers of the Presidents 1961*, U.S. Government Printing Office, 1963, 269.

58. Mary Welsh Hemingway, *How It Was* (New York: Knopf, 1976), 513–14.

4. The Hollywood Screen and Kennedy's Televised Showdown with Truman

1. Michael Wood, *America in the Movies* (1975; reprint, New York: Dell, 1981), 8.

2. Robert Sklar, *Movie-Made America* (New York: Random, 1975), 283–85.

3. Wood, *America in the Movies*, 10–11, 15–16.

4. Ibid., 12.

5. See David Bordwell, Janet Staiger, and Kristin Thompson, *The Classical Hollywood Cinema: Film Style and Mode of Production to 1960* (New York: Columbia University Press, 1985), 13.

6. This topic has been thoroughly discussed by a number of authors. Places to start include Hellmann, *Fables of Fact*, 1–20; John Fiske, *Reading the Popular* (Boston: Unwin Hyman, 1989), 149–84; and Bill Nichols, *Ideology and the Image: Social Representation in the Cinema and Other Media* (Bloomington: Indiana University Press, 1981), 1–42.

7. For a brief synopsis of these events, see Erik Barnouw, *Tube of Plenty: The Evolution of American Television*, 2nd rev. ed. (New York: Oxford University Press, 1990), 243–46.

8. John F. Kennedy, "A Force That Has Changed the Political Scene," *TV Guide*, 14 Nov. 1959, 7.

9. Martin and Plaut, *Front Runner, Dark Horse*, 461.

10. For a full discussion of the cultural meanings of the Jimmy Stewart star persona, see Dennis Bingham, *Acting Male: Masculinities in the Films of James Stewart, Jack Nicholson, and Clint Eastwood* (New Brunswick, New Jersey: Rutgers University Press, 1994), 23–96.

11. Blair, *The Search for J.F.K.*, 381.

12. Russell L. Merritt, "The Bashful Hero in American Film of the Nineteen Forties," *Quarterly Journal of Speech*, 61 (1975): 131.

13. For a discussion of Grant's persona and its meanings in the 1950s, see Steven

Cohan, "Cary Grant in the Fifties: Indiscretions of the Bachelor's Masquerade," *Screen* 33 (1992): 394–412.

14. Heymann, *A Woman Named Jackie*, 300.
15. Eleanor Harris, "The Senator Is in a Hurry," *McCall's*, Aug. 1957, 45.
16. Peter Biskind, *Seeing Is Believing: How Hollywood Taught Us to Stop Worrying and Love the Fifties* (New York: Pantheon, 1983), 4.
17. Ibid., 3–4.
18. Ibid., 10–20.
19. Truman's mistaken reference to Kennedy by his father's name may be heard on *The Speeches of John F. Kennedy*, MPI Home Video, 1988.
20. "Transcript of the Truman Press Conference on the Democratic National Convention," *New York Times*, 3 July 1960.
21. "Kennedy Awaiting Attack by Truman," *New York Times*, 2 July 1960; "Kennedy Replies to Charge Today," *New York Times*, 4 July 1960.
22. "Kennedy Demands Air Time to Reply," *New York Times*, 3 July 1960.
23. Sorensen, *Kennedy*, 152.
24. "Transcript of Kennedy's News Conference," *New York Times*, 5 July 1960.
25. Richard Dyer, *Stars* (London: British Film Institute, 1979), 111–13.
26. *The Speeches of John F. Kennedy*.
27. Blair, *The Search for J.F.K.*, 539.
28. This analysis is drawn from Biskind, *Seeing Is Believing*, 278–84.
29. Thomas C. Reeves, *A Question of Character: A Life of John F. Kennedy* (New York: Free Press, 1991), 152–53.

5. The Erotics of a Presidency

1. The psychoanalytic literature on romantic love is small but growing. Drawing on both Freud and Jung as well as on his own clinical observations, Harville Hendrix uses the term *imago* in the way I have adopted. See Harville Hendrix, *Getting the Love You Want: A Guide for Couples* (1988; reprint, New York: Harper Perennial, 1990), 38–46. Ethel Spector Person adopts the term "Lover-Shadow" from H. G. Wells in *Dreams of Love and Fateful Encounters: The Power of Romantic Passion* (New York: Norton, 1988), 34. Polly Young-Eisendrath, working from a Jungian perspective modified by a historicizing feminism, uses the term "dream lover." See Polly Young-Eisendrath, *You're Not What I Expected: Learning to Love the Opposite Sex* (New York: Simon and Schuster, 1994), 213. While these and other writers vary in their accounts of the makeup of the internal image, they all agree in seeing "falling in love" as an imaginative act whereby that image, summoned by traits perceived in a prospective lover, is projected out upon that real-life other person.
2. Virginia Wright Wexman, *Creating the Couple: Love, Marriage, and Hollywood Performance* (Princeton: Princeton University Press, 1993), 9.

3. Norman Mailer, *Some Honorable Men: Political Conventions 1960–1972* (Boston: Little, Brown, 1976), 21.

4. John Ellis, "Stars as a Cinematic Phenomenon," in *Visible Fictions: Cinema, Television, Video* (London: Routledge, 1982), 108.

5. Person, *Dreams of Love*, 19.

6. See Slotkin, *Regeneration Through Violence, The Fatal Environment,* and *Gunfighter Nation.*

7. On the "gunfighter western" see Slotkin, *Gunfighter Nation,* 379–404; the number of television series is taken from Richard Lemon, "The Last Showdown," *Entertainment Weekly,* 8 Aug./1 Sept. 1995.

8. See Hendrix, *Getting the Love You Want,* 283.

9. Senate Committee on Commerce, *The Speeches, Remarks, Press Conferences, and Statements of Senator John F. Kennedy, August 1 Through November 7, 1960,* 87th Cong., 1st sess., 1961, Rept. 994, Part I, 958. Kennedy also used this precise term in speeches that may be found on 391 and 951. The idea of America as an unfinished country was of course fundamental to his concept of the New Frontier.

10. "Texts of Kennedy and Johnson Speeches Accepting Democratic Nominations," *New York Times,* 16 July 1960.

11. John Munder Ross, *What Men Want: Mothers, Fathers, and Manhood* (Cambridge: Harvard University Press, 1994), 168.

12. See Person, *Dreams of Love*, 31–32.

13. "Texts," *New York Times,* 16 July 1960.

14. See Hendrix, *Getting the Love You Want,* 22–30, 50–53.

15. Ross, *What Men Want,* 184.

16. For an overview of this debate see John W. Jeffries, "The 'Quest for the National Purpose' of 1960," *American Quarterly* 30 (1978): 451–70.

17. John F. Kennedy, "We Must Climb to the Hilltop," *Life,* 22 Aug. 1960, 70.

18. Ibid., 72.

19. Joseph Kraft, recorded interview by John F. Stewart, January 9, 1967, page 12, John F. Kennedy Library Oral History Program.

20. Senate Committee on Commerce, *The Speeches, Remarks, Press Conferences, and Statements of Senator John F. Kennedy, August 1 Through November 7, 1960,* 87th Cong., 1st sess., 1961, Rept. 994, Part I, 78, 81, 101–2, 133.

21. Henry Fairlie, *The Kennedy Promise: The Politics of Expectation* (1972; reprint, New York: Dell, 1974), 74.

22. Theodore H. White, *The Making of the President 1960* (New York: Atheneum, 1961), 396.

23. Senate Committee on Commerce, *The Joint Appearances of Senator John F. Kennedy and Vice President Richard M. Nixon and Other 1960 Campaign Presentations,* 87th Cong., 1st sess., Rept. 994, Part III, 73–92.

191

24. See Wendy Kozol, *"Life's" America: Family and Nation in Postwar Photojournalism* (Philadelphia: Temple University Press, 1994).

25. See Person, *Dreams of Love*, 16, 20, 351.

26. Rupert Wilkinson, *American Tough: The Tough-Guy Tradition and American Character* (1984; reprint, New York: Harper & Row, 1986), 3, 7.

27. *Kennedy and the Press: The News Conferences*, eds. Harold W. Chase and Allen H. Lerman (New York: Crowell, 1965), 223.

28. Kennedy's use of "crisis" and its impact on the public has been insightfully discussed by a number of recent scholars within a number of contexts. For a penetrating discussion of Kennedy as Television President and of his concern with a masculine style, see Bruce Miroff, *Icons of Democracy: American Leaders as Heroes, Aristocrats, Dissenters, and Democrats* (New York: Basic, 1993), 273–307. Richard Slotkin shows how Kennedy's heroic style drew in part on American frontier mythology and had connections with epic films of the era; see *Gunfighter Nation*, 489–533. Earlier, more extensive treatments of Kennedy's use of crisis may be found in Fairlie, *The Kennedy Promise*, and in Richard J. Walton, *Cold War and Counterrevolution: The Foreign Policy of John F. Kennedy* (New York: Viking, 1972).

29. Person, *Dreams of Love*, 23.

30. For a full exposition of the relation of *The Ugly American* and the celebration in the press of the U.S. Special Forces to Kennedy's New Frontier, see John Hellmann, *American Myth and the Legacy of Vietnam* (New York: Columbia University Press, 1986). Richard Reeves documents in detail how much attention Kennedy paid to *The Ugly American* in formulating his Vietnam policies. See Reeves, *President Kennedy: Profile of Power* (New York: Simon & Schuster, 1993), 46–47, 69, 121, 222, 311, 558.

6. An Assassination and Its Fictions

1. For myth scholar Joseph Campbell's meditations on the significance of the Kennedy funeral rites in the context of world mythologies, see his *Myths to Live By* (1972; reprint, New York: Bantam, 1988), 52–54.

2. White, "For President Kennedy: An Epilogue," 159.

3. Don DeLillo, *Libra* (New York: Viking, 1988), 458. Subsequent references are to this edition.

4. See Ernest Hemingway, *The Sun Also Rises* (New York: Scribner's, 1926), 168: "Romero had the old thing, the holding of his purity of line through the maximum of exposure, while he dominated the bull by making him realize he was unattainable, while he prepared him for the killing."

5. Frank Lentricchia, *"Libra* as Postmodern Critique," *South Atlantic Quarterly* 89 (1990): 431–53.

6. Richard deCordova, *Picture Personalities: The Emergence of the Star System in America* (Urbana: University of Illinois Press, 1990), 140.

7. For a study of the biographical and other nonfiction literature on John F. Kennedy produced since the assassination, see Thomas Brown's *JFK: History of an Image* (Bloomington: Indiana University Press, 1988). For a study of the impact of the amplified post-assassination image of Kennedy upon American politics, see Paul R. Henggeler's *The Kennedy Persuasion: The Politics of Style Since JFK* (Chicago: Dee, 1995).

8. Young-Eisendrath, *You're Not What I Expected*, 76.

9. Polly Young-Eisendrath, *Hags and Heroes: A Feminist Approach to Jungian Psychotherapy with Couples* (Toronto: Inner City, 1984), 12.

10. Young-Eisendrath, *You're Not What I Expected*, 72.

11. Ibid., 23, 24, 78.

12. D. M. Thomas, *Flying in to Love* (1992; reprint, London: Sceptre, 1993), 3. All subsequent references are to this edition and may be found in the text.

13. Kennedy actually did stop to "greet a group of nuns." See William Manchester, *The Death of a President* (New York: Harper and Row, 1967), 136.

14. Young-Eisendrath, *You're Not What I Expected*, 97.

15. Young-Eisendrath, *Hags and Heroes*, 36.

16. Young-Eisendrath, *You're Not What I Expected*, 98.

17. Ibid., 87.

18. Ibid., 88.

19. Manchester, *The Death of a President*, 118–19.

199